Good Works Review

2020

Editor-in-Chief
Robert S. King

Associate Editors
Ruth Bavetta, Jesse Breite, Sara Clancy, Joan Colby,
Marie C. Lecrivain, Rachel L. MacAulay

Production Editor
Diane Kistner

For More Information
www.goodworksreview.futurecycle.org

A Good Works Project of FutureCycle Press
www.futurecycle.org

Cover artwork, "Love in the Time of Covid-19," by Diane Kistner
Cover and interior book design by Diane Kistner; PT Serif text with Macondo titling

Published by Good Works Review (a division of FutureCycle Press)
Athens, Georgia, USA

ISSN 2576-8166
ISBN 978-1-942371-93-9

Welcome to Good Works Review

Good Works Review is a Good Works project of FutureCycle Press. Introduced in 2013, these projects are altruistic collaborations of creative souls (like us) willing to give of their time, talents, and any profits to help improve our world. These projects have no source of monetary funding other than occasional sales of *American Society: What Poets See,* our first Good Works project.

Although we have decided to make this the last issue of *Good Works Review,* we will continue to sell all issues of the magazine, plus any past or future projects, through the FutureCycle Press website, Good Works tab.

This, our last issue of *Good Works Review*,
is dedicated to and in memory of Joan Colby,
tireless editor, brilliant poet, fiery spirit,
treasured friend.

JOAN COLBY

1939-2020

Poetry

Fiction

Essays

Poetry

"Storm" by
Karen Boissonneault-Gauthier

"It's Time" by
Karen Boissonneault-Gauthier

Alex Aldred

Clone

When you left, you left no trace:
no hair-clots in drains, lipstick at glass rims,
spattered phlegm round the edge of the sink
or fingerprints on a vase,
no clipped nail or flake of skin
to form the base for something new.

But there are places, here and there,
where the absence of you presents itself—
gaps in the row of half-used shampoos
and cupboards looted of pasta and cocoa.
A bare shelf on the bedroom bookcase.
Flowers unwatered by the kitchen window.

If I could scrape with a scalpel blade
the faceless spaces from empty picture frames;
if I could spread across a microscope slide
the silence of the house at rest;
I'd find a way to isolate your shape
and reconstruct you by the hole you left.

Maria Berardi

First Snow

The air is moving,
visible pixels,

bitter princesses, careless ballerinas,
the sky a blank daze of cold,

the bits of it like glitter
lazing about, down, down.

White on white
on white. Silence,

then the creek:
a low chuckle.

Maria Berardi

Mushrooms

for Camille Brightsmith

Death vegetables,
moon critters,
first flesh in life's soup.

Tender skin like a baby
changeling, pale
as the underbelly of a rat.

The earth's dark electricity
sprouts bloomless
worm flowers.

Divine food, enchantment,
quick-fix, vision: nothing,
nothing, is wasted.

Earth's breath,
sweet rot, recyclers,
small gods.

Rose Mary Boehm

My best friend writes me a long letter

Don't think he wasn't bright. He won three lawsuits for us when we built the house.
But then I built the house, really. Didn't have an architect, just contractors. Don't think
he didn't become a proper lawyer because he wasn't good enough. And I married
the first one just to get out of the house. My father wanted me to become
a sales girl, and I wanted to study fashion. My first one said, *Marry me and you can.*
He came home pissed every night and wanted to fuck. And if it wasn't me, it was one
of the others. I think there were quite a few. A very crowded marriage.

Both my husbands were supercilious assholes. What on earth made me do it? And don't
think there wasn't love. There was, there was. I think. And now I am incontinent
and he's got Alzheimer's and I can't sell his antique books and he's forgotten
the buyers' names. He has to take 32 different pills per day at different times
and he forgets what he has taken. He's diabetic, his heart depends on at least
25 of them. I can't drive, but then he can't drive any longer either, so...who
would have thought. And it's all my fault, he says, and I think I'll probably use his
razor blades but I can't leave him yet and I'll let you know when I am ready.

Roger Camp

Hide and Seek

At the right height
and a favorable

angle of repose
a hummingbird feeder

can birth
a burning lake

refracted from
its reddish base.

When an ace Rufous
streaks in

hovering opposite
the glass bottle

his Magoo face,
eyeballs me.

Darting glassy glances
sneak peeks

we play a game
of hide and seek.

His iridescence
showers the syrup

like a rain swept street
drinking in mirrored neon.

I watch as he sips
his surface reflection.

Abby Caplin

Kaddish Duplex

After Jericho Brown

Kaddish, the Jewish prayer for the dead
doesn't praise or even mention the dead,

> or tell you how to pray for your dead.
> My father prayed in his laboratory,

prayed for sterile test tubes in his research lab.
Some can love a spinning centrifuge.

> Anyone who loves a spinning centrifuge
> can hang an IV for twenty years.

He set up his wife's IV for twenty years
the way he sorted and filed junk mail.

> The way he stopped cataloging junk mail.
> The way the cat starved by the heating vent.

How it decayed by the heating vent.
Kaddish, the Jewish prayer for the dead.

Abby Caplin

To the Moon

for Bernadette Track

Where O'Keefe painted
a burnished clay barrette,
the sky blooms in celestial
turquoise, a ghost ladder,
plucked from Taos,
plunged into a charged
topography. Half-pearl, half-
lidded moon of mica beckons
invisible ancestors dancing upward
over lacquered hills
to another world,
            while still-breathers
kneel near Rio Pueblo, build
pit fires, fashion patterns of horsehair
onto hot clay, some recalling
the time they fed Easy Rider's
film crew, flirted with Fonda
and Hopper, whose motorcycles
smoked through Taos.
In summer heat, an elder
ferries memories of R. C. Gorman
from her closet—
the gallery of velvets, crimson
and purple, the wardrobe
she modeled for his paintings.
A master potter, her son works
his new cell phone,
adobe home of a thousand
years, storied ladders of spruce...

Doris Ferleger

Another Argument About Creation

When God said, "Let there be light" (Gen. 1:3), the light that came into being filled the
darkness, and ten holy vessels came forth, and each filled with primordial light.
—How "the Ari" Created a Myth and Transformed Judaism

The Ari, blind mystic, could see
the fleet of ten thousand clear vessels

each carrying one infinitesimal drop
of holy light into every corner of every galaxy.

Each blinding drop of light,
contained inside its own vessel,

could not touch any other light.
The situation became untenable.

The ten thousand vessels shattered.
Sparks, like seeds and stars, scattered.

Some say it was the vessels' fault,
each too weak to contain its own

holy light. Others say it was our human need
for night, or God's need to go

dark on us so we'd have to seek out
every glowing ember that flew

across space and settled
into every inside, every outside.

I say the reason the vessels shattered
was because God knew my loneliness,

my need to touch another light
and silken or grassy field of chest and belly.

Jack Foster

The Pugilist's Lament

The wet socket pop
of a million stars
when you know he's landed the blow—
this one's going to change
the surface of your face,
the bridge of your nose bulldozed
a half-dozen times or so
what you get is shook senseless,
pure id, whatever that is.

Some nights you're all but sleeping on the other guy,
looks more like dancin' from the outside.
I know what people think,
'cos I'm big and speak judiciously
I'm a brute. I'm not a brute,
I know what I'm doing;
contusion, bruising, networks of blood vessels
pulped and oozing, your organs wrapped like glass
in layers of fat, sinew and matter
shook up and ruptured;
I know what I'm doing—
This bloodletting, the sour rotten inside
I couldn't get it all out if I tried;
I'd need bigger fists.

And when I'm down for the count,
the big knuckle sleep, the knockout,
I always dream the same dream:
I pick a scrap with God
and because he's God he never falls
and because it's a dream I never tire
and I am bled, the venom inside
is drained and at the bottom of the empty flask,
(my soul) all that remains
is nothing but nothing
for something else,
finally, to go.

Malisa Garlieb

Keen

You think you know all the sounds
your body emits when crying.

I've been around the block.
On a floor/bed/plane. At the mirror.

I'm a natural, not that it's theater,
but even the chaplain wept with me

when my husband died at the ER
check-in. Four months in, my ducts

have dried and the case of tissues
shelters below a desk. Yet sounds

erupt in this beast body: abrupt
coyote bark, hag's cackle, kicked cat.

I wonder what the neighbors hear,
what wretched numen rakes my chest.

Malisa Garlieb

Photo of my Husband

forty years before I met him

He's clean-shaven, puckish in a pink shirt,
collar exaggerated like hounds' ears.
Black leather hangs open on a lean, tall torso.
Furthering the aplomb, he's smiling, one hand hitched
at hip, the other on a steel door. He's emerging,
twenty-one, on a train, done with boarding school bullies.
He believed them: *ugly git.*
It was 1971 and doctors had fixed collapsed lungs to his ribs
with a kind of glue—he could do as he pleased.
And he looks pleased, unguarded, his eyes tunnel-
dark with theatre, art, lovers rolling in.

Meredith Davies Hadaway

Aubade

The slit of light around a door.
Door between my bed and cups of coffee.

My hand cups the glow of your warm shoulder.
The warm that folds our bodies into one.

One body, expelled in every breath.
A breath so light, I pause to hear it scuffle.

Light that slips around the edges.
Edges, gleaming, razor sharp.

Meredith Davies Hadaway

Mångata

[Swedish]: the trail moonlight makes in water

Last night, awake beside
my dying cat, the window glowed
so bright I thought I left a lamp on.

The moon, of course, that full
again—November. My cat sways
on spindle legs. I will outlive her.

But not the moon. It will slide
past the place where this house used to
sleep when all is one day water.

Meredith Davies Hadaway

Soundings

When the old man lay dying,
     his family put in his hearing aids

so he could listen to the last sounds:
     his wife whispering, the slow waltz

of his breath, rain rearranging the roof.
     What we heard—above the roar

of the world rushing on—was his
     laughter. Three sharp bursts. There

was no mistaking it. Then a stuttering
     silence where his voice used to be.

John Haugh

Prosperity Gospel Reunion

He takes his John Deere out at full dark, around nine,
as his beautiful willow-daughter of sixteen returns
with her great-haired boyfriend,
home after their church fish-fry date.

Our softball champion cousin, fresh in from Minnesota, pitches
a board game with gusto she could better apply
to late-night, coed beer pong.
She herds four middle schoolers to table. They forget to bicker

for forty minutes, laughing. My top cop sister begins to let go
of all her mayoral political bullshit. Mom grins, content.
For one of two days we share
each year, it works. We work, except

each of us glance, from time to time,
out murky windows as his tractor's lights
dance away in the far fields.

James Croal Jackson

Cocaine

I am too scared to snort
so I lick powder off the blade—
it numbs my mouth. I want to
trust you when you say
there will come no harm
my way but I'd rather ingest
rust. My lungs already cold
in gentle snowfall. And
I worry about the heart.
Why does it feel like
impending illness
when all I want to
do is snort-laugh
with you all through
the night?

Sharon Kennedy-Nolle

Glimpse

Nightly I stumble off
the back steps, hands out, several trips
refilling the bird feeder, more suet too
dumping dinner leftovers for the possum, raccoon, or whatever hungry
cuts through the yard because I can't stand waste
and I have to save something.
Pass by whatever moonlight
silvers the winter through still buds
of the leaf-crimped rhododendron.
But always, I look up
to your darkened windows,
third-floor gable, cold, black, blank.
One curtain hanging, half off the ring
still twisted tightly like paper fire starter.

The worst ghost
is the one that never comes.

Sharon Kennedy-Nolle

Not the Wild Horses or Bulls

but the Camargue flamingos
come back to the salt flats.
The wild slim hyacinths
on the other side of the dyke
in the quiet krill tang
and riffle against the Atlantic roar.
Plovers, cormorants, and gulls building.
It's spring, everything's coming back
—insultingly—
but you.
With mournful gawk
they take mated flight,
the underside of their wings
where the pink burns.
Weep at every watery edge
where under the unrippled clarity
the brown sueded bed of last fall's leaves still lie.
Try to disturb
your drowned reflection,
amid all this useless beauty.

Mary Kipps

The Summer Boy

Left behind on this autumn shore,
a plastic pail, its dollar-store sheen
bleached by the sun,
anchored at the high tide line
by the damp sand inside.

Each afternoon
this is where she stops,
tries to decide
whether he was worth it.
Every day, a different answer.

Lisa Low

Lonely Woman in the Doctor's Office Waiting Room

Tissues, pencils, and a bottle of Purell
provide the pretense of courtesy while
really replacing unwanted conversation.
Through the pulled glass, I hear their
mumbled talk: shopping a favorite topic;
daughters growing old; a son that works
at a funeral home; illnesses; recipes;
other matters of no great import, essential
to daily life. The television on the wall
jabbers, a warm milk bottle held up to the
mind. The doctor's office door is closed,
filled at the bottom with a mysterious
crack of underworld light. Like a high
holy priest, he works within, reading
entrails on the wall; prescribing medicines
to frightened beneficiaries. "I have to
have surgery," a friendly man announces,
pushed out in his wheelchair by a
benevolent younger brother. "But
it'll be a walk in the park compared to
my melanoma!" I stare at his foot,
sticking from the wheelchair footrest,
wrapped in a sock the color of a bathtub
duck. I am single, lonely, and old, no
longer pretty, and that foot looks like
something I would like to hold. I ask
after its health politely, but he takes
a better look at me, and turns away;
shuts down the warm and friendly.

Lisa Low

One Night Stand

After the band rolled away its guitars
and spread out into evening, we staggered
upstairs, dropping to our knees at the foot
of your rented bed, free to kiss, as if
forever, in the private dark, of a motel
room in Portland, Maine. When I came,
my cheek pressed against the sheets, my
head, heading north, I cried out in pleasure
until even the stars relaxed, and the moon
drove its horns into sky. Afterward,
running my fingers down the slick skin
of your Navy man's belly, I headed
into morning, as sleepy as a flower in
a painted wooden shoe. How different
things are in the morning light! You
turned away; fastened your belt's tin
buckle. To you our lovemaking was
ho-hum; it was an experience had, easy
to be had again. A penny flicked from
an indifferent thumb; a feather blown
onto a passing cap. But to me it was
magical and rare: a beanstalk climbing
into heaven; a mysterious stone rolled
from a desert grave away; a stained
glass window held up to the light, God
himself pouring through. You left with a
skip, my taste on your tongue. I wanted
you back. I wanted it starting all over
again. I wanted our bodies wrapped in a
dark: sweeter than yesterday or tomorrow.

Katharyn Howd Machan

Myrtle Casler: Redwing, 1888

And what if he sails the sea and chooses
Redwing? Finds me in my bedroom door
where Moon Street curves at dusk? Oh,
I'm a woman who could use his touch.
Fingers of filth where autumn bleeds.
My life gray as a rat.

I've never smelled or tasted gin.
I've never satisfied a panting man.
But I imagine wolves at night,
black tongues thick to bruise my throat
and leave me purple, throbbing. Who
says I shouldn't die?

And if he comes by ship and train,
his secret sack of knives smeared brown with blood.
Whispering my name out loud
the way newspapers guess, dark voice,
of sweat and smoke and fog: *Sweet whore,
it's Jack, come just for you.*

Thomas Mampalam

Intensive Care (beds 1—7)

1.

We both watch the irregular
pink drops fill the drip chamber
from the burr hole catheter.

Her son slept on a cot
by the curtained window.
What matters most remains.

Water and blood mix
pink as an unstated apology,
denying time like a broken clock.

I peel back her swollen eyelids
to swing light across twin discs
that constrict with tenuous hope.

A double lunacy enjoins for
battle on a scarlet planet:
a sullen pantomime without end.

2.

On the scan, the hemorrhage
looks like a fluffy cumulous cloud
floating in her left temporal lobe.

Memory no longer speaks.
A hospital is not a home.
A pen is not a scalpel.

Clocks cannot have arbitrary
numbers. No ifs, ands, or buts.
The circle must be closed.

A fluttering breeze could
open a book randomly
to the crucial page.

Philosophy has declined.
Physics has ascended.
Language is a distant star.

3.

A pontine hemorrhage
locks him in. The ventilator
keeps him alive.

The family deliberates
compassionate extubation.
They cannot decide.

In suspended time,
the airplanes are grounded.
Many people wear face masks.

No one moves.
Migrants clog all bridges
that leave the island city.

Outside, an orange haze lingers.
A serial arsonist is suspected.
We wait for terminal liberation.

4.

His right side is flaccid from
a middle cerebral artery infarction.
Without words, where is the thinker?

There is nothing more to do.
This is getting us nowhere,
next in an infinite series.

Prime numbers are infinite.
Primes can be easily multiplied
but the reverse is impossible.

There is so little time left
before we must be at the gate.
The whole trip may be cancelled.

A postman walks to the door
with a self-addressed envelope.
No one is home indefinitely.

5.

A turbaned bandage
after surgery for evacuation
of a subdural hematoma.

In the instant after the accident,
he recalled a young man and woman
who walked side by side.

A seaside promenade
stretched out before them.
Salty air and spices mixed.

Fishing boats undulated
in showers of sparks
over the darkened ocean.

A new continent beckoned.
At the harbor, a great ship waited.
The possibilities were endless.

6.

Sepsis after routine spine surgery.
She expected to go home today
but the streets remain congested.

Smoke accumulated rapidly
across previously clear roads.
Another antibiotic is considered.

As should the arrow of time
and whether the universe
is a sphere or a torus.

The pace of tragedy accelerates.
When we reach our final stop,
no one will expect us.

She prepares to fall sleep
with a book that ends obscurely,
open face down on the bed.

7.

The bed is empty now
like a frame without a picture.
All the lines are neatly orthogonal.

All lines of perspective converge
to a single point on the horizon.
With distance, figures become smaller.

An echo of an inhuman voice
follows a game badly lost.
Another contestant will arrive soon.

Objects in the foreground
have warmer and darker tones.
With distance, figures turn blue.

Dreaming could be the most
meaningful cerebral activity
even if nothing is remembered.

DS Maolalai

Flowers and fruit

after dinner he kissed her
and they tried to make love
but were too full. shouldn't
have ordered pasta,
but it had been an italian restaurant—nothing
they could have eaten
leaving them in any position
to move. and there was laundry on the bed
which needed folding.
and the dog had to be fed
and then taken out to piss. and he stood outside
holding the leash
and feeling the rain on his face. so many obstacles.
later they watched tv.
he had beer—she, some whiskey.
and they said they'd do it later,
but that wasn't romantic, so they didn't.
there was a documentary
about flowers and fruit;
how the bees
which pollinate them
are dying.

DS Maolalai

The receipt

like sharing a bed
with a meat-platter
snoring. fantastic—I love
each crease
your body makes. don't know
how anyone
could not want
to stay awake next to you—how anyone
could not want
your belly to slap
on their belly
and to boil you with handfuls
of salt. you sleep
and turn over
and fold—your body. you've put on weight
and so have I. it's natural;
we're comfortable—you all over,
keeping your shape,
and me
just in the guts
like potatoes. I see you
like an old
receipt in my wallet. I carry
your lines
and your folds.

Charlene Stegman Moskal

Nightgowns

Even after he was gone,
the inevitable was a foreign language.

She continued to wear silk nightgowns,
fine lace at the décolleté

that waited till the end of day
to be filled
with remembered   nights

when she would lay next to him
all of him   still intact

with arms that could wrap around
and   two legs

that would slide between hers
and   disturb the sheets.

Now she doesn't move until morning;
the blankets tucked in   tight

Only a shadow says
she has slept   there.

Suzanne O'Connell

The Tale of Four Boys

I said "No, wait," but he did it anyway.
The first boy to lift my skirt found midnight,
dark as bruises on the sky,
no moon, no birds, no hint of sunrise.

The second boy to lift my skirt
found pyramids invincible and roughly hewn,
built stone upon stone at night
by many, many hands.

The third boy to lift my skirt
found a piece of paper tacked to the wall.
The note read: "Night's darkness
is practice for the final resting place."

I lifted my skirt for the fourth boy.
The swift movement generated light.
There were stars, true and wet.
I took scissors, cut a strip of night,
frayed at the edges,
to begin a scrapbook of us,
the pasting together of two lives.

Kenneth Pobo

Anniversary

Years stack up, bubble-glass plates
about to tip over

or orchids blooming
when winter carries an axe to the house.

Kenneth Pobo

Two Figures Fleeing or Adam and Eve

—Charcoal drawing by Odilon Redon

Alone I feed time bits of lettuce.
I don't like lettuce, even perfect lettuce.
Time eats right out of my hand.

The other one, he's perfect too,
sleeps a few miles away under a red azalea.
He tells it to bloom and it does. It will
stay open forever. A turtle revealed
that on another plane of reality
something called seasons exists.
Plants die, come back, it gets cold.
I don't understand any of this. I'll ask God
someday, but for now I have lettuce,
I have time.

A snake walks up to me. I like this
smart philosopher, rub his questions
all over me, eat of the forbidden tree.
I see that I am naked. That's new.
So is vulnerability.

I bring the other one the fruit. He eats it.
He's naked too. God yells.
The garden was a dream, right?
We move into the unknown. It's fall,
it must be, I'll call it fall. Withered leaves,
red and brown, it must be fall.

David Salner

The Hanging of Ben Harden, June 18, 1868

We left the hills and the river valley
and followed the road into the mountains
where the air got thin and cold though it
was June. In a field outside of Tazewell,
a crowd was gathered in their Sunday best.
Men lifted little boys on their shoulders
like there was a ballgame or a revelation
to be witnessed. "They must have heard
we were coming," I said to my friend,
"the whole town turned out to greet us."
Then I noticed the stepladder by a tree.
"Or lynch us." But it was Ben Harden,
the outlaw, they meant to hang. He leaned
on the ladder and smoked a cigar, like
he was just killing time while waiting
for another man's hanging. He sang out,
in a voice like an auctioneer, the names
of the men he'd killed in Kentucky—
including Lucas, his older brother—before
he came to Tazewell and killed a man
for a horse. He bragged that he'd shot them all
in the back—"More merciful that way"—
and he'd do it again. Then beg for mercy
and plead with the boys in the crowd,
"Don't end up like me at the end of a rope."
Then clap his hands, change his manner again,
a whirlwind blowing this way and that.
Later, I heard how a teamster drove Ben
from jail to the hanging tree. He laughed
at the worried teamster. "No need to whip'em, son.
The show won't start till I get there."
Even when they fixed the black cap
so it covered his eyes, he never shut up.
He went up the ladder, jabbering at every step
until the sheriff hollered—"Kick!"—to his men,
and Ben crashed in the grass, because
the rope not his neck had snapped.

I'd say someone cut it part way through
to worry the poor hung man, who moaned,
"Get me a doctor, my knees are broke."
His mood had turned, and no wonder,
from falling six feet in the dark of that cap
and expecting the rope to lift him
into the dark of another world. And that fast
I knew it was me in the dark of the cap.

As the courier set off for the hardware store
to bring back a stronger rope, Ben roared,
"It ain't fair, to hang a man twice!"
This time, two men had to poke him with knives,
drawing blood every step of the way
as he backed up the ladder to his perch.
The night came on with a chill,
which Ben must've felt to his very bones.
He was quiet now. He turned his head
this way and that, looking for mercy
somewhere in the dark of the cap. "Kick it!"
The sheriff boomed out, and the new rope
stretched with Ben's weight, till it held
with a crack in the mountain air...

The last thing I remember of poor Ben Harden—
he wore nice boots. They kicked for a minute
like he could recover his footing and climb
the thin air, one quick little step at a time.

Philip Terman

Of Longing and Chutzpah

1. My Mother's Poems

You look sexy tonight, my husband said.

My mother reads from the poem she wrote
about the night of my conception—
open mic night, Bridge Coffee House.

After my introduction,
she half-runs to the stage and stands
tiptoe up to the too-tall microphone

and proclaims:
my son said I could read three poems,
but I'm going to read five—

to thunderous applause.
Homespun as they were,
she'd recite her poems anywhere,

to anyone,
at weddings and bar mitzvahs—
she was the one who stood up

in the middle of the meal
and read her rhymed verses—
filled with wisdom and good humor—

and it was me she'd call
in the middle of the night
and read them and wonder where

can she get them published?—
tales of her father selling apples
behind his one-eyed horse

through the Depression streets
of Jewish Cleveland,
of her mother getting a ticket

not for driving too fast
but for driving too slow.
I'd watch her type all day

at that long desk in the den,
pages she'd gather neatly
into thick bundles, punch three holes

in their left margins and clasp them
inside a cardboard folder,
design a drawing for the cover,

seal the collection with a title
and store it in the bottom drawer
with the others—

I hear her voice now—
head lowered, eyes squeezed shut—-
proclaim that poem

that embarrasses me back
to my beginnings, her loving become my life,
her sweet pleasure become our poetry.

2. The Shopping Carts

My mother collected them,
pushing her purchases—
ice cream and pretzels, chocolate—
the seven blocks from Giant Eagle to her garage.

She parked them one inside the other
the way they rest at the store as if,
like the good hostess she always was,
she wanted them to feel at home.

If the store manager knew,
he didn't call the police.
Like old horses they kept their place,
as if they enjoyed their new residence,

no longer having to be loaded up
and bullied around the aisles

only to be abandoned at the checkout line.
Until discovered by the son,

always on the lookout
for sugar packets stashed in Styrofoam containers,
mail piled high on all available surfaces,
smell of mold and mildew and unwashed flesh—

the ever-watchful son,
who wheeled them back to the store
by a circuitous route
in the middle of the night.

3. All Our Years of Mother and Son

No matter how large the print,
my mother still can't read Leaves of Grass,

though there it is, beneath her pillow,
in the Alzheimer's Unit, where she sits on the purple blanket
eyes transfixed on the floor: suddenly,

snapping out of whatever solution eluded her,
she stares me full in the face, parts her mouth,
shapes her lips into a semblance of a word,
struggling—what I understand
from all our years of mother and son—

the way her skin flushes with desire,
her eyes widen with wanting—
the child hidden just beneath the adult surface—craving,
as she often did, for beauty over truth—

to assert her determination to escape, pleading,

by all we have between us,
that I must grant this request:

to take her shivering hand in my hand
and lead her back to that world
she brought me into—

all this, and then darkness,
a slight shadow crossing her eyes,

glazed over, knowing somehow—who knows how?—
that she lost again,

now flaying her arms, a wounded bird,
flaying them up and down,
her chest rising, falling,
that alive thing rampant inside her flesh's cage,
that person she was,

that person of longing and chutzpah.

4. The Exchange

Mother, I allowed you to live alone in your decline.
I agreed to place you in what was not your home,
nursed by others who did not love you
so that I could live my life without the burden you bore for me
when I, too, was helpless.
When I, too, could not dress myself, you dressed me.
When I, too, could not feed myself, you fed me.
When I, too, could not clean up after myself, you washed me.
When I, too, could not walk by myself, you held me up.
When I, too, screamed, you sang me to sleep.
And so we exchanged our lives for our lives
and what you did for me I should have done for you.
And now, alone in my house, as you were alone in your house,
Calling for you, as you called for me, and sometimes I would answer.

Coda: *put the book aside in the middle of the poem*

the one that speaks of laurels
moist grass

let your bed remain
unmade the blankets
tossed about as
during love

your face as it is

leave your clothes loose
around your body
however wrinkled

and slide
into those Chinese slippers
that move like leaves
across the carpet

don't bother turning
a light on
or locking your door

simply allow it to creak
in the recent wind
and steal yourself

down the road
that leads out of town

past the dim lights
yellowing empty spaces
behind storefront windows

the last stop sign
the abandoned temple

until all that remains
are pinpricks of light
filtering through the black
yarmulke of sky

look into these   look into these
until you discover
again those words
of the blessing you spoke
each night before bed

for the small breath
of your mother's lips
against your cheek

John Tustin

One of Those Houses

it is one of those houses that looks like
it's made of balsa wood
and it sits atop a hill of crabgrass and caked dung.
the wind is always rattling it
and the criss-crosses of wood in the windows
need paint.
there is a clothesline
and the clothesline is never naked.
the house is light blue
but any photograph of it looks sepia.

a tornado could take it.
so could a three-day rain,
so could many things,
but it still squats in the dirt,
smiling wanly like crooked teeth
in an ugly face.
something will get it.
weather, age, an individual anger
or a collective neglect,
termites,
maybe all of these things.

it is one of those houses
that hold the lifeless or the useless,
the larcenous and the already
forgotten.
the house is light blue
but any photograph of it looks sepia.
nobody important
has ever lived there.

Will Walker

First Light

I bless my past; it got me here.
I stand in a circle of light:

each day a changing ritual,
each night a benediction.

Did some god get me here
or did I do this on my own?

You need a past, to shed
like a cocoon.

To let you walk the streets
naked, to drink each moment

from the morning's newfound spring.
I'm singing an old song

for the first time.
I've known it all along.

Will Walker

This Evening's Prayer

Really, Lord, all I ask—
could you arrange this,
are you an interventionist?—

is five minutes with Jesus,
maybe less, time enough
to say *Dude, fist bump!*

and trade a righteous hug
the way the bikers like to do
on the TV shows, before

they saddle up to settle the score,
crack a few skulls,
and generally kick some ass—

and He could say something
generic and all-purpose,
maybe pseudo-biblical

but preferably in English, please, Lord,
I don't do Aramaic—God, I wish—
maybe *I am with you always,*

righteous, simple, general, but still
special, something to hold me
through the string of long nights

when I lie like a turnip
among a bushel of fellow
root vegetables, dirt behind my ears,

thinking about waiting for the light
with all the other souls
to cross the street and get to

the other side—you know, Lord,
the place of milk and honey,
the Promised Land.

Then I could smile
and say to myself *Jesus loves me*
and roll over and sleep like a baby

and love the squatters in my brain,
the ragged multitudes
with nowhere else to go.

Bless them all, I'd say, my mind
is an abandoned factory
and they have no other place to stay,

so this is home until sunrise
or the Rapture, if it should
break before dawn.

Fiction

*Photography
by CB Adams*

Evan Balkan

Blank Slate

Michelle Truitt's lips tasted like cheap beer. And they were ridiculously soft. Heaven.

But the softness disappeared, replaced by the hard smash of tooth on tooth. Blood—mine—mingled with the taste of Michelle's mouth. And that taste, in the moment before the fist registered, was the culmination of my entire seventeen and a half years of life. Girl, blood, beer: all the elements required to deliver a boy to manhood.

But then a regression: suddenly I was sliding down a hill in my fuzzy costume dodging a flurry of knuckles and boots. Benny's head tumbled after me, its bucktooth leer flashing as it rolled. As the proud mascot of the Fighting Beavers of Brookdale High, Benny had a look that was supposed to project fierceness. But it was really more like the vacant smile of the criminally insane.

When Benny's head came to a stop near my own, I slid it on for protection. I knew what it must have looked like, there on the edge of the lawn, this poor beaver getting the holy hell beaten out of him, all the while grinning and bearing it—enjoying it even, from the looks of that maniacal smile. Someone happening on this scene would have probably assumed some sort of fetish. I shielded myself best I could, praying for a quick and merciful end. Through the eye slits I saw celestial bodies burning away in the night sky. Maybe it was just my own brain shooting neurons in response to each blow.

Either way, this wasn't how I'd imagined the evening going.

•••

Video games in the basement again, deep in the scent of mold and funk that my parents had given up trying to rectify years earlier—around the same time my father had given up on pretty much everything: his wife, his son, his dreams of happiness on the open road. As a result, gutters hung precariously for months at a time; roof tiles littered the front lawn, half hidden in unkempt grass; the wood pile had turned into little more than shells of cored sawdust and papery snakeskin.

I played *Berserk and the Band of the Hawk,* a game that even to my male teenage brain veered into gratuitous violence. The old Dad would have yelled at me to "stop playing that shit." But these days he just mumbled and sighed.

It was my mom who pulled the controller from my hand and ordered me out of the house.

"You've graduated. It's officially summer now. Surely there's some place you can be...go do drugs, go impregnate someone. For God's sake, do *something*!" Her eyes rested on a days-old yogurt cup with a wadded tissue in it. "Get out of this stinking, disgusting room. Go!"

I'd already considered it. My imbecile friend Randy had called three times, imploring me to get off my ass, that he and our friend Doug were headed to Michelle Truitt's party. I could picture the pantomime Randy was going through as he told me this, making rounded mountains of his chest, sign language for Michelle's breasts, legends since the 6th grade. I wasn't immune from lustfulness myself, of course, but Randy's overheated, eye-popping idiocy kept me rooted to the couch in the basement instead of in the back of his car while he and Doug blasted Body Count, a band that did nothing for me apart from make my eardrums bleed. When I thought about the way he—and every other guy in my class—reduced the entirety of Michelle Truitt to her chest, it made me, well...*sad*. But try articulating that to hormonal teenagers; there may be no better formula for getting your ass kicked.

After her mom died when we were in the 7th grade, Michelle turned into some kind of new specimen, a beautiful and rare creature in a cage or aquarium that we could gaze upon but could not touch. When it was eventually gleaned, many weeks later, that in fact Michelle's mother hadn't died but rather had left her family for a truck driver and moved to Nebraska or Kansas or somewhere, Michelle lost all her female friends. They'd collectively decided that she had betrayed them with her dishonesty and prevented their natural rights to console her. She then became one of those girls who had only boy friends, and then boyfriends, a steady parade of them (which made the girls in their jealousy hate her all the more). All that time, I longed to be one of those boyfriends, through every phase Michelle entered and then left: when she started riding motorcycles and played the electric guitar, when she cultivated the Catholic private schoolgirl look, when she shaved the left side of her head and dyed the remaining flop purple.

But before all of this, in the immediate aftermath of Mrs. Truitt's "death," it was me who found Michelle alone and crying in the bottom of a school stairwell. She was crouched in the corner, head in hands against the wall, a mop, bucket, and two barrels of that green powder they throw on top of puke crammed into a corner. I was on my way to the bathroom when I heard the whimpering and stepped closer to check it out. I watched her, mesmerized.

When she realized I was there, she scowled and snapped, "The fuck you looking at?" and sped away.

There are few opportunities in the 7th grade to actually *see* a person, to strip away the external defenses and glimpse a soul. And so bearing witness to that sadness and to that fury—both, within mere moments of each other, well, there is no other way to say it: I was in love.

Now it was five years later and we'd just completed high school, everyone gleefully partaking in the ritual of tossing every shred of paper—every test, every essay, every quiz, every spare doodle—into the air as we ran like mad for the exits, fresh off the final countdown. It's only now, looking back, that I see the cruelty in this, the way that even the teachers smiled indulgently at this ritual while it would be left to the school custodian, an ancient black man named Mr. Harrison, who went by "Ace" and perpetually sucked a tooth-pick, to clean everything up.

The graduation ceremony had been called off because of a bomb threat. So far no makeup plans had been announced and everyone more or less gave up on it ever happening. "Well, at least we went out with a whimper and not a bang" was the running joke.

But Michelle Truitt was having a major blowout. Truth is, I had planned on going, until Randy started calling. "Truitt, dude. Mi-chellllle Truitt," he repeated and I was certain he was sculpting again, so I hung up on him.

But now my mother was threatening to throw away the video games unless I left. This was serious.

•••

The one other time Michelle Truitt actually talked to me, apart from the stairwell, was to tell me how adorable I was. Well, not me, really. But me as Benny the Beaver. Being the mascot put me in a unique social position in the school: not on any actual team, but part of every team. And, accordingly, never actually invited to any team parties, and yet free to attend all of them. I initially took full advantage of this, until I realized that the expectations of me more or less remained the same at parties as they did at sporting events: entertainment, edging along the periphery—part of, but separate; inside, but out, a ratio that grew in direct proportion to the violence of the sport. I could pretty much hang out with the basketball players and be myself. Soccer not as much. Go to a football party and I risked being made to walk a straight line while guys chucked beer cans at me, expected to turn on my heels with each connected shot like those ducks people shoot at carnivals.

Anyway, Michelle: I was headed toward the sidelines after one particularly atrocious outing in which our football squad was annihilated 49-0. No one else was around, most of the crowd, tiny as it was, having dispersed by the third quarter. The teams were already in the locker rooms. I had spent the previous ten minutes desperately searching for a contact lens that somehow got dislodged and was either in a tangle of faux fur or ground to nothing under a cleat. I was walking with one hand over the contact-less eye when Michelle jumped in front of me from under the bleachers. Her eyes were bloodshot and glassy.

"Ohmigod!" she squealed. "I never knew that was you in there. You got some serious moves!"

"Yeah, well, one of those 'moves' knocked out a contact lens. I need to get the other one out."

"Oh, you poor baby. Here." She took a compact out of her purse and held it up for me. Her proximity was thrilling, and through my t-shirt, my fur, her shirt, and her thin sweater, I could feel the contours of her right breast against my arm. I felt myself burning at that touch.

"You are just adorable," Michelle said. "Look at you."

I ran a hand through my sweat-drenched hair. "It's a thousand degrees inside this thing."

She rubbed a bit of fabric between her fingers. "What is this, velvet?" She laughed uproariously, doubling over and crossing her legs in a way that made it seem like she might pee her pants.

"Aardvark, I think."

She laughed again. Then she heaved a big sigh and said, "Man, I wish I had some way of hiding away from the world. In plain sight, but hidden, you know?"

"Sure," I mumbled.

While I held her mirror, she sat on the ground and plucked blades of grass from the earth, a gesture that made her seem like a little kid.

I scooped out the contact and flicked it.

She got up. "Well, see ya," she said.

I watched her walk away, wanting to say something. But, blurry and out of sorts, I said nothing.

•••

Benny was mine to keep. The following school year, Brookdale High would become the home of the Bobcats. The change was mandated when the administration came to understand that the overwrought pep rally enthusiasm shown by the Brookdale boys was born entirely from the sexual connotation of the old mascot. The official reason was that bobcats projected more fierceness than beavers, but everyone understood what was up.

Benny's suit stayed hung in my bedroom closet, the feet crumpled onto the ground near my shoes. The head sat on a shelf at the top of the closet. At that angle, the downcast eyes made Benny look baked out of his skull. But the teeth were menacing, as if at any moment they might leap out of the mouth of their own accord and sink into my skull. It was only at eye level did the smile morph into the crazed goofiness for which it was known. I slipped into the bodysuit and tucked the head under my arm.

"Later," I yelled and made for the front door.

"You're going in that?" my mother asked.

"Graduation party, so...you know," I said.

"Jesus Christ," my dad mumbled.

•••

"Aaaaaaaahhhh!"

This is what I heard when I walked into the backyard of Michelle Truitt's house.

It was her, squealing with delight. "Ohmigod, ohmigod, ohmigod, come here," she yelled.

Her voice had the slurred edges of drunkenness about it.

"Oh, this is too awesome!" Her bloodshot eyes took me in. Then she threw her arms around my—Benny's—neck and squeezed, mashing herself against me. Suddenly, she ripped the head from my own.

"For a second, I thought maybe it wasn't you. I would have been so embarrassed."

"It's me."

She screamed and hugged me again, only this time it was me and not Benny, who sat on the ground at our feet, dumped there by this beautiful, wonderful, wacky person who was squeezing my neck so hard I actually felt something pop.

I squirmed.

"Oh, no you don't," Michelle said and squeezed again, only this time I felt her lips on my neck and then the tip of her tongue in my ear.

A prickly heat spread through my chest and neck and I jammed my lips onto hers, lucid enough to understand that what awaited me would most likely be a slap in the face. What I got instead was her lips in return, and that cheap beer. And then the fist.

It was Derek. Big, stupid Derek Solarno, nineteen years old, still a junior, had been shaving since third grade. He was Michelle's on again/off again boyfriend and, not un-reasonably I suppose, didn't take too kindly to the sight of his erstwhile girlfriend sucking face on the lawn with a half-man/half-beaver in front of a hundred or so drunken teenagers.

The fist landed square on my jaw. It must have gotten Michelle, too; I heard her say, "Ow! you PRICK!" before another punch landed and I was tumbling downhill. Derek must have kicked Benny's head because soon it was rolling after me.

Derek came running down the hill, followed by a bunch of people—minions, I assumed, and curious onlookers. I threw on the head for protection and curled into a defensive position, but the cheap thin fur only provided so much. But despite its flimsiness, it felt like a cocoon, a deep pocket of something warm and moist and animal. It was a sticky night and the inside of the head instantly turned into runnels of sweat and condensation and blood. It was nasty in there. But it was like that movie, that one where this guy cuts open a rotting beast carcass—a muskox or something—and after shoveling out the blue innards, slips inside to hide from marauders.

"All right, you idiots, enough!" I heard. This was followed by shuffling feet. Then I was being lifted off the ground.

"Hey in there," it said. "Show yourself before I tie you to a spit and roast you for dinner."

Michelle uttered a mortified, "Daaaaaaaaaad!"

Mr. Truitt pulled off Benny's head and turned it in several directions, appraising it like a treasure hunter. When the stars fled the edges of my vision, I took in Benny's rough condition: one tooth torn off, right cheek sunken in, left ear smashed to nothingness—I suspect I hardly looked much better, as if the both of us had suffered a botched two-for-the-price-of-one plastic surgery.

"All of you, out. Now!" Mr. Truitt growled.

Everyone complied with sullen adolescent mumbling.

"You—inside!" he ordered Michelle.

He threw his arm around my shoulder and then simply shook his head and smiled. "Come on, son. Let's get you cleaned up."

Mr. Truitt tossed the head onto the kitchen table, where Benny stared at me—blame and disappointment all over his beaten face. Mr. Truitt ripped several sheets from the paper towel roll and wet them at the sink. "Here," he said, handing them to me.

I swabbed my face, peeling off a few layers of mud and blood while Michelle watched.

Mr. Truitt reached into a cooler someone had left behind and pulled out two icy cans of beer. He opened both and handed me one.

Michelle let out a gasp of exasperation and skulked upstairs.

"You're cleaning this shit up first thing in the morning," Mr. Pruitt yelled after her.

She stomped back to the middle of the steps and pointed a finger at me. "What about him?"

"I don't live here," I said.

I immediately regretted saying it. I still held out some hope that, somehow, now that the house had been emptied of everyone else, I had a shot with Michelle.

Mr. Truitt laughed as Michelle turned on her heels and stomped the final few steps to her room and slammed the door.

You want a girl, get in good with the dad. I'd heard this advice a million times, but I'm not sure that's necessarily true when you're seventeen, and it certainly isn't true when the father and daughter plainly despise one another. In fact, it seemed clear that Michelle's loathing of me was the primary point in my favor as far as Mr. Truitt saw it. That, and the sympathy inherent in getting my ass kicked on his lawn.

"You hungry?" Mr. Truitt asked.

"Sure."

He opened two more cans of beer—he was clearly thrilled at the inherited bounty—and, foam dribbling down the side of the can, handed another one to me while he slurped at his own.

I drank greedily, feeling a serious buzz coming on. The alcohol and the beating were really kicking in. I didn't even care when a steady stream of beer dribbled down my fur.

"You like pancakes?"

"Sure."

"Give me ten minutes."

I headed down to the basement hoping to find a bathroom. There wasn't one, but there was a seriously impressive collection of cigarette lighters. The Camel lighters alone were notable enough: more than a dozen of them in the shape of cigarette boxes, little white and khaki heads peeping out of the opening, all cleverly concealing flints and starters. But there were also Coca-Cola bottles, a Noid, a rubber ducky, a Singer sewing table, a Polaroid camera, a bronzed fist flipping the bird, the Statue of Liberty, the lower half of a naked woman, a dozen various guns, pretzel, shampoo bottle, deck of cards, gunship, airplane, lipstick—it went on forever, shelf after shelf, hundreds of them.

"Pretty cool, huh? My pride and joy."

Mr. Truitt stood behind me, lighting up his own cigarette with, I couldn't help but notice, a cheap plastic neon purple lighter you can find anywhere. "Go ahead, grab one."

I lifted the Statue of Liberty and fingered its dull metal surface, wiping away a coating of dust.

"Cool," I muttered.

"Yeah." He cast his eyes lovingly over the entire collection; these were his babies. "You ain't seen nothing yet. C'mere."

He led me to a closet and undid a padlock to open it up, revealing a dozen or so rifles. "Some of these aren't even legal," he said, plainly savoring that fact. He handed one to me. I'd never held a gun in my life, but I cradled it as if I had vast experience with firearms and whistled my admiration. I was surprised by its heft and surprised also by how good it felt in my hands and how a feeling washed over me that I might like to blow something away.

"Watch it, friend," Mr. Truitt said, gently steering the mouth of the rifle away from his face. "It's not loaded, but you never want to aim a gun at someone's head, got it?"

"Yeah, sorry."

He took the gun from my hands and led me upstairs to the kitchen where a stack of pancakes awaited me. We sat down, me still in my beaver suit, Benny's head at the end of the table, watching us.

I rubbed my eyes: This is where Michelle ate her meals—breakfast in the morning, snacks after school, at night before bed. How many times I had wondered what Michelle was doing at the moment I was thinking about her, on a Saturday night, or Tuesday morning, at a table just like this one, and what it looked like, smelled like, sounded like. Here was my answer. To my amazement, I had gotten so much of it right. I hadn't pictured the precise plastic fruit magnets on the fridge, but something like them. I hadn't stretched my imagination far enough to hear the exact squeak of the cabinets when her dad retrieved a glass or the jangle of useless kitchen implements when her dad slid open a drawer, but I was close. This mundane kitchen, where, edging toward midnight, Mr. Truitt and I sat down to pancakes and beer, was more or less how I imagined it was. But where I had been way off was in the absence of some special glow, some celestial force that followed Michelle Truitt wherever she went. In my sweet imagination, I had always seen her moving from room to room, bed to bath to kitchen to out the front door, cloaked in a sort of glow, a pillow of divine light and energy that delivered her, in all of her beautiful, sexy, sad glory to the same school building where I went. If only I could spend just one day with her, I thought, just one day inside that house of hers, that magical palace, then maybe I would understand what drew me to her in such an intractable, unknowable way. But it was clear it would, at least for now, remain a mystery. The house had an aura to it, for sure, as I'd imagined it had. But it was composed of a thin sheen of cigarette smoke.

"Eat up son," Mr. Truitt said.

I shoveled a forkful of pancakes into my mouth and grunted my appreciation.

Michelle walked into the kitchen. She took in the scene of me and her dad eating pancakes together and glared at us both.

"What are you still doing here?"

"Hey, little lady," Mr. Truitt said, and glanced at me. I figured he would have still been pissed at her for the party, but instead he just smiled. It was a gloating smile as if he and his sullen teenage daughter were instead some old married couple engaged in a long-running war and he had just won the latest battle. She exhaled loudly and marched back upstairs. I had to restrain myself from following her. I wanted to try and salvage something—she had kissed me, after all. I wanted to tell her that none of this was my fault and that I was on her side. I'd been conscripted against my will.

"Don't mind her," he said. "She can be real bitchy when she gets her mind to."

"I really should get going," I said.

"Nah, stay. Hang out. After we eat, we'll head downstairs and watch TV."

"My parents will worry."

"What's your number?"

"Huh?"

"Your phone number. I'll call home for you. Smooth things out."

I gave him the number, relieved that my mom would no doubt insist I get home right away and I'd have no choice but to leave. I shoveled down the last of my pancakes while Mr. Truitt walked into the other room clutching the phone. Not two minutes later, he returned.

"All good. You can sleep here," he said.

"What?"

"Talked to your mom. No problem. I explained everything."

I would be sleeping in the same house as Michelle Truitt, so maybe things weren't dead. But she was upstairs in her room steaming and Mr. Truitt was claiming me for his own and before I could even think to protest or ask how on earth he managed to convince my mother that it was a good idea for me to sleep over in some man's house she had never met, he was whisking me to the basement and turning on the TV.

"So, why were you getting your ass kicked?"

"Michelle kissed me and Derek got pissed, I guess."

"I wouldn't worry about him. Or her. She's got a different boyfriend every week."

I felt something warm and nauseating rising in me, as if Benny was rotting from the inside out, infecting me. But it was something else, too: a sudden, radiating anger.

"You know," I said, drunk now and feeling very far away from myself, "Maybe you should be nicer to her. Maybe a little love from her dad might go a long way and then she'd want to be with one guy and not a different one every week."

I waited for him to punch me or light my fur on fire or take one of his guns and put it against the side of my head. Instead, he sucked on his cigarette and then jammed it into an overflowing ashtray. He downed a few more sips of beer. "Probably shoulda let old Derek pound you into dust," he muttered.

He clapped his hand, hard, on the back of my neck. "You sure know it all, don't you? But trust me on this one—" He opened another can of beer and its fizz-pop echoed through the room. He slurped up the foam. "One day, you'll wake up in a place like this and you'll realize you don't know a damned thing. Not until it's too late to do anything about it."

He handed me another beer and I sipped at it even though I was already feeling a roiling in my gut that portended bad things. His hands, I noticed for the first time, were rough, covered in calluses and stained a black at the edges of his fingers. The blackness was lodged under his nails, which were chipped and shattered and in the case of one finger, split right down the middle.

"I'm gonna help you out here, son. You ever hear of table rasa?" he asked.

"Tabula rasa?"

"*Blank slate.* That's the key, son. That is the key to life. Every morning, every single day, you got to look at it and say, 'Okay, table rasa, blank slate.' New day and all that shit. And then make something of it. You do that, hell, you'll never have regrets." He swept his arm around the room, taking in the lighters and the rifles and the desiccated carcasses of stink bugs and the quarter inch coating of dust. "You think this stuff just showed up here? It takes work." He held his beer can aloft like a scepter. "Table Rasa!" he shouted.

"Shut up!" came a muffled reply, working its way through the heat vents.

I looked up toward the noise, toward Michelle, up there, as if in heaven. Mr. Truitt ignored it and turned on the TV. Having no other option, I settled in to watch. It was a reality show that pitted two families against one another in some kind of insane physical competition. It was pretty stupid and the rules were hard to follow, but that might have just been me. I couldn't concentrate. Michelle was two floors away.

Somewhere along the line I dozed off, and then woke with a start. On the TV, there was a video loop of a swollen river churning brown and muddy with a group of goats overtaken by the flow and swept along, paddling like mad, trying desperately to keep their noses above the water, going under and then popping back up, their eyes wild with panic.

Mr. Truitt was asleep and snoring loudly, his hand still gripping a beer can. I tiptoed to the middle level, and then up several stairs. I strained to hear something, anything, coming from Michelle's bedroom. I stood there a long time, listening, hoping. A creak of bed. A sleepy sigh. Otherwise, nothing.

In the kitchen, I found a notepad and a pencil and started to write my thanks to the both of them for a memorable evening. I planned to prop it against Benny's good ear and leave the head there, my gift to the Truitts. But I wound up leaving the note blank.

It was that moment just before sunrise when one side of the sky hints orange and the other, opposite, still holds the traces of stars. It was summer. High school was over. My future was laid out in front of me in a seemingly endless flow of terrifying opportunity. I was walking home, where my parents were. But they had largely done their job and I would be gone soon enough. To where, I wasn't sure. But I knew I'd be gone—someplace without a basement, far away from swollen rivers.

The heat condensed in the air, placing a stamp on the new day. I was still buzzed and sleep deprived and yet I felt good. I stripped out of my costume and, in sweat-soaked t-shirt and shorts, walked toward home, the costume draped over my forearm. The first stand of bushes I passed, I tossed the remains of Benny into it and kept on.

Workers had placed four orange cones on each edge of a sidewalk segment where it had recently been re-cemented. The tips of the cones caught the day's first light. But it was still inky enough outside that the morning felt like mine alone.

I scrawled my name in the cement with a stick. It had barely hardened at all and the going was easy. I was even able to add a nice little flourish to the last letter and underline the entire thing. Then I tossed the stick aside and moved on.

But I hardly got a hundred feet before I turned around and went back, where I wrote Michelle's name, too, right next to mine.

C. W. Bigelow

Naked as Father at Breakfast

Christmas Eve finally arrived after a full week of near silence between us. A storm blowing in off Lake Michigan dropped a heavy snowfall the day before, leaving wind-sculptured piles rising on the cliff's edge like mounds of marshmallows. The battering wind slammed the house furiously and I kept waiting for him to appear, to check the condition of the windows, make sure we were all right, all the things he always did.

A fire blazed fiercely in the living room, crackling as the flames leaped up the chimney, as Mother and I trimmed the monstrous tree without him, which was a first, all the more odd because he loved the holiday season and was normally the leader of our activities.

After frequent glances up the hallway that led to their room, my anxiety became overwhelming, and with each glance the pressure was too much to handle and I finally just blurted, "Where the hell is he?" Tears clouded my vision and all the pent-up emotion of the week threatened to explode in a storm of vulgarities, which—while he may have been amused—it would not go over well with my mother. I gulped my eggnog in hopes of calming down. Daughter like father I figured.

All week long breakfasts were eaten alone while he went through grueling chemotherapy sessions. Sitting in the eerie silence of the kitchen at dawn my neck became tight and sprained from all the quick glances over my shoulder each time I heard as much as a squeak in hopes Father might be coming to join me. And how selfish and delusional I was, knowing full well his hope was to get the first round of treatments completed so he would make it home for Christmas eve.

Mother excused herself. I assumed to find the missing piece of the puzzle.

I spent each morning recalling the special breakfasts we spent together over the years, reviewing a highlight film in my head.

Having had to miss Thanksgiving break due to play practice at school, I was anxious to sit and talk with him, to go over my lines, bounce off my ideas. Not realizing the extent of his disease, I was in total denial.

I wandered into the kitchen. The succulent aroma of the ham in the oven filled the room—it was a warm memory and I gazed about our favorite meeting place.

My first vivid recollection of him was on a stormy morning. I was four years old. The echo of thundering waves woke me with a start, and the whistling of the wind kept me from falling back to sleep. It was a chalky dawn, and misty clouds at the edge of the cliff masked any view of the lake.

Rarely awake so early, a ray of light seeping under my bedroom door drew me like a magnet. I slipped from the warmth of my bed and padded down the dark hallway toward the light in the kitchen.

Standing at the sink, backside facing me, was my naked father, furiously whipping waffle batter in a large red bowl. Mother was asleep. Staring in silence for a moment, fascinated by his strong, tight buttocks; his long hairy legs spread in a sturdy stance that allowed me a clear view of his scrotum swinging back and forth like a pendulum. Curiosity got the best of me. Creeping up behind him, hypnotized by the swinging appendages, I reached up to touch. Touch is all I did, no grabbing, no slapping, but my timing was precarious for he had just lifted the bowl.

An enormous clap of thunder drowned his startled scream. Shocked, turning to see what had touched him, the bowl slipped, and in a futile attempt to catch it, he tripped over me. We crashed to the floor, the bowl landing on his head. Sprawled out, awkwardly propped against the cupboards, with the red bowl perched like a derby and the batter thickly oozing into his eyes.

Blinking through the batter, he reminded me of a clown I'd recently seen at the circus and I fell into a cascade of giggles. Long legs stretched in front of him like tree trunks, hairy belly heaving; he continued to blink, until my giggling became infectious and he joined in while making farcical faces at me through his cake mask.

Instead of cleaning the mess off his face and the floor, he grabbed more eggs and made us another batch of waffle batter in a white bowl. Our giggles serenaded our breakfast. He wore the bowl on his head throughout the meal.

Mother's mouth twisted as she stared at me with empathy. The whole week she had endorsed his decision to stay away from both of us during the round of chemo. Her hopeless expression conveyed more pain than I had ever witnessed in her face and did nothing but confuse me more.

Father's passion was the stage. His booming words were spoken with the passion of an actor. Echoing through the house, resounding and at times startling; it was a source of comfort and entertainment for us.

When I found out he acted in college, garnering the lead in a few school plays, I asked him why he hadn't pursued a career on the stage. He looked down, avoiding my querying gaze while shuffling his feet. A few moments passed before he finally looked at me with clouded blue eyes. "One makes certain choices during a lifetime. My true love was not necessarily the act of being on stage. It was being behind the scenes. Putting together the production—all the business parts—the scenery, the advertising, making sure the director was correct, the troupe was just right. That is my love."

This was breakfast banter as I grew up. Father naked, I in my robe. Dawn was our only witness because Mother wasn't even aware that time of the day existed.

"Merry Christmas!" Father boomed as he entered the room with the energy of an actor vaulting onto stage. Dressed in a blue blazer, crisp blue shirt and stiffly pressed gray flannels finished off with a bright red Christmas tie, he suddenly was the father of our breakfasts. "The most splendid time of the year." He skipped to the window and peered outside. Eyes gleaming with a smile that stretched his cheeks, he continued, "Snow outside. A blazing fire in here. A damn handsome tree and my wonderful ladies. What more could a man ask?" he cried with exuberance as he poured his glass full of eggnog. "A toast!"

We quickly gathered around him, holding our glasses high as we were transported back in time to Christmas' past. I was covered in goose bumps. All the trepidation washed away, all the questions of his health ignored for the moment as I leapt forward to join him in Christmas cheer. I didn't know I was watching a great performance.

"What made you come to the Midwest?" I asked while munching on blueberry pancakes when I was twelve.

"Simple," he yawned. "Anonymity. It's the Midwest's greatest benefit. My mother moved to Florida to be near other relatives after my father died. I certainly didn't want to stay in town, and the Midwest is a mystery to most easterners."

"Your mother is from the Midwest," he chuckled. "Another attraction of the Midwest. It has been a very convenient and pleasurable partnership. Perfect in so many ways."

"Those are odd adjectives for a marriage," I pointed out.

"You'll learn later in life that most marriages would die for such adjectives."

"But do you love each other?" I continued to press, my idealistic views very dominant at that time in my life.

"Our interests may be quite different, but our love for each other is very deep."

Despite his ardor, I wasn't convinced.

Father chose Michigan for the water. "Imagine my surprise upon standing on our cliff the first time. Growing up in the east I had no idea how large Lake Michigan is. Judging from the map I thought you'd be able to see across it." He purchased twenty-seven acres of wooded land on the cliffs along the lake and promptly cleared three of them for the house, which sat perched like a castle overlooking the surf.

"To performing in the greatest play ever scripted!" he toasted, glass held high.

"Which one?" I asked gleefully.

He gazed over at me with a wink. With a deep breath he sighed, "Life, my dear Gwen. Our life. Scripted and directed by your Mother and me; you in the starring role. Hopefully we have prepared you well for all the all plays to come."

Until I turned ten we viewed filmed performances of stage plays and discussed them, while Mother was off working.

We watched Disney movies on Saturdays. We gorged ourselves on popcorn and Pepsi. In my mind, I became Pollyanna.

After ten years of age, he felt I was ready to view contemporary movies. He was friends with a local movie distributor and paid what he had to so we could view first-run films at home. The critiques and heated discussions didn't stop. Once schoolwork was completed in the afternoon, we would move on to the world of film. Monday was viewing night. Tuesday was spent writing the review. Wednesday was reserved for discussion and reviewing certain controversial parts of the film.

"The human condition hasn't really changed over time. We struggle with the same forces as our ancestors, whether they are external or internal. The only difference is the immediacy of the communication available to us."

I wasn't strictly a video child, for reading was stressed just as much and Thursdays were spent reviewing books. My menu was two classics for every contemporary novel. Our discussions took place in the living room by the fireplace. Mother joined these discussions.

Father ran a theater group in Chicago, an hour and a half drive from home. Much of his time during my school days was spent there. On weekends, I accompanied him to the plays.

It was at the Ogden Theatre that I learned the workings of the stage first hand, the settings, the lighting, the directing, the music, and of course, the roles and the actors who fulfilled those parts.

When I was nine, he produced *A Christmas Carol.* He gave me the part of tiny Tim. My hair was cut short, and we spent hours developing my limp. Much to our delight, the rendition got good reviews, and it became a standard for the group each Christmas season.

At thirteen I was given the part of Juliet. Too young to worry about the challenge and the risk, I attacked it with the aggressiveness and professionalism I had inherited from him. I knocked none of the critics dead with that performance, but acting became my passion.

He smiled when I told him the acting bug had bitten me. "Then never back down from it."

Breakfasts became time for rehearsals of lines I had in school plays. But he also made sure I was fully aware and versed on current events, along with providing help with schoolwork.

"You must always know what is going on, Gwen. Participation is a choice, but knowledge is your duty. And as it stands in today's society you will have to be just as knowledgeable, if not more so, than the men around you.

"Someday that may not be the case, but it still is today. Do it and you will be a pioneer. People like to see doers, not bitchers. Don't let the atmosphere get you down. If you get knocked down, get back up and do it all over again. Tenacity is a wonderful trait. People can be overwhelmed by it, annoyed and angered by it, but you rarely find someone who doesn't respect it."

It took me a long time to ask him about his nakedness. It was so natural and I'd become so accustomed to it that I didn't give it too much thought, but as I grew older, I began to realize how eccentric it was.

"It is a freedom we all have. It's my daily reminder that we can do whatever we choose as long as it doesn't hurt others. It reminds me that each day is a brand new start."

I finally got the nerve to show up naked one morning. April Fool's Day of my junior year in high school. Thankfully, it was a fairly warm day. When he turned from the sink, I expected another crashing of the egg batter, but he didn't flinch. "Good morning. I thought we'd do scrambled today, okay?"

I nodded, finding it hard to contain my disappointment as I sat in my chair. We had been eating for a while when he looked up and studied me a moment. I couldn't help but aim my breasts at him like binoculars, to do my best to shock him.

"Damn, Gwen! Do you know you've got a zit on your nose?"

Mother was driving me back to school for play rehearsal the day after Christmas. Up at dawn I was relieved to find him in the kitchen fixing omelets. Naked, as usual, but his thick, dark hair was thinner. His eye sockets were hollow with heavy circles tugging at them. The rug of hair on his chest was totally gray, the firm muscular buttocks had shrunk and were wrinkled, and the skin on his torso was loose like ill-fitting clothes.

The wind whistled sharply off the lake. He turned and gazed at me with a wide grin.

"You are one hell of a beautiful woman."

I stopped quickly, overacting with my hands cocked in mock surprise. "I think that's the first time you've ever referred to me as a woman."

He smiled as he poured a tomato juice. "It's not the first time I've thought it. The first time might have been when you played Juliet. But, it really didn't sink in until you left for school in September. When I pulled away from your dorm and you stood at the curb waving...." He choked on his words. A tear ran down his sunken cheek.

My nose stung as I fought the tears. "I sure miss you."

He smiled. His eyes were the color of his tomato juice. "We've had some great times."

"The best," I sniffled.

And as we looked into each other's eyes, the reality was revealed. It was there all along, but I kept ignoring it. I walked up to him and gave him a kiss on his cheek.

He stepped back and raised his glass. "Break a leg, my love!"

The afternoon was silent, muffled by lazy snowflakes. The park across from my college dorm was empty, growing whiter as I stood under a favorite oak and tried to lose myself in the scene. January had arrived. Until Mother's call, I'd done my best to concentrate on school and wrapped myself in some misguided hope that by not accepting the truth the inevitable would be delayed indefinitely.

Father never voiced his opinion of rainy days, but from the way he hectically planned detailed activities to pass the time, I got the impression he would rather ignore them than face their gloom.

The gray ceiling of a rainy day on the cliffs above Lake Michigan is as restraining as a netting of chains. The sky reaches down to the murky water, forming a shield that inhibits vision and tends to breed circumspection, which when already depressed because of the weather, rarely leads to a positive place. The crashing waves are so resounding, robust and clattering, their deafening roar can be heard miles inland. On days like that, the elements inundate you, and succumbing to their hypnotic power is impossible to resist.

It was mid-January and there was a break in the winter weather. Instead of snow, it softly rained all morning. Swirls of lush charcoal clouds danced in the tepid breeze above the gray mounds of snow that gathered along the shoreline. How ironic that there was a break in the storm while we gathered on the cliff in the early afternoon. Our lives had changed forever, and it was all I could do to stand straight, face into the offshore breeze and hold back my tears.

There was the Minister of Mother's church and many friends from the theater group. I held the urn of his ashes in trembling hands.

I read from *Troilus and Cressida*. I was twelve years old when we read it together and he told me, "I like this play because some consider it a tragedy and others a comedy, while others even like to group it with Shakespeare's histories. Such confusion deserves a reading on a stormy day."

My life, so well planned, well-rehearsed, was in a state of crisis. Mother took me aside before the ceremony. She smiled and sniffled, wiping her eyes with a handkerchief. "He wanted you to remember him the way he was when he was healthy. The reason you weren't summoned at the end was because he wanted your last moments together to be that last breakfast at home."

She took my hands in hers and gazed into my eyes. The stress of his illness had taken a tremendous toll on her, but she had protected me and let me go along in my denial dream.

I threw his ashes over the cliff. They scattered in the billowy gusts. Gazing into the swirling charcoal palette of thick clouds over the churning waves, my sadness and self-pity began to evaporate. The tears and distress slowly turned into a smile, as images of his face floated in the clouds, and I thought about the amazing training he'd given me and how lucky I was that he had made it a priority, enabling me to complete my loop early on. How he guided, but didn't dictate and let me set my own course while helping me to write my own script. And most of all, how he made sure I wasn't left naked.

Judith Beth Cohen

Yoga Cure

Fifty odd bodies surround me, all of them trying to raise their legs. Lying supine, I lift my own in response to the Swami's instructions: up goes my torso, weight shifts to my shoulders as I assume the All Members Pose. As I struggle to remain aloft for the required five minutes, I watch my legs droop and think of my therapist Dr. Dare, that goateed archetypal patriarch of psyche.

"You need something physical," he'd pronounced, munching on stray chin hairs, "an activity that demands so much of your body that you have no time for intellectualizing."

"Thinkety, thinkety," he would chide, certain that my brain was my worst enemy.

After my break-up with Lance, my fickle lover, I was spending too much time with morbid thoughts and too much sherry. Since Dr. Dare had helped me get over my last broken heart, I'd again enlisted his services.

"You have such trouble ending relationships," he said, "Maybe I should give you some practice by refusing to see you again."

"But I also have trouble with beginnings and middles," I said.

"You have a point," he said. "This time, try body work. The verbal game is too easy for you."

He passed me a color brochure showing a yoga camp in the beautiful Laurentians—it would be a vacation as well as therapy. The saffron robbed Swami even looked a bit like Dr. Dare. The object of yoga, I read, was not to strain yourself, but to float into postures and let the limbs be as fluid as water. Closer to a storm at sea, I think, as I watch my legs slap the air.

"On your backs," booms the Swami. "Raise one leg, breathe in. Oom," he chants. "Now down, raise the other leg, repeat."

The pace quickens and the ooms come faster, making the session feel more like military boot camp than the road to bliss. His orange toga flapping, the drill Sergeant Swami paces the rows of outstretched bodies, shouting commands.

"Straighten that leg. Lift that leg higher. The knee should not be bent."

From my upside-down position, I scrutinize the other campers. The elderly man next to me grunts, trying to lift legs that won't obey him. I wonder how many have died of heart failure here on the orange carpet, but the Swami isn't concerned. Thinking makes me lose my ooms—legs drooping, I wilt.

"Next, the Headstand. Follow directions."

I clasp my hands together, place my forehead against them, raise my derriere, then walk into the pose, waiting for my legs to levitate as my toes approach my forehead, just as the Swami has promised. Fighting for balance, torso swaying, my legs flap helplessly as I spot the orange toga approaching me. The Swami grabs my ankles and yanks as if I'm a weed he's plucking. I feel his knee against my spine and am about to beg for mercy when he lets go and I tumble down. As soon as my dizziness clears, I make a dash for my bunk.

My boring library job doesn't seem so bad from here, though I do spend long days answering questions like: "Is Jordan a country, I thought it was a river?" "What's youth-in-Asia and what does it have to do with medicine?"

Back in my apartment, I stayed, refusing invitations just in case Lance called. I'd tried practicing Dr. Dare's advice: Make demands, be direct, tell him what you want from him. Why make him guess? But my wishes couldn't be reduced to mere words. I longed for intensity, caring—at least, someone who didn't see another woman on alternate weekends.

"You'll never get what you want if you can't make demands," Dr. Dare said, grooming his goatee.

When I went to Lance's sculpture studio and laid out my grievances, he looked up incredulously from the mold he was pouring.

"You're asking me to give up my work," he said. "Why can't you be supportive of my work?"

"I have my work, too," I said.

Lance glared. He knew I'd hardly touched a paint brush since we'd started dating. I was waiting to be laid off at the library so I'd have more time for art.

"You want all or nothing," he gestured, leaving a white plaster streak across his mouth.

"Not all or nothing," I said. "Unless you think monogamy is all or nothing."

Lance looked deeply wounded. "I've never lied to you," he said. "I'm afraid it will have to be nothing. I can't live life on your terms."

"OK." I said, offering a handshake. "Let's agree on nothing."

A week later, I headed for yoga camp, but instead of the pristine mountain setting I'd expected from the brochure, I found paths lined with plastic turtles and china elephants—the sort you find at garden shops that sell pink flamingos and wooden ladies with large behinds. On my way to the office, I passed an open-mouthed frog spewing forth a stream of water, a half-finished paper Mache llama standing at attention, and a wooden shrine, housing a picture of the Swami. Outside the office, I removed my shoes as the sign instructed and then padded barefoot to the saffron-shirted woman smiling behind the counter. She assigned me a room and handed me a sheaf of dittoed chants, prayers, and rules.

"No smoking, no drugs, no non-vegetarian food. Meditation compulsory twice daily. Violators will be asked to leave camp."

Incense infused the air, clinging to my garments until I reeked of patchouli. On wall posters, the grinning Swami sat next to a "peace plane" painted in day-glow colors. In other versions he demonstrated difficult yoga poses, with Sanskrit quotations underlining his attitudes.

"Om Shanti," the girl behind the counter bowed at me.

The loudspeaker boomed: "All campers to the dome," punctuated by the obligatory, "om shanti."

Only one of my sandals remained in the pile where I had left two, but I gave up and went to my bunk. My two roommates, who'd traveled all the way from South Dakota to study with the famed Swami, were already breaking the "no smoking rule."

I answered their probing questions, clearly the junior member of our bunk.

"You sure don't look thirty, does she Rhonda?" Fern, no more than four feet ten, compact and full of pep at fifty, complained about the wake-up hour and the absence of a mirror. Tall, freckled Rhonda appraised the men she'd noticed, while I studied my illustrated yoga book and tried to ignore their conversation. The wall separating our bunk from the next one was as effective as a blanket tossed over a clothesline. I could hear a couple discussing the progress of their fast.

"Fern's got a twenty-five year old son, can you believe it? The men here are already flocking around her. I don't know how you do it, Fern."

"They can't keep away from me, girls. What am I going to do? She doesn't do so bad herself." She gestured toward Rhonda.

"Her boyfriend's an Air Force captain. Rhonda and I met at the ashram where we go once a week."

"I'm working on my headstand," said Rhonda. "I practice at least twenty minutes every day."

"Even if you spend the night with the Captain?" Fern giggled.

"Did you catch a look at the young Swami?" Rhonda asked.

"He's the one with shoulder-length hair wearing a white toga and dark sunglasses. I thought he might be a rock star on vacation, but they say he just arrived here from an ashram in India."

"I'm still trying to get over the old Swami." Fern rolled her eyes. "He's at least fifty pounds heavier than his pictures. Don't you wonder how he manages to get into the Peacock Pose?"

The evening meal, served outdoors on the concrete patio, brings the campers together. No stereotype fits the mixed group: I spot intellectuals, hear third world accents, and listen to secretaries, high school punks, and nursing home candidates discuss their yoga progress. A grey bearded man draped in beads and a Mexican serape dominates the conversation at my table.

"I was in a terrible car crash," he says. "My girlfriend was killed and my body was shattered, but yoga saved my life. I am sixty-eight years old and I am evidence of what yoga can do for you."

He seems to be speaking directly to an attractive blond woman sitting across from him. Like an ethereal spirit, the white-clad young swami, his hair brushing his shoulders, his dark shades covering his eyes, drifts by our table. I pursue him with my eyes while the older man goes on with his lecture.

"You must not, however, believe everything they tell you. One Yogi told me to give up sex. First get it down to once a week, then once a month, then once a year, then nothing."

He looks lustfully at the blond woman. "His trouble was that none of the girls liked him —he was too ugly."

I notice the speaker leaning against the blond at evening meditation. His bare, skinny legs poke from under his knee-length serape, but the next day they're both gone; I guess that romance trumped yoga.

Twice daily, we meditate. Cross-legged on the floor, I face the altar where the Swami sits on a raised dais, draped in orange, a sleeveless white undershirt revealed on his one bare shoulder. His plump, bronze arms reflect the light, his gray hair waves thickly over his ears. I close my eyes and try to still myself, to empty my mind, but perverse curiosity pulls at my lids. I scan the room and engage momentarily with another open-eyed cheater until we look away before our resistance becomes a conspiracy. The Swami's chant breaks the stillness:

"A-shee-rash-a-mon, a-shee-rash-a-mon, a-shee-rash-a-mon, pah-he-mon." He belts it out passionately, his eyes closed, forehead rippling. In response, we campers chant, but I find myself drifting, just as I did at the endless Shabbat services my parents had forced on me until I reached fifteen and the age of confirmation and became a confirmed agnostic. During the rabbi's sermons, I would study the women's hats. When mourners stood to recite the Kaddish prayer for the dead, I would look for the grieving, disappointed if I saw no tears. So, what am I doing here among these spiritual seekers? Though I couldn't disobey my parents at twelve, can't I defy my therapist at thirty?

The Swami's sermon begins: "My Experiences in India before I Became a Yogi."

"I used to have an enormous ego," he says. "When I was told 'you must bow down. The Master is coming', I said, 'me? Bow down?' So I stood, and you know, the Master, he came and bowed down in front of me." His giggle goes off like a siren trapped inside his belly. Instead of amens or hallelujahs, we giggle in response. "After that, I always bowed." More giggles from the crowd. "You must get an EGODECTOMY. Get rid of the ego. It is not an easy thing to do. I have not done it, but you should have seen me before if you think I am bad now."

Slightly hysterical, nervous giggles punctuate his conclusion; I erupt as spasms of giddy laughter form, dissolve and re-emerge. The spells soon grow beyond my control; my maverick sounds explode in the silent room; my hands desperately cover my mouth in a pathetic attempt to muffle my involuntary noises. It's sixth grade all over again as my sneezing, choking giggles disrupt a spelling lesson when Mrs. Sikin enunciates that hilarious word, spit forth in a burst of saliva: "boozom." No wonder I never learned to spell.

Leaning against the wall, the young Swami notices me and smiles but his eyes are inaccessible behind his dark glasses. The next day, he leads the yoga class, talking us through the poses in a melodious voice that massages my supine body. The drill Sergeant has been replaced by a pan-like sylph who sings his instructions. On the deck, under a blue sky, my body turns liquid in response to his poetic coaching. My legs move, glide up easily and stay there longer, light and weightless. Screwing up my features for the Cow Face Pose, I worry that he'll be repulsed when he glances my way. During the Wind Eliminating Pose, I hold my breath against the symphony of odors. Suddenly he stops class for a demonstration. We watch speechlessly as he unwraps his white toga waiting in suspense to see what he'll reveal but under his mysterious drape he wears disappointing red-cross swimming trunks.

From the balcony above us, the rasping voice of the old Swami intrudes: "You are doing it in the wrong order. Follow the order I give."

Unruffled, the disciple leads us through the final relaxation Corpse Pose as if the interruption had never occurred. Sliding into a near trance, my arms and legs are floating. His voice seems to stroke each of my body parts: neck, yes, shoulders, lovely, chest, (bosom), please, then abdomen, buttocks, and finally, pelvis. The energy flows from his words up my spine, and it's as if there's no one there but me and the young, sexy, Swami.

"Carrot juice for sale," the old Swami calls, bringing the class to an end.

Waiting in line for carrot juice, I'm giddy—the woman next to me glows orange in the sunlight. "I've had nothing but carrot juice for a week and I feel marvelous."

I'm tempted to comment on the Swami's profits from what he saves by having campers fast, then pay a dollar fifty a glass for juice, but I refrain, still under the spell of the young yogi.

In the sauna, sweat pours from me, proof that the toxins are being expelled from my system. I force myself to meditate, repeating a mantra, any mantra over and over again.

"The owl and the pussycat went to sea," I chant, as I imagine Lance pursuing me here, bursting into the meditation room, begging me to take him back, promising to change his ways.

"I guess I haven't had an 'egodectomy'," I confess to Fern and Rhonda.

Together we mock the old Swami and praise the young one as our life stories dribble out with our perspiration.

"Your Lance could use a week at Yoga Camp. A strong knee in his backside might be just the thing," Fern says.

"Can't you just see my Captain trying to get into a Shoulder Stand?" Rhonda says.

Laughing so hard I can hardly breathe, I picture Dr. Dare standing on his head in the corner of his office. "Please hold my legs," he asks me, "so I can maintain my pose."

As they dress for dinner that evening, Fern and Rhonda discuss the men. I watch Fern unwrap a bandage-like contraption from her chin that I'd mistaken for a toothache remedy.

"Rhonda, why don't you go off with that nice guy named Charlie." She pats her unbound cheeks.

"I've had enough bad Charlies to last a lifetime," Rhonda says as she steps into the shower.

Off into the evening my roommates go to meet their admirers, leaving me behind. Who am I to question Fern's chin strap? Wandering the paths between the animal statues, I nearly collide with the young Swami. He smiles and nods, slowly, hesitantly. I wait for him to speak but nothing comes. Though he turns away, I feel we've shared a silent joke. As I watch his white form gliding away, I begin to follow him. What will I say? I could ask if his system is free of toxins, if he practices celibacy. I might discover what his dark glasses conceal. He turns and nods as I come up behind him. For a while we walk in silence. Then we speak at once:

"You like yoga, yes?" he asks.

"How long have you been here?" I ask. "It's not what I expected."

"This is no ashram like I have ever seen," he says. "The Swami paid my way so I have no choice but to stay. You want, I help you with asanas?"

The carpeted meditation room is empty; the altar just a plywood block. One small light glows while the young Swami strips to his trunks. I undo my jeans and sit in my tights.

"The Corpse Pose," he instructs. "Relax your legs. Stretch, then release. Relax buttocks. Stretch, release. Now lift one leg."

Gently, he takes hold of my ankle and holds it straight, running his other hand behind my knee to check on my form; I hold my breath.

"Now, the other leg." This time his fingers touch my thigh and linger.

"You need to firm muscle here, yes?"

"Sit up," he says suddenly. Then he moves behind me and runs his hand over my back. As he checks my posture, he fondles each vertebra. "Tight shoulders?" he asks, his hands kneading my neck. I lean against his chest, feeling his groin close as he works my neck muscles loose. It seems to last for hours, and despite the hint, the erotic promise, he never breaks from his teacherly role. When he signals that the lesson has ended by donning his toga, I sit, unable to move. He backs toward the door and bows.

"Namaste. Please excuse," he leaves, his white garment glowing. Fern and Rhonda won't believe this, I grin to myself.

The next evening the old Swami leads us on a Meditation Walk, the highlight of our stay, but the young teacher is conspicuously absent.

"This is to be a silent walk," our guru instructs. "Inhale, take a step. Exhale on the next step."

We move out behind him, following his staff and his flapping orange robe. Some are wrapped in blankets, others have knapsacks strapped to their backs. We might have marched off the pages of a Sunday school Bible: the shepherd and his flock. Beyond the camp we move, inhaling rhythmically, past rows of summer cottages where parents and children point and jeer at us. Ignoring the onlookers, the Swami swings his toga defiantly and turns up a street. We pass a small lighted building where a religious service is taking place. Through the window I can see men wrapped in shawls, wearing skull caps, praying. Inside: the children of Israel; outside: us New Age seekers. For a second, I'm tempted to duck away and join my own people, but it has been so long. Though I fit neither group, I stay with the Swami's minions.

Up another road we troupe as the sound of racing engines closes in on us. A horde of kids on mini-bikes is following us, laughing at our strange pied piper. In and out of our crowd they zoom, parting us, then disappearing into the woods, shouting taunts at the Swami. Enraged, he halts the march and breaks the silence.

"Stop this, you will kill someone," he shouts at the trees.

"These same kids have done this before," he yells, "If they come back, catch them. Don't let them go."

We move forward and the bikers reappear, but not one camper moves toward them. It's as if we have formed a conspiracy to torture the Swami. Conversation and laughter are muffled into the folds of blankets. Darting into the melee, the Swami grabs a child, forces him from his bike and demands the kid's name, but the terrified boy struggles free and flees into the woods on foot. With the Swami dragging the confiscated bike along, we proceed.

"Inhale, exhale," he commands.

The engine noises return and again the frustrated Swami calls: "Catch them, catch them."

Again, no one moves. Just as the march verges on total disintegration, we round a bend, and triumphantly the Swami announces that we've reached our destination.

"Sit yourselves on the ground and face the pond," he says.

Though he has carefully timed the walk to catch the sunset, we can still hear mini-bikes whirring faintly from the woods.

"Focus on this peaceful lake," the Swami instructs, "Form a picture of it in your mind. From now on, whenever you meditate, bring to mind this cool, still water with the sun setting behind it."

Mosquitoes buzz my hair as I struggle to cover my exposed flesh. I hear my companions slapping bugs as the Swami makes his final speech, his "peaceful lake," just a stagnant pond choked with dying plants.

"Now you can go back if you wish. The Meditation Walk is ended." His familiar giggle returns. "There is an ice cream store on the way home," he adds.

From nowhere, the missing young Swami emerges and falls into step beside me.

"Was that you on a mini-bike?" I ask him.

He looks at me quizzically.

"I meditate in the woods every evening—more peaceful there."

"I go home tomorrow," I say, hoping he'll care.

Free of his sunglasses, his eyes seem to show interest. His lips curl slightly but his hands are concealed in the folds of his garment.

"You are lucky to be so free," he scurries ahead to catch up with his mentor.

I retrace my steps past the little synagogue. Through the window I watch the swaying, chanting men. Then, seized by an impulse, I enter soundlessly and try to disappear amongst the worshipers. "You must go upstairs with the women," a man hisses. He looks with disapproval at my jeans and running shoes. Clutching my blanket like a prayer shawl, I climb the stairway. Everything seems miniature, so unlike the cavernous synagogue I remember from childhood. I take a folding chair and join the handful of old women who look over the balcony down at the swaying men. The familiar Hebrew chants, mournfully repeated by the women, pull at me through some vestigial, tribal reflex I can't control, making my eyes fill with tears. A kerchiefed woman points at my bare head. Though I thought only married women covered their heads, this is an Orthodox service, so I take a tissue from my pocket and place it foolishly on my hair. When we rise to honor the torah scrolls, it drifts to the floor, making the woman smile at me. The velvet curtains open, the men lift the heavy Torahs, and tenderly carry them as if they were grandchildren. They march up and down the aisles as congregants press their fringed garments against the scrolls, then kiss the fabric that touched the sacred texts. Standing with the women in our segregated section, I can only watch. When the service ends, the worshippers ignore me, all but that one kerchiefed woman who wishes me, the wandering pagan, "Good Sabbath."

Mike Cohen

Where We Will Sit

It was simple. An election was a competition. Yet Judge Frances Waxman Bloomberg, Fran to her intimates, seemed stunned to draw a reelection opponent. A lawyer named Sanford Grim sought to oust Fran from her judicial post, claiming a courtroom slight in the presence of his clients that Fran neither remembered nor intended.

In past elections Fran could count on her father, Eli Waxman, himself a noted lawyer, to write or arrange for whatever checks were necessary to ensure that his daughter retained her judicial seat. In Eli's world the two words *compete* and *win* were synonymous. Every day Fran lived in the bubble of Eli's mantra: "We never lose."

This time there would be no Eli Waxman to help, impaired as he was by stroke and dementia. And her opponent was rolling in money.

"Grim's got $150,000," her consultants warned, "unheard of in a judicial race."

"And Waxmans choose to compete," Fran said. Her answer was rote, listless. She found little solace in the slogan.

The need for money beset her, interfered with her sleep. In one nightmare the voters had rejected Fran, and she found herself suddenly transported, as dreams can do, to the Waxmans' family living room. Standing uncertain and bruised, she related her defeat to her father, Eli, tears of humiliation coursing from her eyes. And lurking in the corner was her younger brother, Albert, at fifty broke, unemployed, and divorced, living in his parents' home, so impishly pleased at the misery of his older, successful sister.

It seemed so ironic that shortly before Grim's declaration of candidacy, the University Law School had sought Fran out and, to her delight, invited her to join its faculty. She was ready to say "yes" but could not. What would Eli have thought if she backed out in the face of competition?

It began when Frannie, at twelve years of age, in tennis whites, had waited for Eli to enter the kitchen.

"Who's up for a quick set?" Eli asked.

"Not me," Albert demurred, chopping walnuts.

Eli took no prisoners. "Momma's boy," he said.

"So what," Albert fired back.

Fran volunteered to fill in. "I'm ready." Fran's eyes begged. Eli was silent.

Shirley cut through the banter.

"Frannie's your athlete," she said. "How many do you need?"

As they played tennis singles, Eli, the relentless teacher, called out commands across the net to Fran like a Marine drill instructor.

"Turn your body, plant your feet, not the back foot, silly; the front foot! Swing through the ball, swing through. Run. Run. Run."

Eli's commands hurt, each one a reminder of how badly she played the game, each command like a punishment in her chest, each missed ball the end of the world. Fran pressed herself. This was her special time with her father, her chance to show him how good she could be at something important to him.

Fran's club matches with girls her age were also accompanied by Eli's sideline ranting.

"Get your head up, don't let that guy see you down. Gut it out. Run. Run."

Sometimes she did not win, and the mortification of losing seemed to accumulate in her Fila bag along with her playing togs, shoes, and spare rackets. Yet, miraculously it seemed, at fifteen she turned the corner. Fran became too good, too strong, too fast for all her competition, even Eli. They played now as mixed doubles teammates, winning father-daughter tournaments first in the club, then city and even state tournaments.

And still Eli hollered at her play:

"Block the lane, get up there up to the net. Jesus. I can't believe you let that ball past. Jesus." Eli's relentless criticism drained the pleasure from the game, left her feeling as if she must say "sorry" at each passed shot, at each double fault.

Yet Fran never stopped competing. Her reward: making the college team. She told both her parents of her accomplishment with her eyes on Eli. At the same time she declared her decision to major in education, to become a teacher.

Shirley nodded but Eli cocked his eyebrows in dismay. Fran could not meet his glance.

"What's the matter with being a teacher?" she asked.

"Those who can, DO," Eli said. "Those who can't, TEACH. Which are you gonna be?"

Crestfallen, Fran wanted to respond, *But you have been teaching me.* Instead she suppressed her disappointment, studied hard for four years, and went to law school. All the while she continued to play father-daughter doubles with Eli, thus affirming her unwavering commitment to victory.

After joining Eli's law firm as a trial lawyer, Fran also played as a doubles partner with senior judges who could do her a favor. *Political tennis,* she reasoned. Decades later, with Eli's help, Fran was appointed by the governor to a seat on the superior court. Her pleased tennis-playing colleagues continued to insist on their regular game.

And Fran never lost.

It was uncomfortable dealing with her mother, Shirley, as she struggled to meet the demands of Eli's care. Yet there was little choice. Fran conceived a ploy to convince her mom to open the election coffers: *I will need a large amount of money or Pop will be disappointed.*

Fran had phoned Shirley in a futile hope to be able to ask long distance but Shirley changed the subject.

"We can't afford all the help around here, and your father worries all the time that our house is being taken away."

"That's crazy, Mom; you know you have plenty of means."

"Look, I write the checks," Shirley said with exasperation. "I am not some dotty old lady. I know what your father is costing." Fran heard her mother huffing like a steam boiler.

"Who says you are dotty?" Fran said. She thought of what Shirley would want to hear.

"We can all do our part, don't you think?" Fran suggested. "Let's discuss, have a family meeting, like old times. Friday night after court?"

"That's fine. Of course," Shirley said. "A family meeting with Albert. And with your father. He always loves to see you. It calms him down afterward."

Fran, on her side of the phone, fidgeted at her mother's characterization of Eli's capacities. On her last visit Eli had looked through Fran as if she were a sheet of clear glass. She considered telling Shirley about the campaign's media cost, but thinking better of it, she used the moment to divert attention from herself.

"I think we should make these decisions about Pop's care together. We need to lean on each other."

"That's fine," Shirly answered, "but I'm not going to go broke. Your dad would never forgive me."

After the call Fran wanted to discuss her mother's fabricated money problems with Albert but chose not to. During her last judicial campaign, Albert was arrested for possession of small stashes of cocaine and marijuana purchased for his collection of aging cronies. Behind the scenes Fran hired a good lawyer to keep Albert out of jail and to kill any story in the press linking the two of them. At Albert's imploring, Fran had not told Shirley and Eli of the episode, but she did not trust Albert to reciprocate by now supporting her.

Opening the front door of the Waxman lakefront home where she was raised, Fran confronted the unavoidable family photo gallery. In the middle: little Frannie in tennis regalia with Althea Gibson, and an older Fran next to Billie Jean King.

She walked through the living room, past Eli's prominent trophy case displaying a dusty silver-and-walnut club doubles championship trophy that Fran won decades ago with David, her former husband. After her divorce Fran begged Eli to remove it, but Eli stubbornly continued to exhibit the cup, flanked by a post-match photo that he had taken of his daughter, cheeks flushed, holding the trophy in the air as if it were the captured flag of the enemy.

Fran found Albert in the kitchen unloading the dishwasher.

"Here comes the judge," he chanted Flip Wilson-style.

Fran attempted a peck on Albert's cheek, but he grabbed her around the waist like a girlfriend. Albert wore bleached cotton baggies, sandals, and a sun-faded, yellow Hawaiian shirt with a white-and-blue marlin leaping over and around the shirt from front to back. Albert's receding hair was cropped tight to the scalp. He looked like a young version of Eli; only the garb differed. *My brother could have made millions as a Palm Springs decorator,* Fran thought.

"Oh, Fwannie," he sighed as he continued to hug her. It was an old gag of his. Fran relaxed. Her brother's touch seemed affectionate enough, but his face only showed that she mildly amused him. Albert released his hold.

"Shirl is on a new kick. She won't leave Eli alone, even for her book club." Albert spoke with mock exasperation, talking about Eli and "Shirl' as if they were his children and the home were his.

"She says she is going to have to be Eli's nurse. I've seen the bank accounts. They're rolling in dough. It's crazy around here, just crazy. Some food?"

"Maybe a glass of wine," Fran said. "I could use a red."

"I'm not sure what we've got." Albert had begun frying onions and fresh garlic cloves in olive oil, and the room had the warm, rich smell of a farmhouse kitchen.

Fran opened the cupboard. At the front cans of Ensure, Eli's dietary supplement, and saltine crackers crowded up to the door. She reached way back into the shadows and fished out a square, half-full bottle of kosher Passover wine.

"A nice red," she said. "Mogen David, anyone?" Albert made a gagging sound.

"Maybe I'll run up to the store," Fran said. "Things look a little light in there. Where's Mom anyway?"

"Sleeping; she's pooped but I promised I would wake her up when you got here."

"I'll go check on her," Fran said.

Tiny as a child, Shirley lay lightly snoring on her king-size bed, still dressed in her Fila gym suit and her Reebok tennis shoes. Lying on her back, her mouth slightly open, she was a frosted version of Fran, neat and wiry. Only her forearm skin was crosshatched and sagging.

Fran sat down on the bed, waiting for her mother's eyes to open. Shirley glanced about, lost, wild, then regained her sense as Fran kissed her.

"Hi, Frannie. We need to get you something to eat," Shirley said, looking worn down, exhausted.

"I'm okay," Fran said. "Albert's cooking something. Sorry to wake you up."

"I would have been up in a minute. I can't sleep anymore." Shirley did not say this to gain sympathy; it was just a fact. "I need to put on some lipstick."

"You look great, Mom," Fran said.

"No, I don't. You, on the other hand, are radiant. Let's go see your father. He will be thrilled you're home."

Eli's room was ensconced at the other end of the hallway from the master bedroom that he and Shirley shared for forty years. In an easy chair sat Eli's night nurse, a woman Fran's age with reading glasses on a chain around her neck. *People Magazine* lay open on a side table over which shone a reading lamp. A fan riffed softly, keeping the air in the room cool.

Eli slept; his nose stuck straight up in the air. A parrot's beak. A down comforter was tucked under his arms, leaving his hands, palms down, exposed to the air. The backs of his hands were bruised, purple-brown.

"Dorothy, this is my daughter, the judge," Shirley said.

"Hi," said Fran, her voice barely louder than the fan. "Just call me Fran."

"No reason to whisper," Dorothy said in a normal voice. "Mr. Eli sleeps like a rock."

"Until ten p.m.," Shirley said, "then he thinks it's the middle of the day and he's back at the law firm. Thank God for Dorothy. He would keep me up all night."

Fran bent over Eli and, as with her mother, kissed her father on his forehead. His skin smelled like baby oil, his eyebrows the only hair on his tiny head. She patted his bruised hands.

"Hi, Pop," she said. "It's Frannie." Eli continued to breathe, his mouth opening and closing. Fran could not tell whether he had heard her or not.

Albert was at the stove as Fran returned with Shirley to the kitchen. The moonlight shone into the kitchen nook.

Fran sighed as she stared at the lake. She would not be able to talk with Shirley alone. *I will be forced to ask for money with Albert horning in,* Fran thought.

"We should get started soon."

"Mom needs some food," Albert said. "She ate like a bird today." He added slices of potatoes to his pan. "I've made you some garlic fried potatoes, Mom. And here's some kippered salmon and bread. Now, are you going to sit down and eat some of my gourmet fare, *s'il vous plaît?*"

"I'm not sure," Shirley said. "A cup of decaf, and maybe something later."

"Where shall we sit: living room, dining room, or here in the kitchen?" Fran asked. There was no place in which to avoid Albert's influence. The Waxmans had festooned their home with his artwork; some was framed, some simply stretched canvas, with gray and red pigment swirling around hunks of texture and dots of yellow. *I will be kept at bay until the two of them get seated,* she thought.

Albert shook the pan like a short-order cook in a diner. "Are you going to eat or not, Fwannie? Here, smell this." He waved the steaming pan in his sister's direction.

"Again, thanks but not now," Fran said. "If Mom wants something, we can meet here at the kitchen nook or maybe the dining room. Isn't there more room at the dining room table?"

Fran's frustration was momentarily offset by watching her brother cooking. As kids they hung around the kitchen, dodging the aimless movement and overlapping squawks of cooks and servers squeezing by each other with plates of steaming food. Albert learned all of Shirley's culinary tricks. Fran, uninterested, learned none.

Albert had set up a tray on the kitchen counter for Shirley.

"If Mom's gonna be the only taker, just set the table in the kitchen nook," Albert said. "That way we can look out over the lake. Really, Fwannie, these spuds are great. You must have some."

Fran felt that Albert was deliberately keeping her from talking about her campaign. She had to answer.

"I don't care where we sit. We can eat in the kitchen if you want, although the dining room table is easier for Dad's wheelchair."

Fran had her own seat at the dining room table at her father's left. Albert had always sat on Eli's right, his second choice.

"Fwannie, it's okay," Albert said, "if you need to sit in your old seat next to Pop." A paralysis was rising in the room like a fog over the lake. Fran decided to dive in before they were enveloped in its viscosity. She turned to Shirley.

"I came here, Mom, because I need to talk to you about my election campaign."

"I am worried about you," Shirley said, "you look thin as a rail. Let's get a little something to eat, then we can talk afterward, you know, when Dorothy brings Dad out. We can sit in the living room around the coffee table. But eat a little first, honey."

"The potatoes are getting cold," Albert said. He had garnished the fried spuds with a spritz of lemon, parsley, and dusted them with grated Romano cheese. "Tell me where I should put them so we can nosh while we talk."

"Stop moving around, Albert," Fran said. "Mom, just have a seat right here in the kitchen." Fran's voice had taken on an edge. Shirley and Albert stared at her.

"I am just trying to get us some comfort food," Albert said. "I want to put out these great potatoes somewhere. Let's go into the living room if you would rather."

Albert gripped Fran's arm as if to steer her toward the living room, his fingers insistent as if it were the room of his choice, the room with the lights reflecting off his paintings.

"You're pushing me," Fran said, locking her knees. Albert eyes grew round and he pursed his lips.

"Look, if you don't want to eat anything, okay," Albert said, his voice rising. "Don't make such a big deal out of it."

"Honey, he didn't mean anything," Shirley said. "I think we should all calm down. While we wait for your father, I think we should go into the dining room like Fran wants."

"Like Fran wants?" Fran said. "What are you talking about? Fran has a problem on her hands. I want to talk about the cost of my reelection. When do I get to talk about why I am here?" Her hands were shaking in a way they had not shaken since she was a new lawyer.

"We live here, not you." Albert spoke softly, as if he were the master of the manse. "You come flying in here to tell us that you have to deal with a situation. Look around. This is a situation too. I have been dealing with Pop and Mom without you. Me here. Every day. You want money. Well, this is my home too, you know. I want the best for Mom. She has to have the final word on giving out any money. You probably intend to tell her to sell this place. Well, that's not going to happen."

Albert's last statement was so uncalled for and so unrelated to what Fran had been thinking that she was speechless.

"I should have told you," Shirley said, "but I was waiting for your father to join us. I put Albert on all our accounts with your dad and me, just in case."

"Albert, who can't hold a job?" Fran blurted out in spite of herself. "My little brother who can't afford to pay rent or alimony is now to manage your money?" Fran's head reeled with the finality of what was now happening.

"That's right," Albert said. "So put yourself in your old dining room chair as if you won this or that tennis tournament, hobnobbing with Pop like you have all the smarts. That was what you intended to do tonight, wasn't it? Just sit next to Pop like always and tell us how to live here?"

"Watch out, Albert!" Shirley warned.

Albert had loosened his grip on the platter, and some fried potatoes slipped onto the floor. He recovered quickly.

"Dammit, Fwannie, look at what you made me do," Albert said, swiftly scooping up the spilled contents. "Sit in your old damn chair until Pop gets here. Who gives a hoot? Because you are not in charge."

In a tone and voice virtually identical to that of an angry Eli, Albert spat out Fran's nickname like it was a curse meant to bury her under a deluge of perpetual childhood. It was almost too much for Fran to bear: her constant struggle this night, the struggle to be heard, the relentless need for Eli's praise.

The floor crackled with the sound of Eli's wheelchair. Dorothy maneuvered it into the kitchen, Eli wrapped in his red flannel robe, white cotton pajamas covering his worn-out flesh peeking out here and there, lamb fleece slippers covering shrunken feet. The cocooned king in his rolling throne. *And here I am: Frances, the 55-year-old judge, hands dotted with age spots, still the child waiting on bended knee for an approving pat on the head.*

Eli's eyes swept the room. He cocked his eyebrows quizzically at each of his children and then focused on Shirley.

"Is the Oldsmobile ruined?" Eli beseeched his wife. "I think I wrecked the Oldsmobile." Fran remembered the ancient Olds that the Waxmans owned over forty years ago.

Shirley put her arm around the ill man. "The car is fixed just fine, darling. Doesn't Frannie look beautiful?"

That is all we know, Fran thought. *Pleasing Eli. To look beautiful for him. To win an election for him.*

It now seemed to Fran that she just pretended to love tennis so that she could bond with Eli. Tennis was a way to prove herself worthy. She was always back at the baseline, waiting to take Eli's serve. For once it would feel good to do something because it mattered to her.

"So where do I park Mr. Eli's wheels?" Dorothy asked the three Waxmans. "Good thing you got a judge in the family. You can always ask her." She laughed. "Judges know such things."

Fran grimaced. A judge, okay, but in the Waxman household she was just one voice among four, all inflating their personal predicaments into unparalleled calamities: ruining the car, going broke, spilling freshly grilled potatoes.

Or losing to Sanford Grim.

At the beginning of the school term, one of her new law students, a young woman, approached Professor Frances Waxman, the former Judge Bloomberg.

"Judge, are you going to use a seating chart? Or do you assign seats some other way?" The young woman stared at Fran intensely, as if the answer would be crucial to her success in the course.

Fran studied the new student's earnestness. These lawyers-to-be, so competitive, ready to do whatever it takes to be known to their teacher, to please, to get an edge. They all called her "Judge." She smiled, imagining Eli's facial expression had he known of her acceptance of a faculty position.

"Oh, it's not necessary," Fran said. "I suspect that regardless of who sits where, I'll get to know each of you quite well. And soon."

Thomas DeConna

With a Sigh

If it had been a normal day, the afternoon sun would reach treetops and diffuse into colorful shadows, but snow fell at a good clip so there was nothing to see but the sky stretching gray and shapes losing distinction. Wet snow clung to my jacket, mittens, and backpack. It gathered on my ski hat, stuck to my eyelashes, and reddened my cheeks beneath the stubble. After walking two miles from campus, I reached the junction for Interstates 75 and 80, a junction uncomplicated because my options were limited to northbound or eastbound. I knew why I was there but didn't know what to do. I had to decide. In a single afternoon my life had changed, and I needed to know which road to take.

I was aware of the irony. Earlier that day I sat engaged in my English class while we discussed poetry; in fact, I had declared myself an English major. It was February 2, 1972, my freshman year of college, and in my last class for the day, Twentieth Century Poets, we analyzed Robert Frost's "The Road Not Taken." The class came right before the Military Draft Lottery, which would be broadcast via radio across the country. The draft changed a lot of lives. To be more narrow, it changed my life and it gave me a serious choice.

But that Robert Frost poem. The one where the speaker walks through a forest one morning and comes upon a path that splits? "Most people know it, or at least the poem's conclusion. Yes, those final lines have haunted me:

> "I shall be telling this with a sigh
> Somewhere ages and ages hence:
> Two roads diverged in a wood, and I—
> I took the one less traveled by,
> And that has made all the difference."

Typical Frost. Not revealing exactly what he means. So, the class had quite a debate over it.

The classroom was one of those uninspired-looking places with contemporary desks having a pressboard writing surface in the shape of a backwards capital P and hollow, shiny metal legs with a metal basket container under the seat that no one ever used. Being on the building's third floor, the room's windows didn't open, which made the warm days close, and because the old heating system never worked right, the cold days were colder. I'm sure most students didn't find the room heartening, but I did. Not because of its spare comfort but because of its sense of shelter. I liked the symmetry of rows, the camaraderie of classmates, the smell of books, and the infinite world of learning. I imagined myself an ascetic in the way that I would always seek knowledge.

Our instructor, a man well past retirement age and a dead-ringer for the film version of Mr. Chips, stood at the lectern. First, he read the poem aloud—the poem we were assigned to read—in a resolute baritone that instinctively found a way to my core. I felt that he knew each poem, knew its every nuance and meaning, and, through his fervent voice he tried so forcefully to convey his understanding to us. Then, after each reading, he left the lectern and sat in one of the student desks and asked questions about the poem, as if he'd never read it before, as if he hadn't a clue about it.

For this Robert Frost poem, the crux of it rested in its final lines. He asked us if the words were hopeful or not; if the speaker's sigh was one of satisfaction or one of regret. Most students said the poem had a positive message because the speaker made the right choice, so the sigh was one of contentment; others said the sigh was one of regret because a road less traveled was full of heartache. A few students wanted to live with the ambiguity, the not knowing. Perhaps ambiguity is a layer of innocence that allows us to exist insulated in daydreams and half-truths. It was a place where I felt comfortable—just like that class-room—a place where I longed to stay. However, our teacher pointed out that ambiguity is all right for literature and even for parts of life, but sometimes life throws us a serious choice that comes with a catch. There's something to lose, and usually the loss is a part of you that can never be regained. He finished by saying, "You can't always travel with clarity. Sometimes you travel in darkness."

We were supposed to discuss other poems that day including "Naming of Parts," but our debate on "The Road Not Taken" raged on unresolved, and the professor left it that way. He asked questions, challenged our statements, and asked more questions. Yes, my Mr. Chips did a fine job of navigating us through the poems as if he himself were an uncertain wanderer, but I believed that he knew exactly what every poem meant and knew exactly where he was going.

My college was in northern Ohio. My home was in New Jersey. For an only-child who was used to his private space, going away to college was an adventure because so much was new to me, especially dealing with dorm life like sharing a room or standing naked in group showers. Even our grades were naked because in those days semester grades were posted on bulletin boards, not by your name but by your Social Security number. Living away from home was a different experience, and maybe I wasn't ready for it. I didn't like the starkness of black and white.

When I was young, I read novels, plays, and short stories; in college I studied poetry. I thought of becoming a high school English teacher where I could cast a spell of "willing suspension of disbelief" over raptured students. I pictured the image while in the class-room that February afternoon as I gathered my books and belongings. After descending the three flights and leaving the building, the damp winter cold slapped against me and my thoughts shifted to the looming military draft.

My country was at war with Vietnam, and college deferments no longer existed. Honestly, I feared the draft, feared being displaced to a country so foreign and to a situation so dangerous. Of course, I loved my country. I had pledged allegiance to it every morning in public school, had been a Boy Scout, and knew why we lit firecrackers every Fourth of July. Fortunately, during my freshmen year at college, the Vietnam War was winding down, so only young men who drew a number between one and fifty would be drafted in 1972.

I walked down the long hill from my class to the dorm. All of our classes were sequestered within the tree-shaded hilltop, but now the trees were winter bare as spring huddled weeks away. Our dorms were at the foot of the hill, and standing there, looking at the deep valley, a person felt awfully small, especially when, as on that day, dark clouds rolled in and cloaked the sky like thick velvet curtains. When the wind blew off the river no amount of clothing staved that watery chill. I walked faster, knowing the draft started soon, and a bunch of us had agreed to meet in John and Mark's room and listen to the lottery on a local radio station. Looking back on that scene, there was only word for it: surreal.

I did not attend an elite college. None of us came from prep schools and none of us came from money. You could say that our families lacked privileges. Most of our fathers had never attended college, and their jobs could be defined by single words: mechanic, barber, grocer, carpenter, or plumber. Back then the dorms were not co-ed and when I entered the room, eleven eighteen-year-old males filled the place. Each dorm room was sixteen feet by twenty feet with two beds, two closets, two desks, and two chairs. The cinderblock walls were painted light blue, but despite the pastel color and large windows, the room on that day, with twelve of us packed in, felt as tight as a prison.

"Ah," said John with a bogus British accent, "the poet laureate has arrived."

I was the only English major in the group.

"Feeling lucky today?" Tom, the cynical one, asked me.

"I never feel lucky."

Some of my dorm-mates had carried in chairs, some sat on the beds, and some sat on the floor. The twelve of us had bonded over the school year. We knew each other's backgrounds and birthdays. We were a band of brothers, and that helped to make the unreal situation tolerable. Together, we were safely stowed inside. As a small, single-bulb lamp glowed on John's desk, we kept the overhead florescent lights off, and through the west-facing windows we had a good view of the murky clouds and coming storm.

The room smelled of unwashed bedsheets and unwashed clothes, but the odor wasn't totally unpleasant. It was familiar and masculine as our eighteen-year-old bodies perceptibly altered from adolescence to adulthood. Some of us had grown beards or mustaches. We wore flannel shirts with tartan designs or sweatshirts above our jeans. All of that was normal, but what struck me immediately when I entered that room was the nervous energy percolating through it. No-one sat still. No-one held another's eyes for more than a second. No-one wanted to show his fear beneath the surface because that's where it was solid. It reminded me of middle-school dances where you were supposed to be a super-confident guy going up to the girls, facing one, and asking her to dance. Meanwhile your heart pounded through your skull because she might say no in front of everyone, or she might say yes and then you'd have to dance, which was even more frightening. So now, no-one tried for false bravado. We all knew, either by reading about it or by seeing it, how guys our age who went to Vietnam returned home with missing limbs or inside flag-draped coffins. Or they returned physically unharmed but emotionally destroyed. No-one in the dorm room downplayed the importance of this moment.

These were the same boys who had tossed a football with me in September and ate cafeteria meals with me daily; the ones who helped each other study for tests and who made makeshift sleds to ride down the university hill just a few weeks ago. I scrutinized the closet doors with their walnut finish but knew it was just a veneer; the same for the student desk that never seemed right for study. And John's radio on that desk. A Westinghouse six by ten inch piece of white plastic with an alarm clock you could set for morning classes and a radio that played AM and FM stations. Today it was an AM station with a strong signal, a station that played Top 40 hits, and that's exactly what was happening. Pop music played, as if it were an ordinary day.

It's impossible to explain the situation; I've tried but people just don't believe me. Music played until the lottery began. The draft's process was simple. A man read a date, someone drew a number, and then officials joined the number to the date. Young men born on that date now had their destiny. If you drew a number between 51 and 365, your life stayed unruffled. If you drew a number between one and 50, you were going to Vietnam. No questions, no doubts, no hopes.

Guys milled around the room, talking about immaterial things so that the undertone reverberated off the cement walls and linoleum floor, sounding like a dirge. Then, suddenly, the time was two o'clock. "They're starting," Simon's voice sounded through the thrumming and the room turned jarringly silent. I can't remember if a special announcement came first; probably, and I probably missed it. The next thing I heard was a man reading a series of dates followed by a number: "August 27—34; December 3—56; April 11—350." The announcer's colorless voice reminded me of a priest reciting a common prayer. Listening intently, we all hunched forward. Some boys grabbed their knees; others crossed arms over their chests; some stared ahead; others looked down. How do you react to a situation you've never faced before and would never face again?

Random numbers assigned to random birthdates. Actually, the odds were good to draw a number over fifty. Still, somebody must go. In fact, that year 49,514 young men were chosen. From time to time I thought of being in Vietnam—a place I pictured with rice swamps, vile insects, and oppressive heat. I thought of firing a rifle and ending a stranger's life, shuddering every time because the thought repulsed me. And yet, I was never one to disobey authority. Conformity was drummed into my head at home and reinforced through school, church, and community. Patriotism and duty were as tangible as the American flag that hung from my parents' front porch. The thought of running out on my country was as repulsive as firing that rifle.

So, the military draft unfurled in stages. The first round of dates had been called; no-one in the room was touched. Did I forget to tell you? In between lottery segments, the radio station resumed its programming: Top 40 hits and glib commercials. While the draft segments lasted about a minute, to us it seemed like the passing of a dark century. Then, blithely, the station broke away to ads or music. Absurd? Damn right it was absurd. While airwaves mixed pop music with acne ads, our lives were being fated. Meanwhile, during the intervals we breathed again, moved about the cramped space, and waited for the next round. I never played Russian Roulette, but that situation was close enough.

During the breaks, guys talked about classes or sports or girls. Anything to ease the tension. I caught snatches without really listening.

"Are you still dating Nancy?"

"Yeah. Why?"

"She's waiting for you to ask her to the Valentine's Day Dance."

"How do you know?"

"She told me. Remember? We have biology labs together, Tuesdays and Thursdays."

"Right. Well, she should know she's going without being asked."

"What are you, a caveman?"

"What does she want—flowers and a box of chocolates?"

"Try flowers."

"Aw, maybe you're right. Hey, since when are you such a Romeo?"

"Me? I'm still looking for Juliet."

More commercials and music. Maybe an "oldie" tossed into the mix. And we relaxed, as if the nightmare had passed. But then that dull, authoritative voice: "January 8—206; September 21—123; April 15—."

The silence doubled because we knew the 15th was Peter's birthday. Eyes shifted to him, a slight boy with thick spectacles and blond, unkept hair; a body that could pass for a twelve year old lad, but a person who possessed a keen mind for math and the emotions of any eighteen year old male. We stared, breathless, because the next instant held his life. "Three hundred forty-three."

I heard the number and then actually saw it suspended in air. The guillotine's blade did not drop. We stood and rushed him, whooping, hugging, laughing. Peter laughed too but his laughter broke into hysterics as if something inside him shattered. His face flushed and tears ran along his cheeks. After springing up from the bed, he staggered out of the room. I imagined him heading to the pay phone in the hall to call his parents, and I wondered what it felt like to be that free. The ache in my stomach and weight on my chest were stone blocks that I could only compare to the ones heaved upon Giles Corey in *The Crucible.* But unlike Corey, I wished that someone would lift the weight.

The chanted numbers ceased, and then a commercial for a General Motors car twittered through the cinderblock room. The advertisement lauded the freedom of the open road. I stepped into the hall. Peter had just hung up the phone and was walking to the side exit door. On weekend nights that door served as a passage for girls to sneak into our rooms. Girls couldn't walk through the front door with a campus monitor sitting behind a desk. If they tried, the monitor gave a benevolent smirk and grandly waved them away. And for the guys inside the dorm, whisking females through a side door made the illicit event even more exciting. Looking back, we were naive to think that school officials didn't know what was happening. How could they stop the most natural force of nature? "They just turned a blind eye to it, and besides, that side door was never locked.

Without seeing me, Peter stepped outside and gulped the cold, cloudy air. Watching him in his confirmed liberty, I thought how close our campus sat to Canada. Of course, I had thought that many times before, especially during the days leading up to this one. And I knew that people were prone to pick up hitchhikers in those days, especially college-age vagabonds with a backpack and a smile. I reentered the dorm room. Although invisible, you could feel it: vitality and yearning welling within us, being on the verge of finding our places in the world.

Time passed. Hours, because of the foolish format of music and lottery. The day dragged on and I remember thinking of Mr. Summers from Shirley Jackson's "The Lottery," and how he wanted to move things along so everyone could go back to work or to their normal routines. If ever reestablished, how treasured those normal moments would be!

Time and time. The man's voice slithered into our flesh and announced more dates and numbers. We held our breaths, and one by one most of the twelve young men were called and reprieved. Tom, John, and I remained. For those who had escaped the draft, I was overjoyed; however, the waiting and the wondering worked like poison inside of me, churning my stomach and numbing my brain.

"Anybody hungry?" Peter asked.

Almost everyone answered, Yes.

Mark said, "The cafeteria?"

We knew the cafeteria was open, but we also knew that no-one could leave the room. We owed it to each other to stay.

"Should we send out for pizza?"

Having pizza delivered came with an extra charge in paying the driver. By picking up the pizza ourselves, we had always spared the expense, but that day was different. After we all tossed in loose change and a few dollars, John made the call.

"Sitting at number ten this week," the radio DJ declared, "is the old hound dog himself, Elvis Presley, with 'I Just Can't Help Believing.'"

Even though I was too young to remember the bedlam surrounding Presley's being drafted into the Army, I knew the event had made world headlines. As the song played and Elvis's smoky voice spread through the chilled room, the lyrics about a man who wants a flighty girl not to leave him tumbled through my mind.

Minutes later the announcer recited the next round of numbers: "June 27—330; March 1—203; February 10—361." No one's birthday was called.

I don't remember the next part of the afternoon too well. Suddenly there were pizza boxes opening and steam licking the air. Peter had gone to the vending machine in the dorm's lobby and returned with a dozen Cokes. He had something to celebrate.

"Here's an oldie that will take you back." The DJ sounded so damned happy. "Five years ago today this was sitting at number one: 'I'm a Believer' by the Monkees."

Actually, the song did take me back to another place that somehow reminded me of the dorm room, but at the same time it was completely different. My hometown personified suburbia. Bordered by middle-class homes that emptied into a main road, the downtown was nothing more than a handful of streets with buildings standing no more than two stories high. The town had a three-teller bank, a delicatessen, a one-screen movie theater, a bakery, a diner, a hardware store, a beauty shop…you get the idea. And, oddly enough, there was a record store—the kind that no longer exists.

Inside, this Mom & Pop place seemed to have no real shape to it because the main area had rows of tight aisles that opened to other makeshift sections. Cardboard signs dangled from the ceiling, suspended by string, and they marked musical categories: Jazz, Rock, Classical, and so on. The store had dozens of waist-high tables that held scores of wooden crates and within those crates were hundreds of vinyl records—albums and 45 singles. Thin pieces of plywood with black marker ink in block handwriting partitioned the records: Beatles, Elvis, Sinatra, Big Bands, and so on. What made the place special, though, were two soundproof booths where music was piped in. Inside each booth, green painted benches allowed space for four people to sit, and the people could request to hear up to ten songs—all 45's—filtered through four wall-mounted speakers. The idea was to listen to new releases before you bought them. Once in a while my friends and I actually bought a record, but mostly we listened to the music and said our polite thank-you's before leaving. The owners, a middle-aged Italian couple didn't seem to mind. They smiled and laughed a lot and always told us to come back anytime. Of all the times there, one afternoon stands out, and now and then I play it in my mind like the records that once played in the booth.

Kevin, Pat, and I were thirteen years old, and following a plan that Kevin had devised, we met up with three girls whom we had known for years because they lived in our neighborhood. They were also thirteen, an innocent age, yet the girls—Joanne, Debbie, and Gail—were steadily transforming into that next stage of feminine mystery and knowledge. Three years earlier we all played Whiffle ball on the street; now we sat close on the wooden benches inside the booth and listened to ten singles in a row. That gave us just over thirty minutes to be in this strange yet brave new world.

That Saturday in February was an ice-blue winter day, the kind that comes after a snow, cold and cloudless, when everything looks fresh and pristine. Inside that record booth, heat radiated from our bodies and steamed the glass enclosure. The girls exuded a soft perfumed scent, and their hair smelled of flora shampoos. Their lips glistened. Because the room seated only four, the six of us squeezed onto the bench seats, male and female arms and legs pressing against each other. From the stack of our records, a Rolling Stones song hit the turntable: "Let's Spend the Night Together." We had never heard such brazen lyrics. The lurid words and thumping music jolted us. Gail, a cute red-haired girl, sat next to me. For years we had kept furtive eyes on one another: playing ball, swimming in the community pool, sledding down a snowy hill. In the booth, her maturing chest, beneath a blue blouse the color of her eyes, rose and fell, and we looked at each other in a new, uncertain way. I leaned towards her, and she leaned towards me. I wanted to kiss her, but it didn't feel right with other kids there. And maybe she thought what I thought: that we had time; that the world was waiting just for us.

I believe that moment was the beginning of my adolescence, the starting point of all possibilities. And I remember thinking that my life will only get better, the way it was promised in the poetry of songs. But what followed the Summer of Love in 1967 were the deaths of King and Kennedy in the spring of 1968. It would have been wonderful to stay in that warm womb of a record booth, safely sealed in from all the elements and all the choices that the future would force upon me. The record booth, the classroom, and even the cinderblock dorm room proved to be invulnerable yet tenuous shelters.

"Damn," said John who stood by the windows, "it's snowing like a bitch out there."

Swirling snowflakes gleamed against car headlights. It was too early for the programmed street lamps to switch on, so the ashen sky and stark campus looked darker than death.

James said, "Let's stack those pizza boxes for the trash."

"We have time for one song before the top of the hour," the DJ said. "The New Seekers are riding the number two slot this week with the longest song title in history: 'I'd Like to Teach the World to Sing in Perfect Harmony.'"

Later *Coca-Cola* used that song's cloying lyrics for a TV ad. Inside the dorm room and through the plastic radio, music played while we sat silently because we had nothing left to say. For those who were safe, well, I could only imagine what they were thinking. For me, I knew that crazy afternoon was happening, but everything felt distorted. I wanted it to end. A few hours ago I was discussing poetry in a literature class.

The music stopped. "Now, folks, back to the military draft." The invocation started once more. "September 4—356; May 21—310; August 17—." And then, everyone's eyes veered to me. I was paralyzed.

"Eight."

Bodies suddenly surrounded me. Friends were talking, clasping, attempting some kind of comfort. But like a rock dropped in water I was falling, submerging into an unknown world. How long did I stay there? I don't know. Eventually I surfaced again. The guys were sitting down, hunched over and staring at their hands, frozen. The radio station shifted back to music.

"The next record is by a fella named Don McLean, and we haven't heard the last of this song because this piece of vinyl is rising with a bullet. It's called 'American Pie.' Well, bye bye."

I don't remember leaving that dorm room. I don't remember going to my room or stuffing clothes into my backpack or walking the campus streets or even the city streets until, after two miles of trudging through snow, cold, and darkness, I reached the Interstate junction. From there, I needed to hitch a ride. Interstate 80 would take me home where I'd report to my local Selective Service office. It was the right thing—the patriotic thing—to do, and I guess most people had chosen that path. But going to Vietnam scared the shit out of me because chances of leaving that war unscathed were not good. Interstate 75 would take me to Canada, a place I had never been and knew nothing about. But I'd be safe there. It was the coward's way out—I'd been told—but then again perhaps courage means taking the road less traveled.

Within the storm and darkness, with headlights of cars and trucks jabbing by, I stood long at that junction and looked in both directions as far as I could. I had lived within shadows, but now ambiguity couldn't shelter me. I wanted—needed—to know the answer, like Frost, like my poetry professor. At that time, I believed that all roads lie within us, but I also wanted to believe that a stronger force guides our most critical decisions.

"God, help me," I whispered and bowed my head. "Please help me."

So, I'm telling this story—ages hence—and I'm telling it with a sigh. At that junction, I took one step and then another, not with satisfaction or regret. Only resignation.

Carolyn Geduld

The Artists

The morning after his mother died, Martin was interviewed by a CBS affiliate correspondent. He was wearing a lapel microphone. The interview was taking place in his parent's log cabin. In the background, portraits of his mother nearly covered the walls.

"Your father was Kent Barry, the well-known deceased painter, who was famous for his portraits of your mother. What went through your mind when your mother passed away in the nursing home?"

"Actually, I was glad my father did not live to see this day. He would have regretted not being with my mother during her last moments of life, as I am." Martin swiped his tearing eyes with his palm.

Before his own death, Kent had painted Nan for seventy years. In all that time, he had never had another subject. Martin had never known him to show real interest in any other human being, including his children. His father claimed that something about his mother always eluded him. Whatever it was, he was still pursuing it in his 88th year.

"The purpose of my art is to capture the mystery of your mother on canvas."

He would say this to Martin whenever he finished a new painting, shaking his head at what he regarded as his latest failure. They would both stand in front of the work, arms crossed over their chests, as if whatever it was Kent was looking for would become apparent if they stared long enough.

Before his powers declined, Kent had an urgent need to find, at last, the pigment, shape, or angle that would open his wife to him just as her mouth opened to his insistent tongue. Then, he might truly know her as a husband ought to know his wife. She had always been a quiet woman, which was part of her allure. Kent had painted hundreds of portraits of her since he met her when she was fifteen years old, and he had persuaded her to undress for him. Over the years, he had been fascinated by the way her heavy breasts changed shape as she changed position or raised her arms.

"It's not your mother's physicality that really interests me," he would explain to Martin, while dabbing at a canvas with a paintbrush. "I want to paint her soul, her essence, that part of herself she keeps hidden from me."

Nan would be posing while he said this. It was unclear if she paid attention.

"If I ever know all there is to know about your mother, she might no longer be fascinating to me. I might lose interest in her and painting both. It's the hunting that drives me. Not necessarily the gathering."

"It sounds like being careful what you wish for," Martin would say.

Kent had retired from the university located in the same town as the nursing home. He had been a member of the Fine Arts faculty for his whole career. His paintings of Nan had been exhibited frequently in the gallery in the Fine Arts Building and in the more established galleries in town. The university museum had purchased two of his larger works, and art museums in Indianapolis, Evansville, and Louisville had also made purchases. The Art Institute of Chicago had one under consideration.

Critics placed his style in the Thomas Hart Benton school although without the working-class social consciousness of that genre. The interest in Kent's work was in seeing how his skill at portraiture had developed over time. As reviewers had commented, to view Kent's work was to view the history of an obsession.

When he was not painting and Nan was going quietly about her chores, Kent could not leave her alone. He insisted they be in the same room, as near to her as possible. If she was washing dishes, he would stand next to the sink. He did not need to touch her. He needed to see her close up.

She, on the other hand, seemed to exist without reference to him or their children. She rarely looked back at him. Instead, she silently focused on the work at hand—cooking, sewing, laundry.

"Nan!"

He would call "her name sharply when he had been patient long enough. She would blink three or four times, as if awakening, and then look in his direction.

When in bed with Nan at night, Kent could not tolerate a completely darkened room. There had to be some light. He had to be able to watch her sleep. He kept a small lamp turned on beside the bed, awaking frequently to gaze at her. Often, he would put his face a half-inch from hers, even though his vision blurred at that close range.

There had been occasions over the years when Kent would go into a rage when he thought Nan was deliberately evading him. He would lash out. There were times when he had to strike her to get her attention. Each time, she fell over soundlessly.

"You made me do that to you!" He would thrust a furious finger in her face.

When he was calm, he would disrobe her and pose her so he could paint the bruises. These were the works that were in the most demand. He titled them "Nan Beaten 1", "Nan Beaten 2," and so on. Kent had been careful to never let his son or daughter, Jean, see the "Nan Beaten" series. These had only been shown to dealers at private showings.

Martin, who lived on his parents' property, was a photographer. His main subject matter was nature, especially the surrounding woods. But the only way to have a relationship with his father was by developing an interest in his mother as an art object. Like Kent, Martin had exhibited portraits of her. Now that she had Alzheimer's, he photographed her more frequently.

He would always show his work to his father.

"I have some new photos of Mom here."

"Oh?" Kent would always look.

"I used the Opteka 85mm f/1.8 Manual Focus lens on these."

"Uh huh."

"These here have more contrast than those."

"Uh huh."

"What do you think of these two?"

"Mmmm."

Then they would have the same argument they had been having since Martin was a boy with his first camera. Over time, it had become a way for Martin to have an opinion of his own while fighting for his father's meager attention and grudging approval.

"Photography has as much in common with portraiture as a mirror does. Whatever it is, it is not art," Kent would say.

"A mirror does not have a human being directing and manipulating the reflection. That is why a mirror image is not art. A photograph is art."

"Those photos of your mother capture her appearance, not her soul. Her eyes look outward, not inward."

"If Mom is looking outward, it is because she had more interest in the world than you ever gave her credit for. That is what my work says about her. This is a woman curious about her surroundings."

"That's what is wrong with your work. You mother was one of the most internally focused people I ever met. A photograph cannot convey that."

"And you think your paintings do? Reveal her inner life?"

"More so than any photograph could."

Despite their controversy, Kent and Martin were planning to have a joint exhibit of their portraits of Nan since her diagnosis. The title of the exhibit was to be "Nan With Alzheimer's." It was to be sponsored by the American Alzheimer Association and to travel to six cities across the country.

But then Jean stepped in when, during one of her visits, she saw Martin with his camera.

"What are you doing?" She asked.

"Photographing Mom,"

"Stop! Don't do that!"

"Why not?"

"You are not respecting her dignity."

The argument continued when Kent took down all the paintings of the healthier Nan from the walls of the cabin and replaced them with the "Nan with Alzheimer's" series. Some of the wall space also contained those of few of Martin's photographs that were to be included in the exhibit. He and Martin had discussed several placements to see which order of hangings would be the most effective.

Jean was appalled.

"These are grotesque. You cannot allow the public to see them. It's unethical."

"Unethical?" Kent's eyebrows raised.

"Unethical, yes. Because Mom does not consent to this." Jean waved her hand at the walls.

"A tree doesn't consent when I photograph it," Martin said.

"A tree is not a human being. I doubt that Mom ever really consented to what either of you forced her to do, but this...this...is a kind of blasphemy. A kind of elder abuse."

"My paintings have always honored your mother. And this series is about the humanity, the soul of someone with dementia."

"What soul? Mom is a shell of a human. Her soul is gone. That is what you are painting. I suppose you would say you are honoring a corpse if you paint it."

"Exactly," Matin said. "Art dignifies whatever is its subject. Even a corpse."

Kent looked with interest at the way the afternoon light deepened his daughter's furrowing brow. He would have to sketch it when she was gone. When Nan died, perhaps he could paint a series called "Jean's Rage." He would have to include an ambiguity, perhaps in the way he painted her mouth, to reproduce the intriguing element in the Nan portraits.

"I hate these," Jean said.

"Good. An intense response to art is what the artist wants. Even a hateful response."

"He's right," Martin said. "A negative response from a viewer is better than no response."

Jean stormed out. Later Martin would sketch the interesting rigidity of her back as it spurned him.

When Nan began to wander into the heavily wooded area outside their door, Kent tried watching her more carefully. It was easy for heathy people to lose their bearings when hiking there. For someone in Nan's condition, walking away from home was treacherous. Even though Kent locked the doors at night, somehow Nan was getting out while he slept. It was clear that there was no recourse other than having her cared for in a locked door dementia facility.

What Kent missed the most after moving Nan out of their house was posing her. She had never objected to sitting in the same position for hours with only one or two breaks. At such times, her expression was dreamy or trance-like. She could be right in front of him, yet at a great distance, too. He was transfixed by the contrast.

By the time Nan was moved from their rural home to the nursing home, the mystery had deepened. Now his ambition was to capture on canvas the gap between the past Nan and the even blanker present Nan. Kent and Martin both recorded the gradual masking of her spirit as well as the deterioration of her appearance—the thinning of her hair, the fading of her features, the hunching of her back.

Kent visited his wife frequently. He could sit with her for hours, just staring at her, memorizing her, locating the little glint in her cornea that was a dab of titanium zinc white with a touch of cerulean blue and dioxazine purple. If he sat her near the window in her room, he could see the interplay of the changing light on her skin as the time passed. When he thought he had seen what he needed, he would hurry to his old Subaru Outback and drive the two-lane route before the light failed, and it was useless to go to his studio.

But after a few months, Kent had second thoughts about the nursing home.

"You know, your mother doesn't walk much anymore. Mostly, she stays in bed or sits in a chair. Now that she doesn't wander, I'm going to bring her back home. The light is so much better in the cabin. At home I can pose her again."

"How are you going to take care of her at your age?" Martin asked.

"I'll hire a caretaker. She'll probably wind up having to take care of both of us." Kent chuckled.

At the end of the month, over the objections of Jean, Kent and Martin arranged for Nan to leave the nursing home and return to the country. The social worker who discharged Nan contacted an agency that would send someone three times a week to bathe Nan. Between Kent and Martin, her other needs could be managed.

Kent was delighted. If he worked quickly enough, there might be some good additions for the exhibit.

Once she was home and back in bed again at night, Kent was too excited to sleep. He stayed up looking at the angle at which her head rested on the pillow, the motion of her eyes under her closed lids, the way her breathing moved her chest. He made sketches while propping himself up in the bed. He could envision other another series called "Nan Asleep."

One morning around 5 a.m., he had to get up to urinate, although he had been up twice before in the night for the same reason. This was not unusual. He took a step onto the small braided rug Nan had made for one of his birthdays. Suddenly, he was losing his balance, falling backwards with his arms flailing. His head hit the night table. Then he slid to the floor. He didn't exactly lose consciousness. He was only aware of something being terribly wrong. He tried to cry out to Nan. Although it seemed like he was yelling loudly, he could not hear the sound of his voice.

Neither could he get up. Something was the matter with his legs. After a brief struggle, he gave up, exhausted. His head lay uncomfortably on the edge of the rug, which had bunched up when he fell. He could not move. Martin checked in before leaving for work around 7:30. That he remembered that fact was proof that his mind still worked. He knew that Nan was likely to continue sleeping. He would have to lay there on the floor until his son arrived.

When Martin came in and found his father unable to move, the first thing he did was grab his camera and take a few shots. Then he called 911. It would take the ambulance a half-hour to find the isolated cabin, which Kent had originally purchased precisely because it was so far from a paved road and so private.

Martin knew that if his father had had a stroke, he would need medical treatment within three hours to have a chance at recovery. He had no idea if the ambulance would arrive within that window of time, since he did not know when his father had fallen. He had no idea whether his father would live or die.

Taking out the array of lenses he always carried along with his camera in his backpack, he began taking photographs of his father: extreme close-ups, close-ups, and middle-distance shots. Then the same from other angles. Changing the lens, he stood back and photographed his mother still asleep in the bed in the same frame as his father on the floor.

He saw Kent following his actions with his eyes. Was his father approving or objecting? Kent had to think he was seeing approval. He had to think he was giving his father the highest respect possible by turning what might be the old man's last moments into art.

It was not without a thrill that Martin imagined having his own exhibit, no longer under the shadow of his father's paintings. He would title it "Nan's Alzheimer's and Kent's stroke."

Then he took his phone out of his pocket and sent Jean a text.

"Dad fell. Looks bad."

Irving A. Greenfield

A Midsummer's Day

Harry Stinton opened the door that led to the terrace to air out the two-room apartment on the tenth floor of the Esplanade, an independent living facility on Staten Island, where he and his wife, Cynthia, lived for the past five years. Stinty, as he was called by his friends, and Cynthia were the Esplanade's only famous residents: he, an artist and photographer whose works were displayed in various museums throughout the world; and she, a sculptor with the same reputation as her husband's. Both were in their nineties, and this day would be special for them, as well as for the Esplanade because it would end with the filming of a made-for-TV documentary about them.

But Stinty's mind was full of misgivings, dark thoughts, shadows of what his and Cynthia's lives might be like if, as she had earlier, continued to lose control of her bowel movements. Cleaning her, then showering her and doing laundry at four in the morning left him very much less than cheerful and very tired.

Standing on the terrace with his long-fingered hands braced on top of the red brick wall that separated it from the empty space around it, Stinty looked out into the predawn gayness, a grayness that was as much inside of his skull as it was outside, visually. It wasn't Cynthia's first accident, and he knew it wouldn't be her last. A few years back, while they still lived in the house they owned in an enclave off Bay Street that gave them a view from their studio of the Narrows and beyond into Brooklyn and Queens, she fell and needed extensive surgery that left her a semi-invalid and required them to move to the Esplanade. It was a move neither of them wanted, but one that was necessary.

Stinty glanced back at the opened doorway. The smell of feces was probably gone, and from what he could see from where he was on the terrace, Cynthia had fallen asleep again. But for him, there was no such grace.

Slowly, as the dawn's light became brighter, the Watchung mountains thirty or forty miles away in New Jersey came in to view. When he was a very young man, he climbed them many times. That was when he was eighteen or nineteen years old, before WWII and his stint with the OSS during the war.

He left the terrace and sat in the big, black lounge chair in the living room, closed his eyes and tried to focus on the day's activities that would begin with him going down to the secondary dining room, which had been a bar and cocktail lounge when the Esplanade in an earlier iteration had been a hotel, before it was converted to an independent living facility for seniors.

After a few minutes, Stinty felt his eyelids droop, and he knew that he was falling asleep.

He slept from five to seven AM. The short sleep refreshed him, and as he stretched and looked at Cynthia on the bed, he realized that she too was awake and looking at him.

"I'm sorry," she said in a tone that was almost a whisper.

He waved her apology aside, as if his action could magically erase what had happened, and asked, as he always did if she were awake, "Are you going to join me for breakfast."

"I want to get myself together," she answered. "After all, today is a special day for both of us."

"So it is," he said, bracing his two hands on the sides of the chair to push himself off of it.

"The TV people are scheduled to arrive around ten," he explained, "and it will take them a good hour and a half to set up." He crossed the room to where his dresser was situated, open the top drawer and removed a pair of blue socks; then closed it, and opened the drawer below it and picked up a pair white cargo shorts and a white tee shirt. "I don't know whether I should wear shorts or regular pants for this last shoot," he said.

"I think you'd be more comfortable in shorts," Cynthia answered.

Holding the tee-shirt and cargo shorts in one hand, Stinty sat on the bed, took hold of Cynthia's left hand, and almost said, *shit happens* but actually said instead, "Let's make this a banner day for us."

"Absolutely," she answered.

Kissing the back of her hand, he said, "You know, I'll never let go of you."

She nodded.

"Well, it's time for me to get moving," he said as he stood and released her hand.

Stinty arrived at the table for breakfast at ten minutes after eight. Dorothy Pinzer, a thin eighty-something widow who wore white metal frame glasses was already there. He'd have been surprised if she weren't. He sat where he always sat, the center chair, close to the dining room's rear wall. From that place, he could see who entered it. To his right was the empty chair Cynthia occupied at lunch and dinner.

"Are you excited about the afternoon's events?" she asked in her squeaky voice.

"A bit more than usual," he answered, as George, the table's waiter, placed a glass of prune juice and straw in front of him.

"It must feel wonderful to be so honored," Dorothy said. "I mean no one else at the Esplanade..." She trailed off, then shook her head as if displeased with something and managed to say, "I forgot what I wanted to say."

Stinty nodded because he thought it was the right thing to do. Then as he began to suck up the prune juice through the straw, it occurred to him that he made the wrong choice. Short pants would not do. His legs too spindly to be photographed. He wanted to look more dignified when he was being filmed. His lightweight blue denim jeans would be more suitable for the situation.

George returned to the table with a toasted blueberry muffin sliced in half and a small round container of cream cheese.

Just as Stinty thanked him and indicated he needed hot water for his tea, he saw Philip Ross, another tablemate, enter the dining room. Phil's arrival completed those residents who left their rooms for breakfast. The five other people who shared the table with them were there for lunch and dinner.

Phil's steps were crabbed, and he used a bright red walker with two large front wheels and two much smaller rear wheels to keep himself from falling. He was smiling when he reached the table, settled on a chair facing Stinty, and said, "What has the poster boy to say this bright morning."

"Not a hell of a lot different from any other morning," Stinty answered.

George came to the table with a glass of orange juice for Phil.

"The usual," Phil said looking up at George.

Stinty's attitude toward Phil was neutral most of the time. Before he came to the Esplanade, Phil was, by his own admission, a professional gambler who won several fortunes and gambled them away. Cards were his metier. Poker in any form and Pinochle were—as he called them—his "babies." He was the self-appointed dealer for the twice-daily card games that were part of the activities program for the residents of the Esplanade.

"So," Phil began while waiting for George to bring him a bowl raisin-bran and a container of milk, "are you ready for the big show, the payoff?"

"As ready as I'll ever be," Stinty answered, trying to keep his feelings of annoyance out of the sound of his voice.

"Yeah, well, the management of this place has gone all out," Phil said. "They want as big a piece of the action as they can get."

Stinty shrugged but kept silent.

"I heard somethin' about you unveiling a new painting and a photograph. Is that true?"

"True," Stinty answered.

"Wow, then it's certainly going to be a big day," Phil responded.

George returned to the table with Phil's bowl of cereal and container of milk.

"Cynthia must be excited," Phil commented as he poured the milk over the raisin-bran. "I mean, after all, it's not everyone who..."

Stinty's forbearance snapped. "Phil, why don't just eat your breakfast and..."

Phil cut across him and with a smile he said, "Touchy touchy, aren't we this morning."

"Let go of it," Stinty snapped. "You're pushing where you shouldn't be."

Phil's palms went up. "No offense meant," he said with a smile.

"None took," Stinty answered grudgingly.

"No matter," Phil said between spoonfuls of his cereal, "it will be a grand day for all of the residents."

Stinty accepted what Phil said without comment. Then he stood, and without saying anything, left the table. By the time he walked into the lobby, he disliked Phil—more, he admitted to himself because he let him "get under his skin." The sad event earlier in the morning rattled him more than he realized. He was fearful that there would be more of the same in the near future and even more afraid about how he would cope with them.

By lunchtime, the other residents who shared the table with Stinty and Cynthia were at the table. The fare was light: bacon, lettuce and sliced tomato on toasted flatbread to make a sandwich with a side of cut strawberries and wedges of pineapple. Everyone was excited about the events later in the afternoon.

Sandra, a heavyset, brassy-looking, woman in her mid-eighties, said that she 'd heard that the reason for the light lunch was that in addition to the grilled frankfurters and hamburgers that would be served, there would also be small steaks on toasted buns and french fries.

"I heard that too," Jack Devlin said, speaking slowly as if each word was weighted with a special significance.

"What about it, Stinty, is it true that we're going to be served steak?" Phil asked.

"It's news to me," Stinity answered with a shrug. "All I was told is that there would be frankfurters and fries, several different flavors of ice-cream, various kinds of cookies, and red, white and rose wines."

"It so wonderful!" Dorothy exclaimed.

Paul Holtz, another man at the table, also a widower, said, "The management wouldn't be doing any damn thing unless they were getting something out of it. This place, like the ten others they own, is a cash cow."

"You're right there," Phil said. "but this is where a famous artist lives. On TV that's worth tens of thousands of dollars, maybe even more."

Paul looked questioningly at Stinity.

"I don't doubt that Phil is right," Stinity said, answering the unvoiced question.

"This morning I told him he was the poster boy for this place," Phil said and added, "He didn't like it, but it's true. Without him, there wouldn't be a TV crew here, and we would probably have only cookies and soda if that."

"I thought we were over that hump," Stinity said, his voice tight with instant anger.

"I didn't know it was a hump," Phil answered.

"I think you've more than a touch of 'the green-eyed monster' in you," Stinity growled.

"Maybe so," Phil admitted. "But that doesn't change the truth."

Stinty was about to answer when he felt Cynthia's hand on his bare arm. He glanced at her.

With a nod, she whispered, "Let it go. He's getting his jollies from goading you."

"You're right," Stinty whispered back.

"The trouble is that Phil is marching to a different tune," Paul said.

"And what would that be?" Phil challenged.

"You know it as well as I do," Paul answered.

"No I don't know it," Phil said. "I want to hear it from you, from anyone at the table."

Stinty couldn't resist Phil's challenge and said, "I'm center stage, you're not."

"You think you're an incarnation of Rembrandt," Phil snarled.

Stinty shook his head. "You have it all wrong," he said. "It's all me, whatever talent I have or don't have."

"Big fucking deal!" Phil shouted.

Suddenly Stinty saw Lois, the Esplanade's manager and her assistant, Joan, coming toward them and realized how much disturbance he and Phil had created. "It's enough," he said as he stood, took the hook of his cane off the back of the chair and with his other hand squeezed Cynthia's shoulder.

"What's happening here?" Lois asked.

"Nothing worth bothering you," Stinty said. "Just some words that got out of hand."

She looked at him for a few moments, then at Phil before she said, still looking at Phil, "Whatever it is or was, let go of it."

Silently, Phil nodded.

"The same goes for you," she said turning her attention to Stinty.

He too nodded silently.

"The camera crew will be here shortly," Lois announced. "I don't want them to find either one of you in a state of turmoil."

"That wouldn't do," Phil said sarcastically.

"No, it wouldn't," she said sharply. "Whatever it is that is bugging you, is yours. You keep it."

Phil stood, and grabbing hold of his walker, he said, "Why don't you ask Stinty what's bugging him?"

"Nothing is bugging me," Stinty volunteered.

"Bull shit," Phil said. "The moment I saw you this morning I knew..."

Stinty cut him off. "You knew and know nothing."

"So you say," Phil answered, and as started to walk past Lois and Joan, he added, "Like any good gambler, I can read people."

Stinty said nothing but felt as if he'd suddenly been overwhelmed by something he didn't understand, something threatening.

"Are you all right?" Joan asked.

"Yes," Stinty responded. "'Fit as' the proverbial 'fiddle.'"

"What about you Cynthia?" Lois questioned.

"A little shook up," she admitted, "but I'm sure it will pass."

"Go out to the deck before it becomes crowded," Lois said.

"That's where we were heading before you and Joan came into the dining room," Stinty answered.

"Enjoy your day," Lois said.

"Yes, enjoy it," Joan added.

Stinty thanked them, and he and Cynthia walked to the open door and the deck a step beyond it.

The deck's wrought-iron fences provided anchors for multicolored balloons and daisy-chains of colored paper. The band and camera crews were in place. Two easels were set up between where the band was and the open door to the dining room. On one of the easels was Stinty's last painting—dramatic edition of a sunset, a burst of yellow and red surrounded by almost black cloud that graded to a variety of grey—and on the other was a nine by twelve inches photograph of a hawk riding the air currents just as the sun was beginning to rise.

Stinty and Cynthia sat close to the cameras. Neither one said anything to the other until Stinty spotted Phil. Then he asked, "Wasn't there a film called *A Face in the Crowd*?"

"Yes. It starred Andy Griffith, Patrica Neal, and Walter Matthau," she answered adding, "But I don't remember anything about it."

"Neither do I," Stinty admitted.

"What made you ask about it?"

"The title just popped into my thoughts," he lied still looking at Phil, who wore a pair of green glasses and appeared to be speaking on his cellphone.

A waiter came towards holding a tray of half-filled wine glasses.

"Take your pick," the waiter said.

Stinty turned to Cynthia. "White or Rosa?" he asked.

"Rosa," she answered.

He lifted the glass off the tray and handed it to her; then he said, "Red for me."

They clicked glasses as Cynthia said, "Congratulations, you earned all of this."

He acknowledged what she said with a nod and a smile.

The band began to play some the songs from the forties and fifties. Some of the residents started to dance in the open space in front of the band.

"Let's show them some fancy footwork," Stinty said, offering Cynthia his hand.

She smiled and nodded.

As they walked to where the dancers were, many of the residents began to clap.

"A nice foxtrot to get going with," he said as they began. He held Cynthia close to him. Then he managed to move her twice around him before the darkness inside of him erupted. He twirled her in front of him and for a moment let go of her hand. Instantly, she went down.

"No," he shouted kneeling alongside of her. Everything stopped. The band stopped playing. The other dancers stopped dancing. No one spoke.

Stinty felt the weight of the sudden silence. It cowered him.

"You lied," she whispered. "You said you'd never let me go." Her eyelids fluttered; then, she stared vacantly up at him.

Suddenly shouting and screams erupted.

Stinty tried to stand, but his knees buckled.

"You killed her," a man shouted.

Stinty recognized Phil's voice. Again, he tried to stand and couldn't. All he could do was wait...Wait until the police came as he knew they would, and they would take him away...

John Calvin Hughes

Summer's Lease

When I was twelve, I spent the whole summer with my grandmother, Jean, and her husband, Ed, not just the usual week or two. Something was going on between my parents, something wrong. It seemed to me like they might be headed for a divorce. They didn't fight or anything. At least not out where I could see it. But everything felt gritty and tight with the tension of the unspoken. Without much discussion about it, my father drove me up to Jean's, and my mother stayed home. He told me stories and sang songs the whole way. He was almost certainly trying to avoid any talk about whatever was up between him and Mama. We got to Jean's and I was sent on into the house, but I stood by the window and watched mother and son. Talking. Jean did most of it. Everything seemed okay between them, but she gave him what I thought at the time was a meaningful look as he got back into the car to drive home to my mother. And then she leaned in through the window and wouldn't let him drive off until she had said some more things to him. In the car, he had given me a book. It was titled *Oh, Promised Land,* by some Mississippi writer, and it turned out to be about early settlers in the state. It was a pretty good read, at the time and for a twelve-year-old, lots of towering trees and red dirt and brave, good-hearted men and women, but I didn't just read it. I scoured it for hidden meanings related to my parents' marriage and my status thereto like some absinthe-addled, deconstruction-maddened literary critic. Waste of time, it turned out. Daddy just liked the book and thought I might too. And, to tell the truth, I did.

Grandma Jean's husband, her second husband, Ed Moore, was perhaps the most cheerful person I had ever met. Every day the three of us rose early and ate breakfast in the still, pale light of dawn, with the windows open and the leftover cool of the night seeping in. I followed Ed or Grandma Jean around all day as they did their work, trying to help or trying to stay out of the way. We ate a light dinner around noon and then napped under ceiling fans through the heat of the day. Around four, Ed would sometimes take off in his truck and be gone until after dark, doing I don't know what. Other times he'd pull cane poles out of the barn and he and I would fish the still pond past the chicken houses and watch the light fall out of the woods in the distance. In the evenings, we sat on the porch and Grandma Jean sang old songs and every once in a while, Ed pulled out his autoharp and played "The Old Rugged Cross" and other such hymns as he remembered from his strict Baptist upbringing until Grandma Jean would cluck her tongue and make him put it away.

One day, three boys came up to the front door. They looked to be about my age, a little older maybe. Grandma Jean said they were the Henley brothers, Zach and Cody, and Jimmy Harlan. They showed up every now and then, she said, hoping for cookies or a piece of pie or anything else that Jean and Ed might give them. Jean enjoyed being the lady who gave out treats. Also, Ed told me later, that what Jean really enjoyed was aggravating Mrs. Henley who didn't believe in giving her kids sugary snacks. Jean handed me a Tupperware bowl full of oatmeal cookies she'd made the day before and pushed me out the front door.

The boys were surprised to see me, and for a moment it looked like they might turn and run, but each took a cookie and mumbled their thanks and backed down off the porch and stood in the yard and ate them. They stared at their feet, shuffled said feet. I sat in one of the rocking chairs and asked them if they didn't want to come up on the porch and take a seat. Sit a spell and talk. They looked at each other with puzzlement as if I'd given them a particularly knotty math problem. Finally, one of them, Zach it turned out to be, did come up and sit. I offered him another cookie and he took it. I shook the bowl at the other boys, and they came back up onto the porch to take another one, but turned around and sat on the steps eating them, whispering, and looking over their shoulders at their boon companion and at me.

I was thinking that Zach was a pretty shy boy who didn't talk very much. Then he asked me if I liked fishing. I told him that Ed and I sometimes fished his little pond.

He snickered and said, "Don't catch much, I bet."

"We don't catch anything," I said. "But maybe some minnows."

"So, anyway, me and the boys here are going fishing tomorrow down to the Widow's Creek, if'n you want to come along."

I said I would, and he said it was date, and he stood up and tipped an imaginary hat and tapped the other boys on the shoulders and they all waved and ran off down the road. The next morning, Ed took me out to the barn to get a pole. He gave me the best one and winked at me. Then we dug up some worms and put them in a little bait bag he'd fashioned out of an old sock.

"Don't stay out there all day," he said kindly. "Try to make it back for dinner. And watch out for them boys."

"Why?"

"Shucks, one of 'em's liable to propose matrimony to you and I don't want to have to explain to your folks how you done run off to Niagara Falls."

I giggled and ran down to the road where the boys were already waiting for me in the creeping dawn. We walked down the dusty road for a mile or more and then lit out across a fallow corn field. By and by, we stepped off into some woods and half an hour of traipsing among tall, dark trees put us at the creek. It smelled cold and green and wet. The sun was a beautiful orange twinkling through the dark leaves. Zach led me to a spot I guess he liked and he laid out his implements.

We baited our hooks and dropped them into the swirl. The other two boys went downstream a bit, out of sight. We could hear them talking and laughing.

We fished with basically the same poles and the same bait, but in a couple of hours Zach had caught five nice crappies and a decent size trout. I had caught one crappie. We put them on a stringer and dropped them into the water. I followed Zach upstream about a hundred yards or so to a place he and his friends must have been before, a kind of hangout place for them, I guess: an old coffee can half full of cigarette butts, some empty coke bottles, candy wrappers, a couple of broke-ass lawn chairs, wherein we sat down. Zach took off his tee shirt and pulled out a paper bag. He had a peanut butter sandwich, cut in half, and two apples. He handed me half the sandwich and took the other half and leaned back in the poor chair and chewed with his eyes closed. His skin was smooth and tanned and his eyelashes were long and black as night. When we had eaten the apples, I began to wonder what time it was and if I should ask him to take me back to Grandma Jean's.

The other two boys came scrambling up, carrying their stringers of fish and ours. They'd had even more luck than Zach.

"Y'all ain't swimming yet?"

I stood up and looked at the creek. And, indeed, there was a perfect swimming hole right there: wide, slow, and, I guessed from the look of it, deep.

"I don't know about that, Jimbo," Zach said, looking at me out the corner of his eye.

"What?"

Zach tilted his head toward me and shrugged.

Jimmy and Cody looked at each other and laughed, then stripped naked and jumped into the water. I walked down to the bank and Zach followed me. We watched the boys splashing and laughing and diving deep and coming up sputtering.

"Sorry," Zach said. "Let's go."

The boys in the water were whispering and glancing sidewise at me.

"Don't you want to go swimming?" I said.

"We don't have to."

"It's hot," I said.

"It is that," he said.

I pulled off my shirt. My chest wasn't that much different from the boys'. I dropped my shorts and stood there in my underpants. The boys in the water were quiet now and no longer pretending not to look at me. I took a deep breath and stepped out of my panties. I started to jump into the swimming hole, but I hesitated. Every eye was on me. I turned toward Zach standing behind me so that he could see me, and I said, "Are you coming too?" Then I jumped into the water.

It was shockingly cold. I was breathless and goosebumpy, but the water was silky and slow and then Zach jumped in. I didn't see him come out of clothes. The boys horsed around, dunking each other and racing, but no one bumped me or brushed up against me. We swam for about an hour and then Jimmy and Cody got out and ate the little dinners they'd brought with them. Zach and I swam some more and he asked me about where I was from and what I was doing at Ed and Jean's house. I told him about Helena and where I went to school, about some of my friends, but I didn't mention the on-going troubles of my parents.

Cody hollered at us: "Let's go home!"

Zach looked at me. Then he said, "Y'all go on. I'll catch up."

The boys laughed and turned to go. When they were out of sight, one of them called, "Zach's got a girlfriend."

The trees overhung the river and fashioned a ragged canopy so that the sunlight fell dappled and bouncy onto the water. I had gotten used to the temperature of the river. I had never swum naked before. I felt—something. I want to say "liberated" or "free," but that's not quite right. I think what I felt right then was "grown." I felt like I was an adult, which, of course, includes such things as liberation and freedom, but also contains, I don't know, let's say, power. I felt powerful. I felt in control. Which, I guess, was a weird thing to be thinking, inasmuch as I was butt nekkid and far from home and with a boy I didn't really know. Looking back now, I suppose I was right there on the verge of victimhood, if Zach had turned out to be a psycho or something.

I wasn't really swimming, just treading water and pushing myself against the water. It was an amazing difference, to swim without pants, to feel the water between my legs. How did the micromillimeters of bathing suit fabric hold off this feeling of water right on my pussy? I was thinking I never wanted to wear a bathing suit again. I turned and turned with my eyes closed like a water ballerina entranced. Zach kept his distance, but watched me.

Power. He wanted something. Something of me. I tried to imagine how far and into what reaches his imagination was wandering.

I moved a little closer to him and he moved a little closer to me. We circled each other like boxers. We were within inches of each other. He stared into my eyes. His breath came quickly. Of course, it could have been the effort of treading water for so long. I closed the distance between us and I felt his cock against my leg. It was small, of course. He was twelve, but it was hard. He kissed me. Our lips were tightly closed, like we were kissing our parents, but he kissed me nonetheless. I pushed him back and looked deeply into his eyes. He wanted something, but maybe he didn't yet know what it was. I liked him.

I let myself sink under the water and pushed myself down, down, but I couldn't find any bottom and the water got colder and colder until I frightened myself and came rushing to the surface, gasping.

"Ain't there no bottom to this?" I said.

He smiled and said, "Not that I've ever found, but I don't wanna be going that deep noways."

We climbed out and chastely dressed without looking at each other. At least, I didn't. We gathered up our poles and grabbed up the stringer of fish and headed home. When we got to June and Ed's, they were on the porch, waiting, I realized later, for me to get back instead of napping as they would have usually been. Zach held up the stringer of fish and they applauded him.

"Did you catch none yourself, Darling?" Grandma Jean said and winked at me.

"One of them," I said, though I didn't take her real meaning at the time.

I had, in fact, caught Zach. We spent the summer together.

It was the great ballyhooed Golden Summer of legend. We ran the fields and prowled the greeny woods and the glens and the dales and all the other Wordsworth kind of stuff, except we weren't driven to poetry. I think we were driven to love. At least, I was. Tommy, Zach's brother, and Jimbo grudgingly left us mostly alone. We did go fishing with them a couple of times a week (though we did our swimming without them). Running the fields, rolling down hills, lying on our backs looking at the burned-out, white sky of full summer. Sometimes he would lie on top of me and we would kiss that tight-lipped hard kiss that we did. Sometimes I lay on top of him. And I did kiss him, but mostly I just looked at his face, the scatter of freckles, that little button nose, those lashes black as split silk. In the heat of the day we sheltered under the trees where the silver voices of the birds and the sawing of crickets lulled us into a green drowse.

One night after Jean and Ed had gone to bed, I crept down the long hall and squeaked open the front door and Zach was waiting for me in front of the house. I don't guess Jean nor Ed would have cared that I was going out of a night. With Zach. But the tiptoeing and the sneaking and the creaky front door jacked up the level of excitement and enjoyment in the enterprise. I didn't know what Zach had in mind, but he was proving to be a fine guide to the elemental pleasures of country life.

He took my hand and we headed toward the road. We walked in the fine powdery dust, like walking in talcum. When we reached the crest of the ridge, he pointed at the horizon and the moon was just rising, the fine white edge of it, like a fingernail, just appearing as we stood there in wonder, like Adam and Eve, curious and willful children in an empty world.

Then we climbed a rail fence and headed toward a barn, dark and looming in the night. There was a ladder propped against the side and we climbed up. I was a little scared, that the roof wouldn't support our weight, that we would fall off, I don't know. The roof was tin, I guess. Some kind of metal anyway. Zach lay down and put his arms behind his head, so I did the same. The sky was clear, and the stars were bright and hard like the tips of spears. The blackness of the space between the stars looked more like a substance than an emptiness, almost like you could touch it. I moved the back of my hand against his hand and he took it and squeezed it. I thought he would kiss me now. Wasn't that why he brought me up here?

Yes, I know we were only children, but I thought we were on the trembling verge of adulthood. We had kissed, we had touched, we had lain atop one another, he had pushed against me in what I suppose now was an instinctual way simulating sex. Dry humping, I guess you'd call it. I don't know. Maybe this lizard part of his brain knew how to fuck or maybe boys just know how instinctually. In any case, I kept expecting him to push our making out to another level. I was ready to follow wherever he wanted to lead. That night, as I lay on the metal roof of that barn, I hoped he would climb onto me and do something we could never come back from. Every night that summer I had masturbated in Grandma Jean's spare bedroom and, of course, I understood the mechanics of intercourse, though it seemed unreal to me at the time because I couldn't actually imagine what actually doing it would be like. But I was there. I was a more-than-willing participant in whatever might happen. I was a Stockholm-syndromed victim of love.

What happened instead was that great blazing stars fell on Arkansas.

It was a meteor shower and for hours we watched rocks from outer space tear through the hard atmosphere and burn up like angels falling out from the doors of heaven. It went on forever and eventually I drifted off to sleep. It was close to dawn when Zach shook my shoulder and said we needed to climb down now and get on home. On the porch, just before I went in, he kissed me. But this time, before his lips touched mine, he gently thumbed my bottom lip down so that my mouth was slightly open, and when he did kiss me, his mouth was a little open too and I felt like I was on fire, like stars were falling on me, piercing me with their hard points, sticking into my body, and I was like a Christmas tree, struck by lightning, burning, shining like a spinning galaxy rushing away from the world out into the emptiest of spaces, beyond any imagination. His hands were on my shoulders and I wanted him to move them over me, to explore me, to spread me like a map, to find the undiscovered countries and untapped rivers and lakes within me.

Right then it occurred to me that he probably masturbated every night too. He was a boy after all, and while I might be a strange and unusual girl who sometimes did it, boys did it all the time. At least that was what I'd heard. Most nights I lay in Grandma Jean's spare bed and rubbed myself against my pillow, picturing Zach, remembering him kissing me, lying on top of me, feeling his hard little dick against my leg, my stomach, and now I wondered what he pictured or remembered as he touched himself. As he kissed me that night, I thought I felt his tongue very close to my lips, my open mouth. Was he ever going to go any farther?

•••

The next day I ran out of the front door and jumped off the porch holding the last biscuit with butter and jelly dripping out of it onto my hand. I gave it Zach and we walked around to the back of the house while he ate it. He bent down to the spigot and took a long drink. He wiped his mouth with the back of his hand and pointed south across Ed's cow pasture.

In all our wanderings, we had never gone in this direction. Today we hugged the edge of the woods and, at one point, we found a tangle of blackberry bushes pushing out into the pasture. I ate two good handfuls. Eventually, we came to a dirt road and headed off east. By and by we came to a little settlement of tarpaper houses. Chickens and children pecked and played in the dust. Not much was going on, no grownups were out and about. At a house at end of the road, a man sitting in tattered lawn chair in front of the place stood up and waved a hand at Zach.

"How are you, young man?" the old gentleman said.

"I'm fine, Mr. Fennel. This is my friend, Darling. She's staying up at Mr. Ed and Miss Jean's place."

"Mr. Ed and Miss Jean. That's nice," he said. "How are you, Miss Lady?"

"Tolable," I said and curtseyed.

"'Tolable'," he said and laughed. "She's a sharp one, Mr. Zach."

"I believe you're right, sir," Zach said.

"'Darling'. That's a right nice name, you got yourself there, young lady. You just wait here a minute, I'm gonna show you something."

He went into the house and in a short minute came back with a fiddle and a bow. He settled himself into his chair again and slapped the bow on the strings a couple of times, wrenched the tuning knobs some, and lit into a lively number. All the kids gathered around and went to dancing. They were joyous and their braids bounced with colorful ribbons and pieces of cloth. The tune was bouncy, it might be called a reel, I think, and then Zach started dancing. His was a strange blend of sixties arm flailing and country foot stomping that was somehow happy-making and heart-rending and I thought right then that I loved him, that all the kissing and skinny dipping and empty-wanting-to-be-filled feelings I had notwithstanding, I truly loved him. I loved him because he was a good kid, a genuinely good soul, a decent and lovely person with a heart of pure gold, and I worried that I'd leave this place and never see him again, and never again find someone so pure and so open and so enamored of me.

When the song came to its abrupt but satisfying end, the children all jumped and shouted and called for another one, but a woman came out of one of the houses and yelled at the children to get gone and stop scaring the chickens and the kids scattered and Mr. Fennel set the fiddle on his knee and bowed his head. The woman gave me a particularly mean look and went back in, letting the screen door slam shut.

Mr. Fennel looked up at us and his smile was genuinely heartfelt and his eyes were genuinely sad. He raised the fiddle to his chin and played a slow tune and it was full of so much—I don't know—longing? Sweetness? Sadness? My heart was full, I felt like I was on the verge of tears. Zach stepped up to me as if asking me to dance and I put my arms around his neck and he put his hands on my hip bones and we rocked in place, barely moving our feet, and looking into each other's eyes and I know mine were brimming with tears and then he pulled me to him and my face was in his neck and the tears fell and the dust and salt mingled on his shoulder and I thought I could never again be so miserable and so happy in life.

The song came to its sad end, and Mr. Fennel stood up and shook Zach's hand and he bowed to me and he went into his little shack. Zach took my hand and we walked back through the settlement the way we came. The children looked up from their play and a couple of them wiggled their fingers at us in goodbye.

We spent the rest of the morning wandering the hills south of Ed and Jean's. We found some high spots from where we could see the late summer landscape spread out before us, brilliant green alfalfa and corn under the blazing sky. Honestly, I felt like we were the lords of all creation, a beautiful world just for us, an Eden. In the prettiest places, the deep greeny black shades of the trees, Zach kissed me with our new open mouth kisses and held me so tightly against him that I wanted to put my hand down his pants. Even now I wonder what formidable social constructions of girlhood stopped me?

It must have been close to noon because I was getting hungry. Zach's house, it turned out, was closer than Jean's, so we went there looking for some dinner. Zach's mother was standing on the porch with her arms folded across her chest. She looked all kinds of pissed off.

"Mama this is—"

"Shut yo mouth." She pointed at me. "Is this the little hussy you been runnin' around with these past few days? And nights?"

"Mama—"

"Don't bother. Get yo behind in the house, right now. And you, you go on back to town where you belong, you little tramp. I don't need my boy traipsing all over Baxter county with some floozy. Go on! Get yo nasty little butt outta here before I take a switch to you!"

I turned and ran and didn't stop until I was on the road to Jean's. I walked slowly, crying, thinking, hoping really, that Zach would come after me, walk me home, say nice things to me. But he didn't. I figured he couldn't, really. He wasn't a grown man, he couldn't just tell his mother to go to hell, defend me, take my side against her. He was a kid, my age, ridiculously caught between childhood and—whatever would come next.

When I stepped up onto the porch at Ed and Jean's, I was still sniffling and so I sat in one of the rockers and tried to compose myself. I didn't do well. I started crying again, and that gave way to some straight up wailing, and then Ed and Jean were out there, asking me what was going on, looking me over and patting me down for injury. They took me inside and to the kitchen where Ed pulled me up onto his lap and Jean wiped my face with a wet cloth.

When I stopped crying, I told them what Zach's mother had said and the names she called me and that I didn't know if I'd ever see Zach again and that I loved him and then I cried some more against Ed's chest.

Jean, who'd been kneeling by me, went to stand up but Ed took hold of her arm and they comically struggled against one another, she trying to stand, he holding her down. She finally tipped over out of her crouch and sat down on the floor with Ed still grasping her arm.

"Let go of me, you old fool."

"I am not even about to. You listen to me, Jean Moore. You're not going over to that woman's house and start nothing."

"Finish it, is more like it."

"And do what? What Christian thing will you do, huh? What godly thing will you say? Are you going over there to turn the other cheek? And what will Darling here learn about how to deal with the raging heathen?"

"Please don't go over there, Grandma Jean. Please," I said.

She stopped struggling and sat on the floor looking up at me in Ed's lap.

"No, child, I won't go. I promise." Then she looked at Ed and something passed between them that I, as a child, was not privy to.

•••

I didn't see Zach for a week. The summer was coming to an end. And then all of a sudden it was the last Friday I would be there. On Sunday, my parents were driving up and get me and I would go back home and start getting ready for the school year, shopping with Mama, picking out outfits and shoes and binders and such. After breakfast, I sulked around the house, following Jean while she worked until she shooed me out. I walked down to the pond and dropped little pieces of biscuit in the water and watched the littlest of the fish come up to the surface, bumping their heads together trying to get them.

I stared out across Ed's pasture and Mr. Henderson's toward the gray-green line of trees beyond. I'd like to say that I was conflicted, but I wasn't. There was no conflict: I absolutely did not want to go home. I did not want to go back to school. I did not want to see my friends. It wasn't like I wanted my friends *and* Zach. My parents and Zach. I just wanted him. I wanted to stay here, with my feet in the dust, my breath in the trees, my limbs in the water, my hand in his. I was in the tight fist of a breathless crush and I wanted more than anything to languish there. No Romantic poet ever loved the land and the boy more than I.

I walked back up to the house and in the through the kitchen door. Grandma Jean smiled at me and said that my boy was out front. I ran down the hall and busted out through the screen door onto the porch. Zach and Ed were out by Ed's truck with their heads together, talking something over. I didn't like the look of it, but Zach smiled at me and I knew everything was going to be okay. Ed clapped Zach on the shoulder and headed over to the barn, giving me a distracted wave. Zach had a small, soft sided cooler which I assumed had some dinner for us, and we took off down the road. When we climbed the embankment up to the blasted old corn field, I knew we were headed for the creek. I thought it would be nice, one more dip into that cold, cold water with Zach, once more to feel him hard against my leg.

We took a different route there than before and ended up at a place far upstream from the swimming hole. There we met Cody and Jimbo who were just arriving. They were carrying two giant inner tubes, like out of tractor tires or something. The boys all slapped hands and Zach gave them something I couldn't see and the other boys turned and headed out through the woods, calling to us to have a good time and not get drownded.

"We're floating today," Zach said.

"To where?"

"To wherever."

"Sounds good to me." I was thinking I would be fine with floating off together and never coming back and following the snaking trail of the creek down to the ocean and then off the edge of the world.

We manhandled the tubes down to the water and got situated in them. Zach held the cooler in his lap. The current grabbed us and we headed south. Our tubes bumped against each other and drifted apart and then together again. We talked. About nothing. About everything. Sometimes we would hold hands and float together, sometimes one of us would get farther downstream than the other. Under canopies of overhanging trees, in the bright sun where the creek headed out through somebody's pasture, past cows curiously watching us.

After a couple of hours, we came to a huge sandbar at a turn in the creek. There we pulled the tubes up onto the sand and took the cooler and sat under a clutch of willow trees and ate. Peanut butter and jelly (Zach's favorite, I'd learned) and overly ripe pears.

Zach walked down to the water and washed the pear juice and peanut butter off his hands, then came back and tapped me on the shoulder, saying "Tag, you're it" and ran. I jumped up and took off after him. He made several good moves around a fallen and rotting tree, but I caught him and took off myself.

Turns out I was faster than him.

And finally, I had to let him catch me so we could continue to play.

We got really hot running in the sand, and so we stripped out of our clothes and got in the river. There was no deep place for swimming so we had to just sit on our bottoms in the current and cool off. We'd been sitting there a few minutes, me trying to catch my breath from the icy water, Zach staring off into the trees on the other bank, when he started singing, soft at first, shyly, then full-voiced, echoing off the trees and filling the countryside with music.

"I'm a rolling stone all alone and lost, for a life of sin I've paid the cost, when I pass by all the people say, just another guy on the lost highway.

"Just a deck of cards and a jug of wine, and a woman's lies makes a life like mine, on the day we met, I went astray, I started rolling down that lost highway."

He smiled at me and I smiled back. He continued. I think there were four or five verses. He knew them all. When he finished, I clapped and said it was good.

I told him I didn't know the song. He said it was by Hank Williams, that his mama had a number of record albums by Hank and that he'd listened to them all many, many times. He said that sometimes his mama asked him and his brother to sing the songs off the albums instead of her just playing them on the record player, and that they obliged her. His brother Cody, he said, had the better voice, but they enjoyed singing together and entertaining their mama.

"We know all the words to just about ever song ole Hank ever wrote."

I asked about the song he'd just sung, and he said it was called "Lost Highway," and that like most of Hank's songs, it was sorrowful and that it predicted, according to Zach's mama, his early demise at the hands of alcohol and drugs.

"He died of alcohol and drugs?"

"From what I hear tell."

"Just how young was he?"

"In his twenties, I believe."

"Wow. That's bad."

"Wrote a lot of songs, though, in that time."

"Will you oblige me by singing another?"

He grinned and sang a tune called, "I'm So Lonesome I Could Cry," and the title was no lie. It was powerfully sad and Zack could a put a real hurt-sounding twang in his voice. When he concluded, we got out of the river and went and stood over our clothes, waiting for the sun to dry us. Zach gave me a look and then fell down in the sand and went to rolling. He was still river wet and the sand stuck to him all over, and when he stood up again, he looked for all the world like a sugared doughnut. I shrugged and then got down in the sand and rolled and rolled until I was dizzy. I stood up, a little shakily, and we stood there looking at each other. He crossed the short distance between us and put his hands on my shoulders and kissed me. I stepped into it, pushing my gritty body against his. We kissed a long time and rubbed against each other, but the sand took a fair amount of the pleasure out of that. I stepped back and said, "I gotta to wash this sand off." He nodded and we walked down to the water and splashed ourselves clean.

Without waiting to dry, we put on our clothes and Zach dragged some dry branches together and lit a fire. We sat across the fire from each other and fed it little sticks and pine cones and dry leaves. Zach stepped off into the woods and came back with a branch off some evergreen bush. When he put it on the fire, it smoked like crazy, a wild, eye-stinging, but fragrant smoke that even to this day when I smell it carries me back to that sandbar and to that boy.

We lay back on the sand, and I fell into what I can only describe as a waking dream, neither asleep nor awake. Then I heard Zach calling to me. He was down by the creek, getting the innertubes into the water. I walked down there and I caught him to me and kissed him. He gave me a look and I thought he was about to say something. What?

We lay down on the soft, wet sand next to the water and kissed like there would be no tomorrow.

As indeed there would not be.

And I thought, *Now*. Now he will do that which he must have dreamed so many times of doing with me. But he just kissed me and pushed against my belly, as he'd done before. We weren't going there, wherever there was. I didn't care. I just wanted him. Not what he'd do, not what he wanted or what I'd fantasized about. Just him. Just Zach.

We floated the rest of the afternoon until I thought we must be in Louisiana. Maybe it was true and we were never going back, to Ed and Jean's, to his mother's, to the bittersweet longings of childhood. The shadows were lengthening across the creek when I saw Ed standing on a bridge and waving. We pulled the tubes out of the water and up to the road, where Ed and Zach loaded them into the back of Ed's pickup. Then we drove back, Ed and Zach talking the whole way about the creek and the relative differences in tube and fishing boats for navigating the trip. Every mile toward home filled me with despair. Is despair too strong a word for a child's fears of losing everything? Ed dropped Zach and the tubes off just down the road from his house. I guess he didn't want to face off with Zach's mother. I know I didn't. Zach shook Ed's hand and thanked him for his help in arranging the float. He came around to the passenger side and leaned through the window as if to kiss me. I turned my face to him, but he just said goodbye.

I fought tears all the way home. Ed drove in silence. He was a good man, a better man than I knew at the time, I think.

On Sunday, both my parents drove up to get me. They were smiling and happy and talking out of my earshot with Jean and Ed. I wasn't interested anyway—whatever had been bothering them looked to be done. But so was my summer. So was Zach. He didn't come. I was thinking he saw my parents' car and knew—what? Our summer was over? That's what I knew. I loaded all my stuff into the car, kissed Jean and Ed goodbye, and climbed into the backseat. I tried to maintain a good disposition, but I heard my father say to Jean that I must have had a great summer because it was clear that I didn't want to go back home. Jean didn't reply, but looked at me and gave me a wry smile. We drove off down the dusty road toward the highway. I didn't watch the side of the road going by, didn't look for Zach standing in a field or among some trees watching my passing, my passing away out of his life forever. I stared at the back of the seat and fought tears.

Ellen Tovatt Leary

Almost Divorced

The simple fact that the dog did not bark told her that it was Michael at the screen door. Also, of course, he had phoned from the Seven-Eleven down the road. She had just enough time to get out of her flannel pajamas and fuzzy slippers and into—what? Not something obviously chosen for the occasion, but something nonchalant, and yet attractive. A long, dark green, wrap-around skirt and a black top. She held two earrings up to her ears and looked in the mirror. No. Maybe not. She didn't want to give the impression that she had gone to any special care to look attractive. She gathered her hair back in a barrette, put on a dab of lipstick, and opened the kitchen door.

"Hi! Come on in. I'm making coffee. Annie! Calm down!" she said to the dog who was wagging her tail, vigorously.

"Thanks, I just had some at Earl's. But you go ahead," said Michael. He came into the room and bent to rub the dog's ears.

"How's my girl? Eh? Howya been? Howya been? Been chasin' chipmunks?"

The black lab's tail knocked over an umbrella that had been set against the wall.

"She's been chasing more than chipmunks, I'm afraid," said Joanne. "Yesterday she brought home a baby rabbit."

"No!"

"Mmm. I had to bury it. I'm keeping an eye on her so that she doesn't dig it up again."

"Oh, Annie!" said Michael as the dog nuzzled his hand, whimpering with joy.

"Annie! Stop it! Go lie down," she said to the dog. "Are you sure you won't have a cup of coffee?"

"No thanks."

"I haven't had breakfast yet," said Joanne. "Got up late." She set a cup and the pot of coffee on the table and went to the wood stove to poke the embers. It was chilly for April, but the lilacs were beginning to bud.

"Am I coming by at a bad time?" asked Michael.

"Not at all," said Joanne, "I was going to bring the machine to you when I went into town next week. But if you need it immediately..."

Joanne pulled the door shut, picked up the umbrella and set it back against the wall. She went to get a container of milk from the refrigerator.

"No...but I figured as long as I had to be at Earl's for the car this morning, I might as well save you the trip," said Michael. "If it's no trouble, that is."

"No. No trouble," said Joanne. "I found all the pieces, I think."

"Great. I really appreciate it," Michael answered.

"No problem. Sit."

Michael pulled a chair out from the kitchen table and sat down.

"I meant the dog," said Joanne.

"Oh," said Michael as he started to rise.

"I'm kidding," said Joanne. "Sit down. Are you sure you won't have a cup of coffee?"

"Well, as long as it's made," said Michael as he sat back down at the table. The dog immediately lay down at his feet, her tail, thumping loudly against the floor.

"You wouldn't have a…cookie, or something to go with it, would you?" asked Michael.

"What's the matter? Yvonne got you on a diet?" asked Joanne as she set another cup and some spoons on the table.

"Yeah. All that gluten-free-wheat germ stuff. You know. Health food. It's OK, I guess, but…you know."

"Well, I made a batch of banana bread last night," said Joanne, opening the door to the refrigerator again. Inside was leftover pizza from the night before and a chocolate Easter bunny with its ears missing.

She shut the door quickly and placed a plate of banana bread on the table.

"Whoa. Great!" said Michael, taking off his plaid wool jacket and laying it over the chair-back.

"I noticed one of the stairs to the door needs fixing," Michael said, helping himself to a thick slice of the banana bread. "I could come around, maybe next week some time, after work and see what I could do with it."

"I already called Gino to come and have a look at it," said Joanne. She sat down at the table and poured them both coffee, pushing the sugar toward Michael.

Michael looked disgusted.

"Gino? Are you still in touch with Gino? I always thought he was…you know…"

"What?" asked Joanne.

"Half caf, half decaf."

"What are you talking about?" asked Joanne.

"You know," said Michael, flipping his hand back and forth, "AC-DC."

"First of all," said Joanne, "I find that offensive. Secondly: it is not true. And thirdly: even if it *were* true, what the hell does that have to do with fixing stairs?"

"What does he know about fixing stairs," said Michael. "I *built* the damn thing, you know."

He put three heaping teaspoons of sugar into his coffee and stirred vigorously.

"Are we talking 'stairs' here?" asked Joanne.

"What do you mean?"

"Are you jealous?"

"Of course not," said Michael. "You can see whoever you want. Just don't have him fuck up the goddamn stairs!"

Joanne looked at him.

"Well…I didn't want to bother you," she said.

"No bother."

Joanne nodded. They drank their coffee.

Seeing him across the breakfast table, as she had done so many mornings before, Joanne wondered, again, why they were getting a divorce. Like childbirth, she thought. All the pain sank to the back recesses of your mind and only the good part remained. Except Joanne had never experienced childbirth. She had only heard about it from her friends.

They had tried, for a time, to "get pregnant," which was how people phrased it these days—although she would be the only *pregnant* one, she thought. But somehow it never took. Thermometers and cool baths and a D-and-C later, they decided to stop short of fertility drugs and just let nature take its course. The course that nature took left them with no children of their own. They had Nicole, Michael's daughter from his first marriage, who had spent half of her time with them, growing up. But now she was grown and about to get married.

Joanne got on extremely well with Nicole, even during her teenage years when she spat venom at anyone within range. Nicole benefited from the fact that Joanne had grown up with her own stepmother and knew that stepmothers had to tread very difficult terrain. Virtual minefields. They could not be mothers and they could not be friends. They had to walk a thin line between the two. Joanne walked this line very well, having experienced the other side.

Looking at Michael now, with his broad shoulders and his muscular arms, Joanne thought that he looked better with his gray hair than he had looked when they had gotten married—when he had a thick, full head of black hair. Like James Brolin, she thought: the gray in the hair and the creases in his face just emphasized his masculinity. It wasn't fair that they did exactly the same thing for her. She brushed strands of her hair back from her face, self-consciously, wishing she had chosen a color other than black for her top; A brighter color, to give her a little lift—a little help this early in the day, with the bright, spring sunshine streaming in the window.

"I'll get the sewing machine," she said. "It's down in the basement." She got up from the table, sucking in her stomach.

As soon as Joanne disappeared, Michael helped himself to another piece of banana bread and got up to look around the living room, followed closely by the dog. He picked up a framed photograph of the two of them with Nicole as a young girl at the seashore. Nicole was about seven at the time the picture was taken and wore a floppy sun-hat and over-large sunglasses. They were all smiling for the camera. He stared at it for a moment before putting it back in its place.

Joanne returned from the basement with a large box. She had pinched her cheeks for color while she was out of the room and they glowed with an extra pink that Michael found a little startling.

"Here it is," she said.

"You know, the place looks very nice. Different," said Michael. "You changed things around."

"Yes," said Joanne, nodding. "Do you approve?"

"You no longer need my approval," said Michael.

"I mean…do you like it?"

"Yeah, it looks nice."

"Thanks," said Joanne, "Feng Shui." She set the box on the kitchen counter. Michael gave her a blank stare. Then he looked at the sewing machine box.

"Great!" he said as he sat back down at the table. "Joanne…?"

"Yes?"

"Nothing."

"What?"

"How've you been?"

"Great. And you?" She sat down and picked up her coffee.

"Not bad. Not bad. Can't complain."

There was a pause.

"How's Yvonne?" asked Joanne.

"She's fine. She's working now."

"Really?" said Joanne with interest. "Doing what?"

Michael hesitated.

"Maternity massages," he said, sheepishly. "She likes it," he shrugged.

"Uh-huh. How interesting," Joanne responded. "They come to your house? Or does she go to theirs?"

"They come to us. Women. By the dozen," said Michael, eyeing Joanne with a tilt of his head that presented his chin first, braced for the sarcasm.

"Hmmm. How interesting," Joanne said again.

"You know *Yvonne,*" Michael continued, emboldened by success, "she always lands on her feet."

"Or someone else's feet, as the case may be," said Joanne.

Michael gave a sort of snort, shook his head, and looked down at the table.

"Yvonne did nothing to break up our marriage," he said.

"She didn't exactly give it a shot in the arm," said Joanne.

"What did she do?" asked Michael with his palms up.

"Nothing," said Joanne. "She was just *there. There* in her little black tights with her little tight buns while I was at home with hot flashes and a red nose."

"Joanne, someone is *always* there," said Michael. "It wasn't Yvonne's fault. It was *us.*"

They drank their coffee in silence. Outside, a catbird called to its mate.

"Someone told me you were working at Penny's," said Michael, finally.

"Who told you?"

"Randy. She said you looked good."

"Just to make a little extra money," said Joanne, pleased to have gotten a good review.

"You never did know how to manage money," said Michael, a familiar edge to his voice.

"The rates went up on the mortgage," said Joanne.

"I thought we had a *fixed* rate?" said Michael.

"Did you come here to fight?" asked Joanne.

"No," said Michael, "but we had a *fixed rate* mortgage."

"I had to re-mortgage during the winter," said Joanne. "The car broke down."

Michael pursed his lips and made a conscious decision to let the matter rest. He sighed.

"I just don't like the idea of you working in the mall late at night. That's all," he said.

"That's no longer your concern, Michael."

"I know. I know."

The phone rang.

"Saved by the bell," Joanne said as she got up from the table.

"Hi Mom," she said into the receiver, "I'm fine. But I have company right now. Can I call you back? OK." She hung up the phone and sat back down at the table.

"Your mother?" asked Michael.

"No. *Your* mother," said Joanne.

"She still calls you?"

"Why not? I was her daughter-in-law for seventeen years. Do you think those relation-ships just disappear because we are divorced?"

"Not yet," said Michael.

"Not yet, what?"

"We're not divorced yet. We signed the papers, but we didn't get the final thing back from the court. We're *almost* divorced."

"Whatever," said Joanne.

"I didn't know she still called you," said Michael… "She's not crazy about Yvonne."

"I know."

"What do you mean? What does she say?"

"That she's not crazy about Yvonne."

"That's all?"

"That's all."

"Yeah. She blames her for the break-up," said Michael.

He got up from the table and opened the sewing machine box, looking in.

"My lips are sealed," said Joanne.

It would be convenient to be able to blame someone else, Joanne thought. But she knew it wasn't Yvonne's fault. If you run your car off a road and into a tree, you can't blame the tree, thought Joanne. Once, over lunch with a girlfriend, Joanne had unloaded a litany of things that irritated her about Michael.

"But he's *worth* it," the friend had replied.

At the time she had chalked this up to the fact that her friend had never been married. But now, when she recalled the remark, she could see the simple wisdom behind it. Why was it always *hindsight* that was twenty-twenty?

Michael looked at his watch.

"I'd better get going," he said, coming back to the table and downing the last of his coffee. "I really appreciate your letting me have the sewing machine. I think we paid 50 bucks for it 10 years ago. Today it would cost about $200."

"I just hope it works," said Joanne. "What are you planning to do? Sew while all the pregnant ladies are getting massaged?"

"I like to sew," Michael said, defensively. "My father used to sew."

"I remember," said Joanne.

"I just haven't done it for a while. Is the instruction manual with it?"

"The *instruction manual*? I don't know. Did it have an instruction manual?"

"Of course, it did."

"No. I don't think I saw it when I put all the parts in the box."

"Oh well," said Michael. "I guess I can figure it out…"

"Let me check once more downstairs," Joanne said.

"Sure," said Michael, and sat back down on the chair.

Joanne went down the stairs to the basement, stopped and leaned against the concrete wall. She put her hand over the left side of her chest, where her heart was, and rubbed it as though she had just been struck by a stray baseball. *We've been through this and through this.* It didn't work. Or, rather, it worked for a few months and then fell apart again, she thought. Like a second-hand car. We've had so many trial separations and getting back together again. All those fights and tears! She knew she could not go through another one of those.

"What are the grounds for divorce?" the lawyer had asked them.

"Irreconcilable differences," answered Joanne.

"After seventeen years?" asked the lawyer.

"Yes," she said. There was a pause while the lawyer looked, distrustfully, from one to the other.

"Has he ever hit you?" he asked Joanne.

Michael and Joanne's eyes met quickly, and then they looked away. They were both remembering the time when Michael, out of his mind with frustration during a fight, had swung his fist and spun her around with a sharp blow to the shoulder. He had been so distraught by hitting her that he had sunk to his knees in tears, banging his head on the floor. Michael was a Conscientious Objector: the blow had hurt him more than it had hurt Joanne. Now she looked at the lawyer.

"No," she said.

And so they were granted a divorce. Irreconcilable differences. It was for the best.

But winter had been long. And there were just so many self-help books you could read and diets you could go on. And the tae-bo fitness tape she had purchased sat in the drawer after only two viewings. For the second viewing, she watched listlessly from the easy chair while the instructor said enthusiastically, "That's it! You're doing great! A little higher." And despite her best intentions, she occasionally found herself rewinding the movies and playing the romantic parts over again. Except for the dog and her friends and the obligation to get to work every morning, she knew she was in grave danger of curling up tighter and tighter into her own little ball.

Michael appeared in her dreams with regularity, she knew…although she slept deeply and rarely remembered her dreams. Suddenly, in the middle of the day, opening a drawer, or biting into a tuna sandwich, or pushing her grocery cart, a picture would pop up in her mind, making her draw in a quick breath, and she would realize that, once again, she had dreamed of Michael. He was an ingrained part of her subconscious. She would never be completely free of him.

"Are you going to the wedding?" Michael called down to the basement.

"I don't think so," Joanne answered, looking under things for the instruction booklet.

"Why? Plenty of families have divorces and things now."

"I know but…her mother will be there, and, well, Yvonne will be there and…how will Nicole introduce me? Her *former* step-mother?"

"What do you mean?" said Michael, "Why can't she just say, 'this is my mother, this is my stepmother and…'" his voice trailed off.

"Where's Emily Post when you need her?" said Joanne. "I think it would be better if I just stayed home. And you can stop rolling your eyes," she added.

"Jesus! What've you got down there? Radar?"

"I have a gift for her," said Joanne, coming back up the stairs. "I'm going to give her my garnet necklace. She's always admired it, and it is her birthstone. January. And…who else am I going to give it to?"

Michael raised his eyebrows and nodded, approvingly.

"But I think she will really be upset if you're not at the wedding," he said. "She really cares about you."

"Don't make me feel guilty," Joanne said.

"Why not? You belong there. You were close to her for a long time. You brought her up, practically."

"Michael, please. It's difficult enough for me."

She had checked her horoscope on the day that they had filed the divorce papers. "Sagittarius: the decisions you make today will benefit your life for a long time to come," it read. Who could believe in that *nonsense*? She cut it out of the newspaper and scotch-taped it to the side of the refrigerator.

Joanne held up the sewing machine manual. "Ta-dah! I found it. Amazing!!"

"Joanne. I'm sorry," said Michael. I didn't come here to argue with you."

"It's OK. Forget it."

"It's just that…the last I heard they were planning on you at the wedding."

"Look, Michael," Joanne said, putting the manual in the box and turning to him, "maybe some people can just get married and divorced without causing a ripple in their grocery shopping, but I am not one of them. I am just trying to put one foot in front of the other and go on with my life…and I am *doing* it! I work two jobs and keep the wood stove going and shovel the car out of the snow. I even bought a drill the other day so I wouldn't have to pay the phone guy seventy-five dollars to put the extension in the bedroom. And you know what? I drilled the hole through the goddamned wall and made it work! I'm managing. I'm doing it. But it isn't easy, that's all. And a wedding...so full of promise and hope for the future...well...I'm just not up to that yet."

What she didn't say, and wouldn't mention, was the *hardest* part of living alone. Unshared beauty. The things she used to rush to tell him about: The first sound of the peepers after a snowy winter. The aroma that the grape hyacinths give off just before they show color...perfuming the air with the smell of grapes. The mother skunk with her four, tiny babies by the side of the road. The heron rising from the pond. And then, of course, the loneliness of nights when, getting out of bed, careful not to wake him, she would suddenly realize that he was no longer there.

Michael stared at the coffee cup and worked his jaw muscles.

"Nicole will be disappointed. That's all," he said. Joanne sat down and leaned across the table.

"A divorce is a little like a death," she went on in a quieter tone. "Even if both parties want it. Even if the patient is on life support and has a DNR sign on the chart. When the death actually occurs...the finality of it...it is still so jarring. I mean...Don't you think?"

"I know, Joanne," said Michael. "I was thinking the other day: I've known you half of my adult life."

"Michael, you never *had* an adult life," said Joanne.

No wonder he prefers Yvonne, she thought. She beams affection on him like a sun lamp. Just as intense and just as phony.

The week she signed the divorce papers, Joanne decided that she should take off her wedding ring. She got a tiny, white string-tag and wrote, "save for Nicole," on it. But when she tried to get the ring off her finger, it wouldn't come. She soaped her hand and soaked it in cold water to reduce the swelling. But nothing worked. She blamed the weight she had gained over the past seventeen years and went to bed, disgusted with herself. The next morning, remembering an old trick, she got out her sewing kit. She wound thread around her finger, squeezing it tighter and tighter right up to the ring, until, finally she was able to slide the ring over the threaded part and get it off. That's how they get them off dead people, Joanne thought, ironically.

"Well. By next week the divorce will be final," said Michael, getting up from the table.

"That's for the best, Michael."

Suddenly Michael sat back down and sighed deeply.

"What's the matter?" Joanne asked.

"Joanne...I didn't just come for the sewing machine," said Michael. Her heart rate quickened in alarm.

"Is something wrong?" she asked.

"I came to tell you something," he said.

"Are you all right?"

"Yes. Fine."

"Is it Nicole?"

"Joanne. I'm getting married. Yvonne and I. We're getting married. As soon as the divorce is final, that is," said Michael.

Joanne's face went white. She tried to appear unfazed, but her whole system seemed to drain itself of blood.

"I didn't want to tell you over the phone. And I didn't want you to hear it from someone else," said Michael.

"No. No, of course not," said Joanne. "Well. How nice for you. I mean, congratulations!"

A wave of dizziness swept over her. Her hands felt clammy and she suddenly knew that she was going to faint.

"I'm so sorry," she managed to say as her head went down on the table.

"Joanne! God! Are you all right?" said Michael, jumping to his feet. He grabbed her as she started to slip to the floor.

"Jesus! Joanne!" said Michael, looking around for water at the kitchen sink, but afraid to let go of her. He lay her down gently on the floor. The dog, startled, woke up and wandered over to them. Joanne came to. She blinked her eyes and for a moment couldn't figure out what had happened. She was in her kitchen. That, she knew. And Michael was there. It seemed a perfectly natural scene. Then, as if remembering a dream, the fragments slowly started to coalesce. The reality jarred her back into complete consciousness.

"I'm sorry," she said as he helped her up to a sitting position. She put her hands to her forehead. Her wrap-around skirt had opened, in the fall, revealing her upper thighs and her panties. Carefully, Michael pulled her skirt back around her. The protective nature of the gesture...the ingrained, automatic, husbandly nature of the gesture, touched her so deeply, that she began to weep.

"Oh, Joanne," he said, as he knelt and rocked her like a child, "Please don't. I'm so sorry. I guess I should have given you some warning. But I thought...I don't know. You seemed so sure. That we were doing the right thing. I didn't think it was going to *matter* all that much to you."

"Well," said Joanne regaining her composure, sniffing and wiping her tears with the heel of her palms, "they say 'the third time's the charm!'"

"Yeah," said Michael, grateful for her mood change, "but they also say, 'three strikes and you're out!'"

Slowly he helped her to her feet and sat her in the chair. He opened the cabinet that contained the glasses with the familiarity of one well acquainted with the kitchen and got her a drink of water from the sink.

"Thanks," she said, breathing deeply. "I'm OK now. I really am. I don't know what hit me."

"I guess it was a shock," said Michael.

"Apparently," said Joanne, with a short laugh.

"Joanne," said Michael, "I just want you to know...I believe that the heart is big enough to hold new loves without discarding the old."

"You sound like you've been ordering Chinese food," said Joanne.

"I mean it. I'm not making a joke."

"I know. I'm sorry. I happen to agree with you, in fact," she said.

"I was hoping you would wish us well."

"I do," said Joanne.

"Don't say 'I do,'" said Michael with a smile.

The dog had found some banana bread crumbs on Michael's chair and was licking them up, sideways.

"Are you sure you're OK?" asked Michael, anxiously.

"I'm sure."

"I guess I better get going then. Yvonne will be wondering what happened to me."

He took his jacket from the back of the chair and put it on.

"Don't forget the sewing machine," said Joanne, as she took another sip of the water.

"Right! Thanks!" said Michael.

"Think nothing of it," said Joanne.

Michael gathered up the box from the counter. As he headed for the door, the dog followed him. He reached down to pet her and opened the door, careful not to let her out. He walked down the stairs, letting the screen door close behind him with a click, paused at the broken step, and then continued on his way.

The dog pawed at the screen and whined. Joanne got up from the table and gently pushed her away.

"I know, but it's for the best, Annie. It really is," she said as she shut the kitchen door and locked it.

Zoe Messinger

Baaa-Baresco

I walked into the warm, chocolatey center of the Angelino bistro. I was on fire. Little top hats sat on everyone's table in perfect agnolotti. I was wearing my bandana and blazer—a classy antagonist to the traditional garb.

"Anything to drink," she slurred, as any fox does.

"Wine," I said. "We're celebrating." What are we celebrating? We're celebrating the fact that I turned off my mind, pulled it out of my head, and threw it away. A cynical champagne cork flew through the air from the other side. "Hurry along, foxy," I said, trying to grab her brush before it wagged away. No, I didn't say that. I didn't do that. I couldn't move. I was too mesmerized by the little hats and the pappardelle hanging from the ceiling. Richness hanging above me, in plain view. I was so close to all of it.

The bread came to join me, along with her friends cracker, olive, and multigrain. We were a culturally diverse group. I was the only whitey besides ciabatta, but she was Italian, so she had flare. *Bellissima, bellissima!* The somm made his way over, sheepishly, as any sheep should. "How can I help you tonight?" he asked.

All I heard was baaa-baresco. So I whispered it back into his ear, "Baaa-baresco," just like I heard it. He trotted away, adjusting his shearling bow tie.

I sat back, as the fire burned into the night, as the warm, chocolatey center let down and enveloped me, as the wine decanted down. Sips later, my little hats came floating down onto the center of the table, like pillows, like little dreams. I took a bite and the dancing stopped, the music stopped, the grazing stopped—everyone was suspended in the air—the horses, the carriages, the knights, the ballerinas, the bulls, and me—floating—like a contemporary painting at The Met. I parted my naked lips and opened wide. The delicate mascarpone filling danced through my mouth and down my throat, pirouetting every swirl, her white sheer scarf suspended like the sky on the first day of the last day. She held me hostage, a prisoner to her divinity, like the fox and the sheep, the bread basket—my mind. My mind that I threw away. Somehow she made her way back just in time for dinner. She always does.

Emily Rubin

Water Finds Its Own Level

> *"A blob transforms, leaving behind a squirming cylindrical body. I am a blob!*
> *A milkshake. I am all fury and a little furry too. A butterfly emerges from mush,*
> *what emerges from a latrine except shit and piss and where do the tampons go?*
> *I am finding this human tainted world a pain."*
> —*Journal entry, Ellie Rue Solomon, Girl Scout Camp, 1967.*

Ellie Rue buried the journal at the end of the summer next to the latrine she was forced to clean with a toothbrush after a water balloon fight she instigated went wrong. Upon her return, she gave up on the Girl Scouts and embraced a life of touch football, baseball cards, chemistry set explosions, short hair, and dungarees with rolled up cuffs.

•••

Years later, in her early twenties, in the midst of renovating an apartment in an abandoned Lower East Side building, in another sort of transformation, she was reminded of the cocoon she had so closely watched. Her transformation to apartment living required one more task before she could move in: the installation of a toilet. It was 1981 and she had recently turned twenty-two and had saved waitressing tips to purchase the toilet. It was the memory of the cocoon and the latrine that inspired her to approach the task of acquiring and installing, like the caterpillar hunkering down to allow for the natural order of change coupled with the discipline and patience of the knuckle-scraping precision of cleaning a latrine with a toothbrush.

She was at the bakery around the corner from the apartment, reading the corkboard advertisements for a variety of services.

Babysitting. Call Jenelle. References upon request.

Housecleaning. Call Jenelle. References upon request.

Apartment for Rent: $250. Call Jenelle. References required upon request.

1972 Volkswagen Beetle. Runs good. Best Offer. Call Larry.

The signs had tabs to rip off with phone numbers. Every flyer had the same phone number: 212-598-7070. As she stared up at the signs, a lanky, stringy-haired guy wearing a red baseball cap sidled up to her. He spoke quietly, as if he didn't want the other customers to hear.

"Are you looking for something?"

He had a broad, chipped-tooth smile and craggy hands filled with grease.

"I need a toilet installed."

"Martin Cruz. I could do it for you."

"Really?"

"Where you be living with no toilet?

"Around the corner, on 7th Street."

"Which building?"

"The one between the garden and the rubble."

"I know that building."

"I'm not living there yet, just clearing out the mess. All I need is a toilet to move in."

Martin took a bow, holding his coffee cup above his head in a gesture of deference to royalty.

"Cruz Construction and Plumbing. Toilet installer at your service."

"How much does a toilet installer charge?"

"I hear there are two vacant apartments on the top floor. I'll do the toilet for free if you recommend me," he said.

"I'm new there. I think there's only one apartment left. A guy they call Hump moved in not too long ago."

"I'll hook you up."

"Are you licensed?"

"Not necessary, and a licensed plumber would be out of your price range."

Ellie Rue figured her coveralls and worn work boots were an indication of her limited finances. In the bakery the gurgling sound of milk being steamed for café con leche mixed with neighborhood gossip. Everyone stopped talking as an older gentleman with a plastic bag on his head and several more covering his shoeless feet came into the bakery. Martin excused himself. At the counter he gave the girl a five-dollar bill.

"For Jorge. Make him a bread and cheese. He likes his coffee with six sugars," he said.

The young woman in a yellow uniform took the money without a smile. The plastic bags crackled like a campfire as the old man shifted back and forth and shuffled along the floor. Martin went over to him.

"I got you, Jorge," he said.

A grunt of recognition and a nod with darting eyes was Jorge's response. Martin went back to Ellie Rue.

"He's a poet. Lost his mind when someone stole his thousand-page manuscript," Martin said.

A smell of oranges and peppermint had come in with Jorge.

"He has a kind face, and he smells really sweet. When do you want to install the toilet?"

"You get a porcelain throne from the plumbing store on First Avenue, bring it to the apartment, and I'll take care of the rest. Tomorrow?"

The girl at the counter waved to Jorge to retrieve his food. Ellie Rue watched as he shuffled forward. Coffee and sandwich in hand, he closed his eyes and took in the aromas, then shuffled back to the door.

"Buenos dios, Jorge," Martin said.

Jorge gave a deep-throated grumble and went outside, where he lifted his head to the sky and picked a spot in the sun and settled cross-legged on the ground against the building.

"That was nice of you," Ellie Rue said.

"Welcome to Loisaida. Lo-ee-sigh-da."

"Lo-ee-sigh-da, got it. Is that Spanish?"

"Nuyorican for Lower East Side."

"It rolls nicely off the tongue. Lo-ee-sigh-da."

"P & J Plumbing will have everything you need."

The next day Ellie Rue made the sojourn to the plumbing store. Inside, the smell of grease and steel mixed with cigarettes and man-sweat. It felt tribal and awkwardly comforting as stares and smiles of nicotine-stained teeth came along with the welcoming gestures to step up to the counter. Two guys telling stories raised their voices as she shyly sidled past them.

"Why would someone flush dentures down a toilet?"

This wide-bellied older guy wore a Led Zeppelin T-shirt.

"To punish grandma?" his buddy said.

"Those false teeth got lodged so far down, we had to go through the ceiling of the apartment below to get them out of the pipe."

"Were they in one piece?"

"Yup."

"What did grandma say?"

"Thank you."

"Don't tell me?"

"She did."

The creases in their weathered faces went topographic.

"You should write a book."

"Call it *Pipe Dreams*?"

"More like *Shit Storm*."

They looked to see how Ellie Rue reacted.

"That's funny," she said.

"What do you need, little lady?" a guy behind the counter, leaning forward, asked.

Her head barely reached over the top of the high counter. Behind were shelves filled with tubes, pipes, ductwork, and elbow joints. The counter guy had a tattoo on his neck of a faucet with a large tear-shaped drip. The place looked like a warehouse for robot replace-ment parts.

"A toilet."

She stood on tiptoes to look up and over the counter. Getting closer she saw another tattoo of a skull and crossbones on the side of his neck which had, instead of bones, toilet plungers for the crosspieces. He pointed to the middle of a page in a well-worn OED-sized catalog.

"This is the only toilet that fits a tenement bathroom."

"Okay," she said.

"American Standard. It's $166."

The toilet was more than her month's rent. She counted out precious waitress tips and calculated how much rice and beans would cost for a week. He tapped his pen and leaned over the counter.

"Do you have someone to install the toilet?" he asked.

"A guy from the neighborhood."

"You need a licensed plumber for the inspection."

The building was not likely to be inspected any time soon. The city inspectors wanted nothing to do with buildings they figured would all soon be demolished.

"If he can't do it, I'll come back for a recommendation."

"We don't appreciate cleaning up the messes of amateurs."

"Hopefully, that won't be necessary."

"Do you need it delivered?"

"No, thank you."

Ellie Rue pulled up the flatbed dolly she had brought along. Looking over the bill, she noticed a surcharge of ten dollars.

"What's this for?" she asked.

"A donation to the local union."

"What?"

"If you used a licensed plumber, I would take it off."

"Got it."

She pulled out a crumpled bill. Her stomach groaned.

The salesman spoke into a microphone to alert the storeroom.

"One American Standard. No delivery."

A worker came up from the basement carrying the toilet and loaded it onto the dolly. He helped Ellie Rue get it out to the street.

"Good luck, little lady."

As she stood in the morning sun hitting the brand-new porcelain, two dogs were humping in front of the shop. They turned their heads with worried looks, as if they were up to something illicit, or maybe just worried about being stuck. She left the dogs to their own devices and proceeded to pull the toilet home. At the corner of Avenue A and 7th Street, she felt a spasm in her back and stopped to stretch.

An older gentleman smoking a cigar said, "Looks like you're ready in case of an emergency."

"I like to be prepared," Ellie Rue said.

"American Standard. Good choice," he said.

He chewed on the end of his cigar and walked across the street.

Approaching Avenue B, she passed the domino-playing locals ensconced in a rousing game. They had a pit bull tied to a drainpipe next to the gaming table. As she pushed the toilet, avoiding a large crack in the sidewalk, the dolly skirted close to the dog. The dog shot out like a bullet with fangs. Ellie Rue saw herself reflected in the dog's dark eyes, its jaw an inch away.

"The dog! The dog! Watch out!" one of the players yelled.

A spiked choke collar held the dog back. Front paws aloft like a pugilist, the dog coughed but didn't back off until one of the players put a metal pipe to its chest. Another player threw a scrap of meat from a sandwich to the ground. The dog ate ravenously.

"Embarazada y pero."

Ellie Rue was shaken and breathless.

"She's pregnant. That toilet must have spooked her," the pipe-wielding fellow said.

"I didn't see her. Just trying to get this home."

"You're lucky she didn't take a chunk out of you or the toilet."

"Chevere," another player remarked.

He pushed a row of dominoes that made a fantail wave around the table. Everyone watched and gave a cheer when it stopped.

"Gracias," Ellie Rue said.

The domino players spit and laughed as she continued down the street. At the front of the building, she stopped. The front door opened and the guy Hump whom she had heard about was coming out. He was bear-sized and wore green khaki coveralls much like Ellie Rue's except his were big enough for two or more of her to fit inside.

"A girl and her toilet, now isn't that cozy," he said.

She affectionately hugged the toilet. He and Ellie Rue had not officially met.

"Nice new throne you got there, girlie," Hump said.

He was a gruff, attractive mess. The middle finger of one hand had an oversized splint.

"I have someone coming to install it today," Ellie Rue said.

"You're on four, right?

"You want to *hump* it up?"

"Hey, you being funny? How'd you know my name?"

"Thalia told me to look for you. I'm Ellie Rue."

"That's a poetically sad name for such a pretty little girl. I'm Don Sawlkowski,."

Flustered by the compliment, she tripped over her own feet, stumbling and making the toilet wobble on the dolly.

She grabbed it to steady it.

"Why 'Hump'?"

"After the Hunchback of Notre Dame."

He pointed over his left shoulder to a slight hump. It wasn't very pronounced, more like a bulging shoulder muscle.

"Charles Laughton played that hump to great effect; heartbreaking.

"Hump Sawzall is my *nom de plume.*"

"A writer?"

"Contractor. I write poetry and do some journalism on the side."

Ellie Rue wondered if his poetry was construction cantos, or perhaps plumbing palindromes?

"This is a big day for me," she said.

"First flush is revelatory."

"It's all I need to move in."

Without a word, Hump picked up the toilet and carried it up the four flights. In his gorilla-sized hands the toilet looked like a salesman's half-scale model. With the door to the apartment opened, Hump stepped over construction debris and placed the toilet in the bathroom.

"One toilet delivered," he said.

"What happened to your hand?" Ellie Rue asked.

"Fireworks and LSD don't mix."

He held up the middle finger.

"Looks like a commentary on Independence Day," Ellie Rue said.

"These Reagan years got me down."

Past the front door the construction debris was obsessively arranged. Wood slats stacked in neat rows. A perfectly circular mound of used nails. Slabs of broken linoleum lined up like a fanatic's record collection.

"I've never seen such carefully arranged demolition debris. Compulsive, huh?"

"Just giving respect to the mess."

He bowed and wiped his brow with a bandana. A scuffling and squeak came from behind the bathroom wall. They both stared at the plywood covering the portal of original entry. The scampering stopped.

"Is that a..." Ellie Rue's eyelid twitched.

"Better get a cat, maybe two. That ain't no mouse."

"There's always something going on behind these walls."

"This building has solid bones. You look pretty solid too, a bit bulked up from all the work you been doing?"

"Excuse me?"

"Strong; you look strong."

"I have put on a few pounds since I came here. I can't resist the bakery around the corner."

"What about this guy you have coming to do the toilet? How'd he hustle you?"

"He wants to live here."

"The apartment upstairs across from me?"

"Yes. Why?"

"I took the windows from that apartment and put them in mine. Don't tell him."

"You stole them?"

"Sawzall's Salvage is the name of my construction company. I'll be home later. Tap on this if you need me, I'll come down." He tapped the riser in the bathroom with the metal splint on his finger and left.

In the apartment the sun hit the piles of debris that beckoned to be bagged, but they would have to wait. This day was all about the toilet. Lost in thought, staring at the hole where the toilet would be installed, she came back to the present with a knock at the door.

"Anybody home?"

"Martin?"

"Your toilet installer has arrived."

He stood at the door, carrying one empty compound bucket and another filled with wrenches and hammers, saws, and screwdrivers. He set down and turned over the empty one.

"Glad you're here," Ellie Rue said.

He gestured to the overturned bucket.

"Have a seat," he said.

Martin was skinny-skinny, average height, probably twenty-five but looked younger. He bit his nails down to the quick.

"Are you from Puerto Rico?" Ellie Rue asked.

"Cuba. Operation Peter Pan got me out in '62. I was twelve."

"I'd like to go to Cuba," Ellie Rue said.

"Not an easy place, but no one's homeless. All the kids go to school. I send my family electronics and sneakers."

"I'd like to see what a revolution is all about."

"This country had a revolution too, you know. Did you say anything to the powers that be about me? Let's get your throne hooked up," Martin said.

He held a flashlight over the hole.

"Have a look."

Ellie Rue leaned over the abyss, afraid of what could be in the netherworld below.

"It looks clean all the way down," Martin said.

"Okay. That's a good thing, right?" Ellie said.

Martin pulled a wire hanger out of his tool bag, snipped and bent it into a stiff pointer, and pushed it down the hole.

"No obstructions. We'll be ready to get the water turned on soon."

"Hector, the super, said he would take care of it when we were ready."

"Go get him."

Ellie Rue knocked on the apartment directly across the hall. The smell of Hector's cologne hung around his front door. The smell overwhelmed her as he opened the door, freshly shaved and nattily dressed in crisp green khaki shirt and chinos.

"Is it the big day?" he asked.

"The moment of truth has arrived," she said.

In the bathroom Martin placed a gasket around the hole and shifted the bowl into place. Ellie Rue looked anxiously over the top of Martin's bony shoulder.

"I have to tighten the bolts evenly, otherwise you can crack the porcelain."

"We could use a plumber around here," Hector said.

"We'll talk," Martin said.

Martin went back and forth with the wrench, tightening one bolt then the other like a dentist working the screws in a gaping jaw for dental implants.

"She's all set," he said.

"I'm a little nervous," Ellie Rue said.

"The water is turned off. Fill this bucket from the hydrant."

She stared at the bucket.

"You heard the man, *vamanos*. I'll go down to the basement and wait for your signal before I turn on the water," Hector said.

Ellie Rue and Hector went downstairs together.

"I'll hear the water flowing once you pour it down. The pipes, they talk."

On the street three or four kids were getting soaked in the gushing stream from the open hydrant. While Ellie Rue filled the bucket, a black-and-white pit bull was biting a side stream. It started barking at the bucket, then took a couple of fast circles, trying to catch its tail, and went back to biting the stream. Ellie Rue was wary of the dog, but her fears were allayed when a little girl in a pink bathing suit jumped on the back of the dog and kissed its head.

"I love you, Elsie," she said.

The dog lifted its nose in the air and shook as the girl held on. A woman sitting on a stoop across the street yelled.

"Selena, let Elsie be!"

"She likes it when I ride her!"

"She's a dog, not a horse!"

The little girl got off the dog and twirled around in the gushing stream. Martin leaned out of Ellie Rue's kitchen window.

"Hey, get up here! You can cool off later."

As she carried the bucket up the four flights, the water sloshed like a trail of tears—*tears of joy,* she thought.

"You do the honors," Martin said.

She poured the water into the bowl. The thirsty, gaping mouth easily received the libation. They watched as it disappeared into the abyss. A gurgling came up from the pipes that reminded Ellie Rue of her Aunt Norma's lungs being suctioned when pneumonia got the best of her. The sound gave Hector his cue to turn on the water.

"Give it a minute. You'll see water finds its own level," Martin said.

After a few minutes Hector came upstairs and joined them.

The three crowded into the tiny bathroom and stared down into the white porcelain. There were more burps and gurgles, but then the water rose to a respectable, flushable level.

"Go ahead, give it a flush," Martin said.

Ellie Rue pushed the chrome handle. The water disappeared in a clockwise swirl and slowly the bowl filled back up. The three stared at their reflections in the water, framed like an old-time portrait of proud bandits after a successful heist.

"You're in business," Martin said.

"Why don't they come with seats?" she asked.

"Personal preference; everyone is different. You can get one cheap on Canal Street," Hector said.

"You are the proud owner of a working toilet," Martin said. He started to collect his tools.

"A job well done," Hector said.

"My work here is done," Martin said.

"And I am officially home. I couldn't have done it without you," Ellie Rue said.

Martin and Hector, having bonded even in the short time over the plumbing experience, left, talking about the apartment upstairs.

It must be a guy thing, Ellie Rue thought and sat on the overturned bucket, staring at the toilet.

"Wait, Martin, you left the bucket," she called after them.

"You don't have much furniture. Consider it a housewarming gift," he said.

"I will cherish it. Thank you."

"Buckets are good for sitting and hauling," Martin said.

She pushed the toilet handle, this time with a proud gesture of confidence. The water disappeared and returned. The swirling water was a thrill. The sun came through the window and shimmered on the agitated water. Ellie Rue looked out the window and down to the garden. Doña Carmen, Hector's mother who lived on the first floor, was tending a plot in the empty lot next to the building that she had made into a garden. Ellie Rue's heart swelled, and she thought, *Now that I am here, really here, maybe I can join in on this garden too.* She flushed the toilet again and again, feeling with each successive flush that she had crossed the great divide from homelessness and had landed ashore at home. She needed toilet paper. A new expense to add to her monthly nut. Scary, mythic, defiantly real.

Nick Sweeney

Wheel

(First published in Ambit Magazine [print only], 1999)

The flowers of the counter-revolution all dead, their scent fading with each new moon, I hear fortune at a distance, spinning its wheel. I walk through the streets of the new age among people blinded by things that glitter, afraid to think that one day the gold at the heart of the light won't come to them.

My grandfather found a pebble of amber in the sand at Łeba and sat on the dune cliffs looking at the Baltic Sea. He thought of the Prussian knights owning it and all that lay in it, owning the land, the labor of its people, even owning the glare that came in from the horizon.

He turned to the girl next to him, his sweetheart, my grandmother, neither of them knowing about the shabby dynasty they'd create, and said, "Much good it did them, in the end." The knights came again, of course, brought fire and misery, left ruins and ghosts. They didn't know about that either, though I once heard grandfather say he'd had a dread feeling all along that the Prussians would be back for their pebble. It sat hidden in plain pride of place in one of those pointless glass cabinets people go in for here. Throughout the Second World War, it was secreted in a cistern, then about grandfather's person. From the Oświęcim death camp he walked a widower's walk through the scarred and smoking country back to Warsaw, a city of broken stones, his pebble intact in his pocket.

"A symbol for him of the land," I asked my father once.

He said, "What?"

"Or of the sea?"

"Eh?"

"Of the nation, the people?"

He said, "How should I know?" He swept a harried hand across his brow. "I can't even finish the crossword."

All the same, when he gave me the stone to keep, he said, "Promise you'll take care of it?" I promised, and he read my mind and said, "I don't know why, but you must never lose it." He had other preoccupations by then, was about to do that widower's walk to the hospital to pester his last nurse. I held the stone, imagined it as the hard yellow stuff gripping his vital organs, killing him with its riches.

•••

I have no riches, no money in the bank. "And I don't believe capitalism will save us all," I say to anybody who asks me. I have not much hair and old clothes and a chipped front tooth, a smile that will stay with me like grandfather's amber. I have a face from *before,* young people tell me, made to last in these corner-cutting times.

I was a curious child thrown up by times of darkness and the grim mirth of those who sought to better themselves in a system in which all were meant to be equal. I got a life sentence; I will never forget the rituals that made me, church and school and party in a country that didn't know what it wanted to be.

Out train windows I see that country, mountains, valleys, rivers, cities, towns, the midget houses built over allotments of fertile land on which nothing grows except the ugliest of vegetables, all fixed in time. I see a lit-up Christ over the engine-turning yards at Katowice, His fingers pointing out cattle-trucks slinking by in painful memory. Near Mława I see a line of trees upended, whose topmost branches will grow into the ground in a parody of roots. Giant churches rise out of the land as if rooted there in imitation of the factories and their cooling towers, their gas-burners that light the traveller's night.

I met the only woman I ever knew on a train ride made everlasting by the unfathomable logic of communism applied to railways. It was Gliwice to Lublin; she was thin and sickly with a face so pale the light seemed to pause inside it, she was head-scarved, in a dowdy coat and battered shoes, looking for something to eat, somebody to love. In Lublin we bought bruised apples and ate them as we walked, made jokes, laughed and choked. Lublin's market streets were muddy underfoot and ruined, spoiled fruit stamped into them, wooden slats from broken boxes, an ugly wind blowing us the stench of dead flowers.

We sat on steps, knowing we'd live together and marry, buy a glass-fronted cabinet, and have babies. Life stretched ahead of us, some of its spaces filled in. I thought I ought to warn her that in my family the women we married died young. Instead I asked her name, which turned out to be Iza: Izabela, Catholic name, Gypsy name.

Just as Iza was a sweetheart going begging, Roma children make historic supplicating gestures, offer the sight of borrowed babies; the new era doesn't seem to be doing them much good. The Roma know that democracy suits them no more than communism ever did, and that persecuted people are just as persecuted under climates of smiley liberalism. People say they have shoes really, that they get them back when they bring home gleaming coins.

The children see my smile and try to soft-touch me. "You have no heart," one of them said to me once.

I said to her, "I have plenty of heart, but no money."

There are easy livings to be made, I know, but somehow when the free market came to me, I didn't know how to rise to the occasion and make one. Others get rich overnight, if they don't get caught first. "They must have a secret," people say, but the simple matter is that they're dark in the heart with ambition minus talent. I ride the length of this country of ours, see them scattering the new currency behind them, happy to watch, that smile on my face. "I have no gold," I tell the other rail-riders I meet, young Antipodeans, fresh-faced Scandinavians, haughty Latin girls with matchstick bodies, and at the time in their lives in which our paths cross they're impressed by this, don't know that they will one day turn into their parents and have babies and buy cars and glass-fronted cabinets. "Let the others have the gold," I say, and they back up their agreement with fists punched in the air.

•••

The Prussians got the gold, but they didn't find every piece of it. Heading for Łeba and the sea, I walk my widower's walk to the station and am reassured by the glow in the sky of the north. Tomorrow's a prospect like any other, I remind myself, pregnant with disasters, so I take precautions, pull out grandfather's pebble and, slowly, carefully, hold it up to the light.

Intesar Toufic

Tyranny of the Worshiper

"But I know that you would like me,
If only you could see me,
If only you could meet me..."
The Smiths—*"Unlovable"*
—*Spring 1999. Beirut, Lebanon. Childhood Apartment.*

A seven-year-old boy was sitting on his living room sofa, biting his toenails. His father had just woken up and stood at the living room door in an undershirt, slippers, and boxers. He was squinting, half-groggy, half-enraged, at the boy, his skin and eyes turning shades away from pink and into red.

"Didn't I tell you to fucking stop biting your toenails." He stomped over. "You like feet?"

He stuffed his foot in the boy's mouth. The boy would wear socks to bed every night until many years later. He now hated his feet, as if those 10 toes had betrayed him.

•••

Fall 2012. Washington, D.C. American University.

During an exchange semester at American University, I found God. I found God and found the devil snickering beside God. Because I found Michael, but Michael was straight.

I was 20 at the time, and he was exactly this Arab's type: blond, muscular, deep voice, and something else. He seemed carefree and powerful. Invincible.

I didn't want to sleep with Michael. I didn't quite know what I'd wanted. Any physical interaction perhaps, but something more, something higher.

I wanted him to like me. That I was sure of.

One day in the gym, I found him drinking at the fountain. As a Middle Eastern homosexual, I had learned to savor glimpses of hot men without letting my eyes linger on them. Sips of water in the desert. That day, however, I remembered I was in America: land of the free, home of the brave. I looked at him, beefy legs bent at the knees, broad shoulders blocking the entire fountain. His shaved head then rose to perch on his thick neck and strong back and he returned to the heavy weights room. He proceeded to do barbell squats, the metal rod pressed against his unyielding upper back. That upper back, where gold would gladly melt and dangle from. They're called traps for a good reason.

Minutes later, Michael would go back out to drink again. I mustered up the courage and tapped his traps.

He turned to me, light green eyes oblivious.

For young queers, deceit is survival. Sometimes, it is a means to more than that end. I had a plan, but I had to teeter between friendly and aloof, the way a straight man would. Any extra charm meant my fairy wings would show. Any lacking charm would be a bad first impression. I needed a hook that did not feel like one.

"Hey, how'd you get such big traps?" I asked.

He told me about some exercise, and I did not sense any intrigue in him to further the conversation. He was simply instructing and I was running out of time. When he stopped talking, I thrust my hand forward and told him my exotic name.

"It's Arabic for luck," I explained.

Surprised by my name, his handshake came late, and that was the opening I'd needed. I then asked the *real* question:

"Y'know, in my country, Lebanon, we just got out of a nasty and long civil war. My cousin's a sculptor and he has an assignment to like, make statues in the most damaged cities, as a symbol of unity. And strength. He told me to look for any like, good physiques for him to use as models. Could I get a topless picture of you, and if he likes it you get $10,000?" With each sentence, I felt my mask of friendly heterosexual crumble to expose the adoring fiend beneath. That last cadence ended on too high a note.

He smiled and shook his head—he didn't buy it but was flattered—"No thanks, man."

"No problem." I sustained the blow and kept my smile on, a proud graduate of gay clubs where rejection must be returned with a poker-face, no matter the pain.

But I was hooked. Although I didn't know what I wanted from Michael, I knew that I wanted to see more of him.

Fate was kind, I suppose. Days later, he was in line to sign a petition. Something about paying the cafeteria staff properly. There were three people standing between him and I, his broad shoulders jutted out of the line of mortals. When it was my turn to sign, I simply counted up: one, two, three. Bless his benevolent petition-signing heart: I found his name! *His name.* His name meant his social media accounts. Meant images. Comments. I could see his opinions and plans and use them to gauge my next move.

A small part of me was reprimanding this expedition into Michael's turf of cyberspace. *But,* I self-persuaded, *that turf is publicly accessible. All I acquired was an address.*

More thrilling was that I now had a space for safe interaction. We could talk. I could ask if he'd go to lunch with me, or something. I had the key that unlocked a gate of honey or of acid. Due to his Facebook privacy settings, however, all the key opened was the criminally brief gallery of his profile pictures. Five pictures. Each resonating with me, making me warmer, my heartbeat heavier, and setting off strands of silk to construct webs upon webs of lies and truths and humor and tragedy—*anything* it would take to intrigue and entrap him.

Not matter the technique, it all begins with greetings, which I sent him like a child lighting fireworks. But nothing burst.

The weeks scraped by. I hoped and dreaded finding him at the gym again. I tried bringing myself to message him again, but then I would go through his pictures and feel too tiny, too ambitious. I felt like a loser compared to his godly, rich self. What could I ever offer him? And what *exactly* did I want?

Yet I indulged in my infatuation when Michael uploaded a new picture of him at a party, and I thought how lucky everyone around him was. In it, he was carrying a beer bottle and I found myself slightly envious because it was in his warm, firm grip. He selected it. He enjoyed it. It met his lips, then willingly surrendered to him its contents—itself—without which it became trash.

Like a monk I studied the scripture of his replies to the comments on the new picture. I was unimpressed with his friends. I realized it was such a shame I wasn't there with him. I knew I could entertain him better than all those dude-bros combined. It would be so easy, not because his friends were dumb, but because I know I'm funny. I was trained by Will & Grace and Oscar Wilde; the gay academy of comedy. I was a garrison of exquisite quips, stabbing deep and drawing laughter.

I really wanted him to laugh—to be entertained—because of me.

There was something special about him, a message glowing from his being in a language that was familiar, yet indecipherable.

Then came the yawn. Sleep was pulling me away from dreaming.

I sighed at my laptop, defeated. I was looking at someone I probably was never going to have. I persuaded myself that there were other men who look like him: Broad-shoulders, huge traps, shaved head, the rumbling basso that commands men into battle, and others to surrender.

True, there were others who may look like him who were gay or bisexual. Possibly accessible. *Yes,* I thought, *stop torturing yourself. Stop this sweet self-harm.*

At the end of the exchange semester, I blocked Michael. I was only briefly surprised when my eyes got wet.

•••

Spring 2013. Beirut, Lebanon. The American University of Beirut.

Hussein (Alexandra by night) popped into my university dormitory after having passed the campus police with the well-trained lie of carrying his student ID "next time." I admired his foxy mischief before he plucked the laptop from my hands—charming smile, tired eyes—and onto his lap, and opened seven different sites and arrange clients for the week. It's not procrastination if your sex-worker friend puts your homework on hold to earn his living. Besides, he always came bearing tales of scandalous Arabian nights—of kinky Saudi princes and gilded hotel room shenanigans—and divulged as best as his divided attention allows. But first, I heard a moan. I sat beside him and found he opened a porn site. Before I could object, I was arrested:

An athletic youth is sucking the big toe of a buffer, older man.

It was so unfamiliar, yet made perfect sense: The twink on his knees, sweaty neck moving his head up and down as the tongue sensually worshipped the bodybuilder's wide orange sole. The latter, in office-wear, head cushioned in beefy arms, had an eyebrow raised, smirking in masculine approval.

I got hard, and in that moment I learned what 'throbbing' means. I was so embarrassed at finding this hot but Hussein wouldn't poke fun at me—he chose the video!

"*Layki malla master w slave. W'Allah bi'bal koon mamsaha 'ando!*"/ "Look at that master and slave. *God* I'd love to be his mop!" he fawned. *Master and slave? Is that what they call this?*

A chatbox window popped over the video: a price from a bargaining client. I stopped myself from snapping at Hussein to collapse the chatbox and return to the video.

I *really* wanted to see more. After Hussein left, I watched that video again, and wondered why it turned me on. It felt like the first time I realized that I found men attractive. For some reason, I was not *supposed* to. And I remembered Michael.

I unblocked him. His Facebook name alone ignited me, my hand clicked on the new colors of his profile picture. He was broader. Fuller. In his eyes the calm of God: Whatever they fell on, he owned. So naturally, so effortlessly.

His hooks slipped back into the unhealed scars in my mind. *Are they scars or pockets I was born with?* I wondered.

That language of Michael became clearer. Hussein's video was a bilingual dictionary. *Do I want to lick Michael's feet?*

It didn't feel wrong, but not quite *there*."

•••

Summer 2013. Beirut, Lebanon. Bliss Street.

I was celibate at 21. My friends were beasts of prey, carnivorous for men, and I seemed to be the herbivore of the queer jungle. I didn't envy them for their prey, but for their promiscuity. Their ability to be drawn to many (*many*) more people. Their sluttiness.

Then again, I had higher standards. Hussein can have his fat concierge.

I, on the other hand, was exclusively attracted to buff men. Usually straight.

One sweltering afternoon, the sun draped Beirut orange, and my friend Yahia and I found a very hot visitor on Grindr: Don Angelo. He looked like he was going to the eastern side of Mt. Olympus, got lost, and wound up in Beirut. Seven feet tall, caramel skin, blond, and muscular.

For some reason, Angelo decided to reply to our Grindr messages. We asked if he'd be up for sex. We jumped when we saw his "Yes" like Korean schoolgirls.

Inside the hotel room, we made small talk. Angelo told us about his time as a Dolce & Gabbana model, and the subsequent drug spiral that made him "fat" but taught him who his real friends were. Yahia and I were intimidated, but all the more determined to impress him.

I felt like I'd just won the gay sex lottery and I couldn't imagine what it would be like, except that I'll brag about it and do my best not to disappoint Angelo, Yahia, or myself.

Like the skilled leopard showing me how it's done, Yahia ravages Angelo's sculpted body with kisses, and I must make due with seconds: A lick of thigh here, a kiss of beefy arm there. Then, Yahia sits on Angelo's groin, kissing his lips and eclipsing his upper body from me.

I turn to find Angelo's feet.

They looked nice: nails clipped into thin crescents, high assertive arch. The Roman emperor rests on his king-size bed, waiting to be fanned.

Hussein's video fades into my mind. Michael's majesty fades into my mind.

I crawled to the edge of the bed and bring my face to Angelo's feet. I know they're clean —I cleaned them when we showered together. I'd never seen another man's toes up-close before, but I was not repulsed.

I kissed his big toe.

It didn't feel strange. It was smooth, familiar. It was flesh. I was analyzing. I was scared to indulge in this for fear of what it would make of me. I was staring at this foot like a high diver at a pool. Meanwhile Yahia and Angelo kissing sounds like liquid fireworks.

I wanted some fun too, damn it. I kissed his foot again, leaving my lips there and closing my eyes. Suddenly, I heard:

"Hey baby—no—don't-a do that, si?" Angelo said with guilt.

I looked up before Yahia could find me red-handed (or red-mouthed). Fields of wheat shimmered on Angelo's smiling face. He extended a muscular arm and I ascended to kiss him.

As we kissed, he elated me with his tenderness, he was telling me I deserved love even though I don't look sexy. I thanked him, pressing my wet lips onto his, beards brushing, his hot, olive-oil tongue swirling in my mouth then stabbing into it, again, and again, inflating my confidence until he started moaning. *Just from kissing? Damn, was I that good?*

I opened my eyes and Yahia was thrusting into Angelo, and Angelo's thrusting tongue was not affection, it was physics.

We couldn't top Angelo's sexiness, but Yahia could certainly top Angelo.

I laughed—it was too good to be true—then slowly slipped out of Angelo's loose arms to let these two experts reach their glorious climax. I felt that I had reached my climax first.

I wasn't not jealous.

After that, I was afraid of confronting myself about what I'd done. The temptation and the surrender. Michael and that porn video. I was afraid of confessing to myself how I was pulled to Angelo's foot. Of what kissing it meant. *Am I a slave?* My mind was a circus of demons and I sealed the tent shut in hopes that demons need air.

I blocked Michael, afraid of what I *really* wanted with him, and also afraid of his reaction sequence of: Get creeped out, reject, then block me. Block me with a tap of his almighty finger, flicking me into pitch-black regret at my foolish leap of faith before I'd crash against the stone-hard surety that nothing, *nothing,* will ever happen between us.

Blocking Michael gave a sense of catastrophe averted. It also gave a sense of agency, like *I'm* the one ending it, and double-locked the circus shut. The demons snickered but I held the keys.

•••

Summer 2014. Beirut, Lebanon. Hamra Street.

The boss left me the keys to the office, impressed that I wanted to do some overtime. Doing overtime would make us both happy. For me, though, overtime meant Oday.

I smirked with a swing in my hips, feeling like a slutty secretary as I led beefy Oday to the office. Key into the lock as smooth and magical as this date seemed. *Damn* it felt good: turning this hallowed office into our pocket of scandal. Oday seemed like a godsend: Taller, broader, buffer, played metal guitar while I was the drummer in a major Lebanese punk band. We argued over politics, intensely, before our tongues wrestled it out. And he liked me. *Me.*

The meeting room table is where we both climbed, half-naked. I kissed his olive six-packs, and he kissed my head. His pecs cushioned my face.

He then took off his shoes and his feet are hideous. Asymmetrical clown hands. The blood retreated from my groin and I panicked. I told him to put his shoes back on, but I knew I'd lost it.

As we resumed, I tried to reignite myself. My body said *nope*. This engine would not start. His feet were a deal-breaker and discovering this new—unyielding—quirk of mine could not have come at a worse time. But to stop sex because of this guy's feet? I'd be the laughingstock of Beirut!

I closed my eyes and to tried to enjoy his body. I failed but pleased him. Then I told him I'm hungry. It was a reversed date: sex, then food.

After this, I rejected taking up Yahia's offers for another threesome. I was too embarrassed to ask the would-be third party for foot pictures.

I unblocked Michael. No new pictures. But I missed him. I pretended to speak to him, for the nth time, and ended up charming the wall.

•••

Spring 2015. Beirut, Lebanon. Furn El-Chebbek.

American politicians are announcing their presidential campaigns.

I wondered what Michael's politics are. Is he a kind king of my world? Is he socially left-leaning and tolerant of us queers? Or is he a conservative hardliner, uncompromising, merciless on immigrants, on the poor, on the working-class, on minorities? Getting rich as we all toil, cigar in one hand and Belorussian mistress in the other. Whipping us if we complain.

Cruel Michael and kind Michael were equally sexy fantasies, but I wanted solid evidence of either. I find him on LinkedIn and see that he is working for a Democrat's campaign. Looking so dapper in a suit.

It had been years and he still had the same effect on me. The pull was not any weaker.

But then I wondered: What do *his* feet look like?

I popped my eyes: *OH MY GOD! If Michael's feet are ugly, then maybe I'll stop liking him!*

Lust shattered my fatigue and I sprang out of bed. *I must see his feet.* A harmless ambition, a harmless request, but so strange it can't be part of a conversation between acquaintances. I'd have to deceive again. Oh he had no idea of his power over me, mighty and oblivious, like a giant.

I schemed.

I realized that for once, American politics may play in this Arab's favor. This tedious election was the key to Michael's attention, then intrigue, then his respect, then his trust, then his beach pictures: buff legs crossed, feet against the bowing orange sun.

My fiendish mind purred *"perfect."* I cast a message on Facebook, and presented myself as a humble Arab journalist who would like to know more about the candidate he works for, insufficiently covered by the press. The real bait was the accompanying friend request to access his pictures. Arabs are friendly (Arabs are dangerous). I waited for an answer, but hours of time difference forced me to wait for a day, and then a night. Sleep whisked me away...

As soon as my eyes shafted open I whipped out my arm to find my phone and frantically open my messenger. He'd gladly answered my query, accepted my friend request and then unfriended me. He knew it was me.

FUCK! I was sloppy. I was sleepy. I underestimated him. How *dare* I take him for a fool?

I was embarrassed, crushed—but elated—that he remembers me: this persistent admirer. Adorably fiendish. Flatteringly obsessed. But harmless! *I! Am! Harmless!*

HARMLESS!

HARMLESS!

HARMLESS, GODDAMN IT!

What on Earth is he stupidly afraid of?!

And look at me! I was a fairy chasing this beast and they call us weak and they call them strong. They call us sissies and they call them bosses. This guy couldn't even *correspond* from hundreds of miles away. I was disappointed, but it wasn't not enough to break his grip on me, or rather, my fixation on him. Indeed: we were both victims of the other.

In any case, this was another chess-move in our epic duel. I blocked Michael, hoping that he'll forget about me after due time passes. This was far from over.

•••

Fall 2015. Rome, Italy.

I am with Yahia. He is flaunting his summer-cooked stalwart body and chest-hair while I dragged behind in more modest, less revealing attire. It might rain, I told my lanky self. Men stopped their motorcycles to get Yahia's number. He bragged in broken English. It was funny and depressing.

Yahia is off with date number three, the dinner date, and I once again had our hotel room to myself. I was sitting on the sofa, barefoot, when I found that if I crossed my feet and put them in the rays of setting sun, an aesthetically appealing image formed. I took a picture with my phone.

I checked Grindr. Not one message. Yahia must have siphoned them all. Well, the golden rule of Grindr is: New profile pic, new messages. And what the hell, I'm in Rome. *When in Rome. Be scandalous.*

It wasn't like Beirut where scandal spread like wildfire, forcing you into hiding for a few weeks.

Let's try this foot thing again, I thought.

I took down the picture of my face and replace it with the picture of my feet.

Within minutes, I got a message. A man addressing me as 'Sir' was begging to kiss my feet. He was referring to himself as a dog-slave and proposed raunchy, unorthodox things. I sent him my address.

A rush surged through me and I sprang up. I instinctively *knew* what I must do: I put on my puffy black jacket and black sweatpants. I put on Yahia's sneakers. I had to look. *Big.* My heart was racing like I was being chased by someone, chased and nervous—but *excited.* I was excited and felt it in my *bones* that *this* would be a significant day. That this would be a day I will remember and will set the tone for the rest of my life.

The doorbell rang. I was handed an exam and knew all the answers. Did I study? Yes—no—maybe.

I opened the door and smirked, then put my foot forward and watched—half expectant, half amazed—as the middle-aged man bowed down, lower and lower, bending knees, back, and neck until I felt the press of his lips against the sneaker. Against my toes underneath. A hiss of blood trickled to my groin. *I liked this.*

I escaped my body and watched the dominant in me unleashed.

•••

I am masterful. I'm a natural. I am slapping a stranger and grinding his fingers. I am loud, assertive, and angry and masculine and he knows it and is polishing my shoes with his tongue, whimpering Italian gratitudes like the bitch I tell him—roaring—that he is.

And I'm throbbing. I tease him with the boner, juicing out his sweat and kneading desperation into his voice. Then I skull-fuck him so fucking properly, so porn-award-deservingly, like I'd done it a million times before…

I ask him, when we finish, how I was. He says I was very good. I tell him it's my first time. He bows again, adoring my God-given skill, and leaves after giving my foot a farewell smooch.

Viva Italia.

•••

Beirut now had a new dominant, and the demon circus remained shut. I briefly thought about how this had anything to do with Michael, but I first wanted to fully explore this new superpower, this unused zone of my psyche, this Excalibur I had pulled out. I wanted certainty and I wanted strength and I wanted the sex I was starved of.

Michael remained blocked.

•••

Spring 2017. Nagoya, Japan.

I freshly arrived to Japan, making new friends who were also navigating the omnipresent language. Here I had a clean slate: no past, only a reputable present.

As a cunning Arab homosexual, it had been necessary to have two Facebook profiles: one for family and boring acquaintances, and the other for real friends and fellow faggots. The latter account packed the ex-lovers, the gay tourists, the Drag Race fan pages, and pictures of underground theme-parties where I joined the glimmering constellation of queer youth in Arabia.

Indeed, scandal was locked behind my password and tight social circle, but that seal proved to be porous. The parties eventually hosted mutual friends with cousins, and it wasn't long before word spread in the family. In a messy, painful coming-out, I had to delete this account.

In Japan, the need reemerged for another medium of correspondence (with the uncouth) and another gallery of snippets (of the uncouth). I made a new account, extra-private, complete with a sassy Japanese name. Among the friends I added were ones I made back in Washington. As I fondly remembered my high-heeled days strutting down the townhouses of grey DC, Michael stormed my mind.

I remembered him like thirst from a second, forgotten throat. Michael's hammerhead shoulders as he surveyed the food in the cafeteria—his big arms holding his plate—his eyes calmly selecting what he will devour—Michael towering among the other frat boys—t-shirt stretched so tight—suffering but elated to be worn by him—yellow logo painted across his chest—like he was born with it and the rest wore it in allegiance. At the gym with thick, hairy legs pushing against the resistance cord—against my civility—big white sneaker—supple tip—lifting close to my face before recoiling—catching my dreamer's eye with indifference because he expects awe like he expects oxygen in the air.

Fuck.

Domination had made me more assertive, more macho. But there was still something unsatisfied. The demons did not die. I realized exactly what I wanted to have with Michael: I wanted to serve him. And I knew that he would like me, if he would give me the chance to have my wit tickle him and then hook him, then curl and hook again because my wit is fierce and honed by years of making hot men laugh, laugh just to get the high—the rush—of their pleasure. Besides, I had enjoyed being served. Surely Michael would.

But first I still needed to see Michael's feet.

If Michael had ugly feet, then the curse would be lifted. All emotions toward him would be blown out like a candle.

It dawned on me what an amazing tool this new Japanese account could be. What an unprecedented opportunity I'd had. Not only for his pictures, but for correspondence.

At the time, it was classic angel versus devil taunting one another across my shoulders:

Do I confess my non-sexual—but intense—desire for serving him and add him as friend, or do I weave another lie and add him as a friend?

If I confess, I get his blessings for being honest and *possibly* pictures as a reward. It would be the accepting embrace of a savior. Warm, liberating. But there was a very real risk of getting blocked. Of getting kicked off his cloud with a mere click, making me curse my poor foresight again. And besides, *what* was I going to confess? I could barely confess it to myself let alone articulate it to him. *Dear Michael, I've always found you godly. I'm gay and you probably have never noticed me. Can I be your friend on here? Nothing sexual. Please...*

And none of my friends—the ones trustworthy enough to explain this to—had obliged my request for assistance.

Indeed, I had made the fatal error of befriending decent people.

Of course I couldn't just "let him go" like they advised. It was him who was gripping me. Like a planet around the sun.

I had to lie. I found Michael and posed as a Japanese admirer. No plan. No plan because I had the instinctual faith that the desire of every straight man is to reign supreme in this world. Or another. I would be Michael's other world. I would pull him into my dimension and crown him ruler.

To complete the ploy I had to sound Japanese: I cut myself in the English language gland and articles bled out, among other things.

•••

March 12th, 2017.

木刀
"U r like god. Can i see your feet please god?"

Michael
"What? Who are you"

木刀

"Hello god I am so so hapy you answer Im just found you randomly And u r the best man on this planet. I m sorry if i scare you or make you angry. I am Tomoya from Japan...If you dont send me picturs of ur feet i will be very sad :("

Michael
"Well thank you, but I have never just randomly send picture of my feet"

木刀

"You say for me thank you! :) :) :D But y god no send feet picture :(I fail."

Michael
"lol what do I get?"

木刀

"I sorry, get what?"

Michael
"if I send you a picture, what do I get?"

木刀
"Gift?
My kiss on your feet :D :D m(-.-)m :'(
U r sooo god! I want to waship u!
I m gonna cry"

Michael
"lol maybe if I get money"

木刀

"God...i wish i could become gold for you. Wear me like gold slippa. I don hav bank akount :(:(:(:(Please i beg you!!!"

Michael
"lol then no"

木刀
"God why so bad with me....
One foot maybe?
Or toe?"

Michael
"lol no
Money"

木刀
"If you are here i waship and give to you"

Michael
"lol but i'm not"

木刀
"I dont have bank akount yet God :("

Michael
"so venom money"

木刀
"Venmo?"

Michael
"way to send money. App. but if not, going to block you."

木刀
"No please no block!
I wil try
I will ask frend."

Michael
"i don't want to see picture of you—I want money"

木刀
"I only have yen God!
Pleass come to Japan!
I giff you here!
But please no block
I feel crushed
Like worm under your foot :("

Michael
"well send me money or you're getting blocked"

木刀
"I will try
With my friend
But...maybe god lye :(
U go away
I wil stil waship you"

Michael
"let me know soon or will block"

木刀
"But maybe you lye god!
God r u lye? :') :') :')"

After that, he blocked me. He disappeared from my message box. I spiraled down from his clouds, heart heavy, a tuft of heaven in my claws. I was so close, and interacting with him was euphoric. The same rush I got in Rome had possessed and rattled me. It was electric, born from a place within, so deep, so real, so overpowering.

I knew what I had to do next: I had to tell him I would gladly pay.

•••

March 24th, 2017, Nagoya, Japan.

I created a twitter account solely to send him a message confessing my feelings and the intention to pay him.

I waited several days for an answer. I wrote about this period somewhere in my diary, but I tore that entry away. I wanted those feelings extracted, frozen, and disposed of.

Days passed. I felt heavy but lost weight. Food was purposeless, just stimulating mush in my lazy mouth. I felt like a loved one had gone missing and I was craving any new information about them.

If someone sees your twitter message, a blue check will appear. It will be—I read—to the bottom-left of the message, along with the date. I had yet to confirm this. However, twitter also has the option of not receiving messages from strangers to "keep the creeps away."

And so I became a creep. I didn't want to be. I just wanted a chance. I just wanted to be his friend, *not* make him uncomfortable, but damnit he was not giving me any other option. I'd spoken with him for years, in my imagination. I'd tested the throwing knives I made in my mind's garrison. I'd reply out loud, and he would laugh in my head and I would become happy. However, this meant that I'd thought about him infinitely more than he'd thought about me. I was a mosquito, hell-bent on touching this one giant and Michael was waving me away if paying attention at all.

I felt like I could just call him, just call and say, "Hey Michael," like we've known each other for years.

He'd know it's me and sigh like I'm some overbearing aunt, but he'd be flattered.

A friend said this was obsession.

But how could I not be obsessed when the only way to break this obsession is to *see* that he has ugly feet?

But there was still hope. He had been inactive on twitter. This, I thought, would surely not last.

Besides, I had screenshots of our conversation. I had a weapon now and half a mind to blackmail him with it: *I'll post these all over the internet unless you send your goddamn foot picture you golden idiot!*

But something stopped me. I'd rather he pity me than hate me. Hate would seal the door shut forever. With pity, time would chip away at it.

For weeks, he remained inactive on twitter and I assumed the worst—did someone die? Was I being a nagging brat when he was in so much pain? These thoughts kept me from prodding further.

•••

April 26, 2017. Nagoya, Japan.

He tweeted again. No blue check. Fate was a patient sadist. I wanted him king and he didn't want me his slave. My stomach churned like a sizzling mound of beef. I sat in bed. I needed to push out this heavy nausea. Tears are your body's way of excreting unwanted—harmful—matter.

But what if...

I balled my hand into a fist...

•••

April-May, 2017. My Imagination.

There he is, relaxing on the hotel bed. I'm on my knees and it's so easy. My money is next to him, one arm cushions his head, the other lay on the bed. A faint smile rests on his round, rugged chin. He observes me with those eyes, the eyes of God, the eyes that own. He knew this all along—that this was going to happen—that I am his—and he can get used to this.

I take off his sneakers—then his socks—he's calm—he knows he has no reason to worry —he is intrigued but knows what's coming—wonders if girls feel the same way— enterprising.

I ask him if I may kiss his foot. He says "Yes."

My body shakes, after years of wanting this so bad, I move my head slowly to his mercies.

My lips land on my knuckles, warm and moist. And loving.

•••

Winter 2018. Nagoya, Japan.

After months of exorcising him out of me as ink and tears, I thought I'd gotten over him.

It's not manly to be shy, I reasoned. *His strategy ironically worked,* I reasoned. *I'm chasing a man afraid of me, when he is much more powerful.*

But then I stumbled upon him. In sinister charity, he'd made a public Instagram account.

Oh boy. I knew it wouldn't be healthy to look at his pictures, but some people eat fried cheese. Scathing, sticky, roils in your stomach, as though your own regret could be weighed in dead-slug pounds. The difference is that the body takes care of cheese eventually, but there are no intestines for the brain.

Time would have eventually engulfed the last thought of him. But now he was right there, at my fingertips. The internet had warped the distance between us, as though I (and the other admirers) were grains of sand under his beach towel. So close, but not close enough.

I peeked, of course, to see his fucking feet once and for all.

He was still broad. He grew out his hair, combed back, not douche-y like a Trump, but shorter, thicker, with a few strands twisted in the middle into a crest. Life was going smoothly for him, as expected. Never a hint of mortal difficulty. Always relaxed and powerful.

I was being pulled, ever so lightly, back into the familiar trance of his radiance, back into his orbit, back into his damage. I was so pissed at myself for how helpless I felt and this anger emulsified my adoration and made me see a bigger picture.

Here was an American whose vote in a ballot could be the blade in my guillotine. He is more powerful than me, in this unjust world, and his actions will have more effect on me than mine ever can. He is oblivious, distant, and destructive. He is powerful and epic and majestic. He is America.

But was it him I adored or the idea of him? He was every straight man on the edge of experimentation, toes about to touch the queer grass where I stand and wait with the clasped hands of Job.

But he pushed away. This beautiful man in the pictures wants nothing to do with me. These straight men, so powerful, so cowardly. So many juxtapositions.

Michael, as always, was a painful blessing. He is what I had yearned for and would never have. Maybe that's why I chased him. Maybe that's why I hoped he'd accept money, because it would mean I'd found the master key that could unlock any rejection; that protects me from that which would bring pain.

There he was, killing me, smiling at a burrito that sags adoringly in his warm palm.

There he was, killing me, smiling next to a Democrat politician. But not in arrogance, more in realization. He was pleasantly discovering the conveniences of power, and it fits. It made sense. It's natural, like puberty. The world was made for him to rise in.

He will be powerful. And he might never really know me.

We were both foolish.

But I wrote this.

Victor Walker

Flying Home

The TV on mute, Reena stared at the weather map of yellow suns and puffy clouds on a golf green field. The scores all in the mid-eighties: *Chicago, 84. Washington, D.C., 88. New York City, 83. Scattered showers across the West.*

Pressing the speed dial on her cell phone, she waited for the machine at the other end to pick up. Jamal would still be asleep, of course, even though it was an hour later there. At the tone, she told him when she would be touching down, then ended by wondering whether or not to say "I love you" and decided on "I'll see you soon" instead.

Retrieving the remote, she turned her gaze again toward the screen and began cycling through the Rolodex of cable channels without bothering to stop or switch the sound back on.

Leaving the hotel in the rental she had picked up at the airport, Reena headed east toward the lake, then south onto the Drive. In a few hours the beaches, parks, and roadway would be overrun with Saturday skaters, cyclists, and joggers, but for the moment she had the lake and Drive all to herself.

At The Museum of Science and Industry, she turned off the Drive and headed west through the University of Chicago and Washington Park, crossed underneath the el station at 55th and continued along Garfield Boulevard where weathered but still impressive graystones flanked both sides of the parkway like huge chess pieces facing off across a giant board. There were gaps between many of them, however (where a rook had fallen here, a knight had been captured there), surrounded by hurricane fencing advertising future developments, with such names as Garfield Terrace and Boulevard Gardens. Others were simply weedy open lots littered with malt liquor bottles and fast-food containers, a doorless refrigerator in one, a rusting bed box spring in another. And yet, the cross streets, residential—Lowe, Union, Emerald—were tree-lined and quiet.

Further up Garfield Boulevard on the right, she could see the huge white elephant of the Schultz Building (which Reena had only known as the old Silvercup Bakery), a neighborhood landmark that had once filled the neighborhood with the aroma of freshly baked bread. Remembered how her father, whom everyone in the neighborhood—even her mother—called "Doc," would get her up early Saturday mornings just to drive to the Silvercup thrift store so they would be the first in line for a take-home of just-baked cinnamon buns and freshly iced sweet rolls.

There was no smell of bread in the air now, however. The bakery's windows were dark, and where the Silvercup electric sign had once crowned the rooftop, only a skeletal "tiara" remained.

Reena drove on. Past Sherman Park. Past Loomis. On to Bishop Street. Then two blocks south. A run of modest brown brick bungalows in a four-block stretch, running from

Tyson's Fresh Food Mart and Wooley's Tap Room on 59th to Dotson's Ice Cream & Candy Store on Garfield Boulevard. In-between, on just her old block alone, the Salter brothers, Maurice and Philip; Solice Miles and Karen Brannum; crazy Buster Baker; and her best friend, Gloria Steptoe, rode their bikes and roller skates from one end to the other under the ever-watchful windows and front porch eyes of Bishop Street's extended family.

Their reach, unfortunately, could extend no further than their voices carry. "And so in the fourth grade, just when Reena had made them all so proud by scoring in the ninety-fifth percentile on a citywide exam, she was plucked away from them mid-year and transferred to Pulaski School on the other side of Ashland Avenue, an unmarked dividing line in a city of dividing lines.

Her mother, who hadn't walked with her to school in years, had gotten her up forty minutes early just to accompany her to school, her father, who had to get up even earlier to drive to work, joking that she should simply think of it as her very own Head Start program. And while neither he nor her mother talked about the fact that Pulaski was all-white, her friends were not hesitant about warning her that she probably would have to run home every day if she didn't want to get beat up by the "paddies."

Yet on the morning of her first day, still bleary-eyed, she stumbled down to breakfast only to find a waxed-paper bag with a still warm cinnamon raisin bun inside waiting for her on the kitchen table.

Reena crept down Bishop which looked more worn than she remembered, but less worn than she expected. Would anybody still be there whom she recognized? "Who recognized her?"

You're Yolanda and Doc Dorsey's girl—Reena! "Curtis, come out to the porch and see who's here!"

...and they would invite her in for a glass of iced-tea and a plate of sugar cookies and tell her about everyone who had "passed on."

We heard you're a doctor in New York now.

...and she would have to tell them that she was not that kind of doctor. And that she actually lived in New Jersey.

They would ask if she had any kids. *I bet they're smart.*

...and she would say yes, Jamal was smart and avert her eyes only to see a row of old Christmas cards lined neatly along the mantle and the smiling faces of grandchildren beaming back at her.

Buster is a city supervisor now.

Others, too, would have succeeded in varying degrees. A high school football coach. A loan officer at a downtown bank. A housing developer.

You see the signs for Boulevard Gardens and Garfield Terrace? "That's the Salter brothers. *You remember them?*

...and she would nod back and smile, look at her watch and tell them she had to run. To catch a flight. But to tell everyone she said hello.

Of course she did none of this. She did not park her car, go up any steps, knock on any doors, or ring any bells. Instead, she continued along Bishop, slowly driving past her old house at the speed of a dream.

The flight out of Newark had been early and she had no time to say goodbye to Jamal before taking the bus in to the airport. Sitting by herself in the concourse awaiting her flight, she put down Joan Didion, opened her cell phone and pulled up pictures of Jamal she had taken only a few months before. A handsome, bright-faced teenager with long lashes and a shy smile. But there was also something else in some of them, a kind of ghosting, as if she had gotten a double-exposure and there was another, fainter Jamal peering out from behind the ones smiling back at her.

When Jamal was very small he would pad down to the living room just before bedtime in his Runaway Bunny pajamas whenever he heard her playing the clarinet, and he would follow along with her note for note by ear on his little toy xylophone with its little red plastic mallet. Sometimes they would even share a dish of ice cream afterwards, alternating bites between them before she'd usher him back to bed and tuck him safely under the covers.

"Did you know he's been taking sleeping pills?"

Reena glanced up at the wall of diplomas. Awards. Certificates.

Dr. Varja had come highly recommended by several of Reena's colleagues. ("Sue's really great at getting adolescents to open up and start a dialogue going between both sides.")

Dez, however, had initially been skeptical about bringing in a family therapist. ("It's only natural. All boys his age go through these things. My brothers and I went through them. J. will get through it, too. It's called growing up.") "Reena found it interesting that her ex seemingly had no such reservations when it came to hitting up the club pro to help him shave a few strokes off his golf game.

Long before the end of their marriage, Reena realized she had very little in common with Desmond, save Jamal—and he was now pulling away from both of them. And yet ironically, it was Jamal's pulling away from them in the last six months that had brought them closer to one another than they had been since before their divorce, for they could both see in Jamal what they had once seen and liked so much in each other now being threatened in their son.

"As scary as that might seem, it's not really that unusual. Jamal's not really trying to harm himself. It's just his way of pulling up the covers. Kids call it 'zonking out.'"

Reena understood the feeling.

You wouldn't have known, looking from the outside. As an outsider, all you would have seen would have been the neat rows of squat brick bungalows on either side of Wolcott. Small patch lawns that came up to the sidewalk. Block after block. No driveways or two-door garages. But no For Sale signs either.

And then you come upon it, taking up almost an entire city block. An elementary school. Pulaski Elementary School. 1926. Modeled on Independence Hall in Philadelphia. Its completion coincident with the 150th anniversary of The Declaration of Independence, a glass-enclosed copy of which was prominently displayed in the lobby just inside the main door, it along with Casimir Pulaski's statement to General Washington upon volunteering his service to the Continental Army: *I came here, where freedom is being defended, to serve it, and to live or die for it.*

The first few weeks at Pulaski were uneventful, as most of the white students seemed to look upon Reena as a curiosity and largely kept their distance; and for those first few weeks she kept to herself as well. In class, she did not raise her hand but rather waited to be called on and then answered in a voice not much above a whisper lest she risk saying something wrong—or worse yet, stupid—and thus confirming what everybody told her about what "their" people already thought about "her" people.

Her new school did offer things Copernicus did not, however, an after-school enrichment program, for instance. Students whose parents signed them into Art got big brown portfolios, all sorts of free art supplies, and the chance to have their work selected for display on transit platforms throughout the city. Students enrolled in Music were donated instruments and given a chance to represent their district in a downtown performance in front of The Friends of Euterpe, for which they would be rewarded by getting the entire day off from school. Unfortunately, by mid-year when Reena transferred to Pulaski, there was just one space still available in the enrichment program—in music—and only one instrument left—a clarinet. Only the tuba could have been less cool, and the band didn't have any tubas.

The head of the class, Mr. Norvo, had the whitest complexion Reena had ever seen and the kind of wavy black hair described as "tresses" in the pomade ads in *Ebony* which were Scotch-taped to the wall-size mirror in Iola's Curl 'n' Twirl like the pin-up pictures in a barber shop. Mr. Norvo tried to help her catch up with the others by showing her how to read music, hold her instrument, and breathe—even assigning one of his 6th grade students to help her with the fingering.

It was not unusual either for him to bring one of his own records to class and tell them to listen for their part in a particular song, then "lip-synch" along with it on their instruments. Sometimes he would walk around the class (Reena always thought he smelled of scented candles.) to see how each of them was doing; other times he would remain in front, conducting them as much with eye movement and pressed lips as the wooden ruler he used for a baton.

During the week of the district finals when Reena was home sick for several days, Mr. Norvo paid an unexpected visit to her house to bring her an album so that she would still be able to practice during her absence. It was the first time any white person had ever set foot inside her house—or likely anyone else's on Bishop Street—and as if to acknowledge the occasion of such a visit from a teacher—let along a white teacher—Reena remembered her father giving up his TV chair to Mr. Norvo and her mother bringing out a plate of Silvercup cinnamon raisin buns, warm from the oven, and serving them in the living room —the one and only time Reena could ever remember her mother allowing anyone to eat anything upfront.

Mr. Norvo told them that he thought she was very talented, only to have her father dig out one of his old jazz albums ("Love of music runs in our family.") and play it for Mr. Norvo, embarrassing her no end. Afterward, the two of them talked music for almost a solid hour, Reena finding out how her father came by the nickname "Doc" and Mr. Norvo telling her father that he used to play the vibes in his own college band—Neece Norvo & the Nighthawks.

Neece?

After Reena passed into the 5th grade, Mr. Norvo let her keep her clarinet so that she could continue practicing through the summer. He also lent her one of his prized albums, *Flying Home* with Benny Goodman, Gene Krupa, Lionel Hampton, and Teddy Wilson. Benny Goodman, he told her, was originally from Chicago and had been the first white jazz musician in the country to integrate his band, a "liner note" she at the time did not realize was all that big a deal.

All summer long she could hear her friends just outside her window in raucous competition for the street championships of the block, most of whom believed the only reason she practiced all the time was because "Doc" and her mom made her do so—having sent her off to "that white school" and all. Even her best friend, Gloria, had confronted her one day outside of Tyson's and asked why she wanted to stay in the house practicing all the time. ("Where you ever going to play the clarinet anyway—*the symphony?!*")

But she continued practicing just the same—not for The Friends of Whatever down-town or the day off from school, but to prove she was good enough to be in the school band, and not just for her family or Mr. Norvo or even all the people on her side of Ashland Avenue, but for herself. To prove to herself that she was good enough.

Yet when she returned to Pulaski in September, she found Mr. Norvo's room empty and the Music enrichment program dropped from the after-school. Budget cuts were the reason given. Except the Art program went untouched.

Even before, there had been whispers passed around like notes in class about Mr. Norvo that even she had heard. Rumors like those spread about her when she first arrived at Pulaski, crayoned slurs scrawled anonymously inside bathroom stalls.

At first she blamed Mr. Norvo for having wasted her entire summer, having encouraged her only to leave her all by herself once more. The school's reclaiming of her clarinet—the instrument originally no one wanted—felt like a double slap in the face. And when she came back home that first afternoon, instead of staying after school for practice, she stormed directly up to her room and threw Mr. Benny Goodman into the trash.

"Jamal's quite talented," said Ms. Rydell, his 4th grade music teacher. "We have a special program, you know? For students who demonstrate his kind of special ability."

"Yes, I know. Jamal has a good ear."

"Oh, it's much more than that. He has a sensitivity. It's really quite rare, you know? Music is more than simply playing the right notes and chords. Many of our students have been playing even before they could read. Some of their skills levels are truly amazing. Frightening even." She smiled.

"Jamal is different. It's not that he doesn't have their same skills level—he does. It's just that he's able to surrender to the music as well. That's very rare and very brave." She paused and smiled again.

"You know Shakespeare says that music hath charms to soothe the savage beast?"

Reena did not bother to correct her double error.

"Well, I think that's what's going on with your son, and it comes through each and every time he's playing. Even the other students who are themselves quite excellent can hear it."

"I think you and your husband have something very special in Jamal."

"Yes, I know," she said. But even as she was in agreement, Reena knew she was not going to sign Jamal into any special class, that the worse thing that could happen to him so early in his life was to be set apart for being special.

"Did he ever tell you that they call him names?"

Reena felt herself involuntarily reaching for Dez's hand, recalling all the terrible names a black child could hear spitballed at his or her back.

They had tried to inoculate Jamal from just that kind of thing. Her own parents had never actually sat down with her and explained such "facts of life." They didn't have to. She knew where the Ashland Avenues were. Jamal did not. And even if he had, there were no Bishop Streets he could run back to. He had grown up in a very different world—a world where the lines were not so clearly drawn. No intersecting avenues or numbered streets. Often there weren't even sidewalks. It was a world in which everyone's children were expected to be in the 90th percentile, or higher. Where there were no excuses for excuses. No one to blame but oneself.

So why had a bright and talented 14-year-old like Jamal suddenly pulled the covers up over his head? "What was it that he just could not face?

"He's afraid of hurting you."

Reena could feel her ears expanding.

"Hurting *us*?"

They were her thoughts but it was Dez speaking them.

"He's afraid of telling you about the name-calling at school because he's afraid that you'll think less of him because of what other people say."

"That's nonsense!"

Dr. Varja's gaze turned toward Desmond.

"No. It isn't. A young person's feelings about his or her parents' opinion of them are much more important than society often credits them with being. A boy's fear, for instance, of letting his father down—of not being 'up to snuff' in his father's eyes—can be especially strong."

"You're telling me that my son thinks that what some kids *I don't even know* say or do will somehow make me think less of him?!"

Reena could feel Dez's hand tightening.

"Yes. And I just want to preface what I'm going to say here by making it clear that I'm in no way passing judgment; I'm simply trying to pull this altogether."

Reena nodded but sensed Dez pulling back.

"You've both been divorced for almost two years now, but as I understand it, you were separated for at least a year before that, which would have made Jamal eleven when you moved out. Is that about right?" Dr. Varja looked directly at Desmond.

"Yes, that's about right. Eleven." Dez looked to Reena for confirmation.

"And did you talk with Jamal about why you were moving out?"

"Of course we talked. We all talked about it." Dez looked again toward Reena.

Dr. Varja nodded.

"Did Jamal talk, too?"

Reena was silent.

"Of course he talked," Desmond cut in. "I told you, we *all* talked."

"And what did Jamal say?"

"What do you mean what did he say?"

"I mean did Jamal tell you how he felt about your moving out?"

"He didn't like it. He didn't want me to go."

"But you did."

"I explained—*we* explained—it to him." Dez looked over at Reena once again then back at Dr. Varja.

"I'm sure you tried. But did you also tell Jamal you loved him?"

"What does that mean? He knows we love him."

Reena suddenly felt her own fingers tensing up.

"I'm saying you probably sat him down between the two of you and tried to explain why you were getting a divorce. But Jamal was eleven years old and although he's very bright, you were trying to explain this to him as though he were an emotional adult. He wasn't, and he isn't. Yet. All he knew when you were talking to him was what he was feeling inside, and what he was feeling was confused and afraid, confused as to how you could stop loving his mother and afraid that you could stop loving him, too—just like his mother—if he ever disappointed you. And that the only way he could keep that from happening was to hide from you anything he thought would disappoint you so that you wouldn't think that he was weak and thus undeserving of your love?"

"You mean like the fact that he was being picked on at school by some bullies?"

"It's devastating—especially for a child—when he or she first finds out that love isn't always unconditional, that we can lose it. And that we can even lose the love of the people we love."

Here there was an awkward pause, not unlike the ones that had filled the final few months of their marriage or the silence following their talk with Jamal when they had tried to explain why she and his father could no longer live together. Dez had tried to fill that gulf by telling Jamal that their separation wasn't necessarily permanent—and in any case it didn't have anything to do with him.

"So," asked Dez, "what exactly did these boys *call* Jamal?"

Why did he have to go there? Reena thought. Why didn't he just ask Dr. Varja what they could do to get their son back? To make him feel unconditionally loved once more? Why was he always so damned dense?

Of course Reena already knew the answer to Dez's question, and Dr. Varja knew she knew, and so when she spoke she was speaking not to Reena but to Desmond.

"They called him a 'faggot.'"

"A *faggot*?"

Reena did not feel Desmond's hand slip away from hers (as it had months prior to their separation) so much as just suddenly go limp.

As Reena parked on Wolcott and approached Pulaski, she could hear a party of young black voices even before she could see any black faces, and she found herself taken aback by the new ownership of her old schoolyard, a schoolyard that had never been a playground, a schoolyard where now three black girls—from *this* side of Ashland Avenue—were laughing and double-dutching, completely unaware that their very presence at Pulaski gave real meaning to any paper promises of independence encased in glass. Or any noble words of unflagging support of that independence inscribed above them.

Back in the car, Reena headed east back onto Garfield Boulevard again and looked for Dotson's Candies. The name had changed. It was Biggy's Cream & Candy now. But the dancing candy cane and smiling ice cream cone on the sign she remembered were still there.

"What's good today?"

"Is all good," Biggy said, and Reena smiled. She did not look at her watch, but she knew that it was probably close to noon.

It was the first ice cream cone she had had since she could not remember when, and it *was* good, she thought.

Returning to the hotel, Reena finished packing her travel bag and set it down on the bed. On top of it she folded a light jacket. And on top of that her paperback of *Slouching Toward Bethlehem*. After calling down to the front desk, she checked her room one last time before sitting down by the window and turning on her cell, only to discover that it was down to a single bar, and for the first time realized how closely the charge light resembled a tiny xylophone.

"I just called, honey, to say I'm on my way to the airport now, and I hope to see you soon." She paused, almost closing the phone, then stopped herself and added, "I love you."

Reena walked across the food court at O'Hare. She had eaten nothing all morning except for the ice cream and she felt the need to put something in her stomach before boarding her flight back, not so much because she was hungry as to settle her stomach and the anxiety that often accompanied any trip—not just one by air.

Her first choice was McDonald's, but the line was long and while waiting she realized that they had already stopped serving breakfast several hours ago. Looking elsewhere, she saw that the line was shorter at Cinnabon. As she walked over, she was thinking of getting a coffee and a bun (There was a stand sign advertising it as a special.), but when she got close enough to read the board behind the counter, she changed her mind.

"I'll take a box of 'minibons'," she said and added, as if the young girl behind the register had had the slightest interest, "I'm taking them home with me."

In the Gate 12 waiting area, Reena sat and watched a little boy and girl of no more than five or six, one black, one white, running unattended between the rows (and even under the seats) laughing before she heard their parents calling for them from opposite directions, separating them. But not before they stuck their tongues out at each other in parting.

Several rows ahead, CNN was on a large, overhanging flat screen monitor where two *Dating Game*-attractive anchors (again, one black, one white) engaged in closed-captioned banter like a TV-happy couple before "throwing it over" to their handsome bachelor next-door neighbor whose magic touch-screen map showed suns all across the country, his cheery but soundless twitter, "Another perfect day for golf."

A woman's voice came over the public address and began calling out the row assignments. The girl and boy who had been playing earlier and their parents went by, boarding first. The little girl's father carried her up in his arms; the little boy's mother gripped him firmly by the hand. Neither child looked happy or sad. They simply looked, as Dr. Varja described it, zonked out.

Reena waited patiently to hear her row called before rising. Gathering her ticket and boarding pass, she was on her way over to be checked through when her ring tone, "Flying Home," sounded from inside her purse.

Fumbling for the phone, Reena fished it out and checked the ID. It was Jamal, calling her back.

Essays

*Photography by
Patrick McEvoy*

John Ballantine

The God Question

"There's a thread you follow. It goes among
things that change. But it doesn't change.
People wonder about what you are pursuing.
You have to explain about the thread..."
—*The Way It Is," William Stafford*

I. The boy questions

What is the thread holding the patchwork scenes of my life together? I have wondered about the blue-green thread tying together the young boy questioning Einstein as he wandered to work at The Institute for Advanced Study, he with wild hair questioning God's games and teasing us kids as he walked. My sister and I were troubled, too, by all these adventuresome gods my father, and Homer, told us about on Sunday evenings. The Greek gods were much more engaging than the stern Christian edicts of Sunday school. We chose Odysseus traveling far in a rocky boat after Troy while Penelope spun tales to keep suitors at bay. And what, we wondered, became of those without gray-eyed Athena by their side, and why, I asked my father, was Jesus forsaken?

Why so many gods? Why the struggles?

I was happy when Pan died, letting the Greek gods fade into myths to entertain, not pyres upon which I should worship. Those gods were dead and I, as a young boy, only had to deal with the stern Old Testament man who cut boys in two, or the more forgiving New Testament God who sacrificed his son for the sins we inherited from Adam and Eve. Questions persisted; who should I pray to? Homer's Greek gods were much more fun, fickle, and dangerous if you crossed them. Poseidon consumed many more wayward sailors than God's disciples, turning their backs on Jesus, crucified on the cross.

How could I cover my base with head bowed watching the sun set? Who would save me when I went astray? At 12, I was stuck with the Christian God as I biked to school. All the fire and brimstone spouted by preachers, pretending to know. They did not ask the most obvious question that plagued me—until *Time Magazine* plastered it on the cover in 1966 —"Is God Dead?"

He died for me in 1961 when I lost a small thimble in the living room rug and could not find it. God took it, I swear. When I pedaled fiercely to Witherspoon School in seventh grade, Carl and I debated God's existence, to and from school—how to prove, what did you know about the gods, were those miracles real? And what about those other more mercurial gods? What proof do you have? Some fuzzy belief, a temple, cathedral spires, hieroglyphics etched in stone, a Dead Sea palimpsest—and what about that lost thimble?

These fierce ontological debates raged as we pedaled faster and faster to school. Serious questions that kept us up late at night. Like Einstein, we did not rest when life's forces did not compute. Later I learned of my atheist grandfather and his minister theologian father writing daily letters about God's ways—my grandfather turning to commerce, law, and sophistry, and my great-grandfather embracing music, mystery, and love. Carl and I debated the same questions—why God did so little. How could he leave us a world turned upside down by nuclear bombs, war, and poverty? Why did the gods play with our fate? Testing us, some argued, then asking us to believe.

II. A long family debate

The God question was a long family struggle with real consequences. My great-grandfather, Reverend William Gay Ballantine, was thrown out—or asked to leave—several colleges when he explained in written words how Darwin said we creatures evolved slowly, testing fundamentalist tenets. He traveled to Palestine in the 1880s, surveying what was to become the hotly contested Promised Land. The books in Greek, Hebrew, German, and Latin lining his shelves told him there were no seven days, no forbidden fruit, and no Satan crawling like a snake near the Euphrates. He dug deep into scripture, trying to show how evolution fit into a creation story. His students and parishioners nodded skeptically at his spin on how seven days stretched out to a millennium before Adam and Eve wandered, lost, in the Garden of Paradise, falling finally to birth us. He preached of questioning souls with no imperious god, or one way to salvation.

My great-grandfather argued with true believers—those that could burn you at the stake—about our existence, our purpose. William Gay was tossed out, almost sacrificed because some enlightened souls saw the apple fall and believed it was God's doing and not the birth of empiricism with Isaac Newton. He wrote daily letters from his Professor-of-Theology chair to his son, my grandfather, the legal scribe, who said *pahh* to such sophistry. Long, passionate letters from father to son and son to father.

> *Our laws do not say how to love, or why there is no peace.*

III. Again, the God question

I knew nothing of these family conundrums, or why my ancestors were itinerant ministers. Questions about God were in our bones. The Vietnam War, divorce—sex, drugs, and rock 'n' roll—protests, raised fists, and civil unrest turned my family upside down. The spinning gyres could not hold.

    —My sister found solace as she wandered in Anglican cloisters with
Christian prayers, as she donned the cloth and worried about my lost soul.

    —I held to my swearing off God for taking that thimble. But at 19, I tried
to say no to Vietnam, lying in my conscientious objector essay that I
believed in some supreme being. "Do Not Kill" thy enemy; do not send me
to Vietnam. But those rumpled draft board men with enquiring eyes looked

directly through my deceit. There was no way I was a conscientious objector
if I did not believe.

I knew my goose was cooked when I sat in the Unitarian Church on Brattle Street one Saturday evening with other draft dodgers. We donned assorted God rationalizations, some supreme being invocation for "getting out of Vietnam." No truth or God in our words. I would fight in World War II, but not Vietnam or Iraq. Going to war was my choice, not theirs or some god's. I danced with the God question at 21, but the draft board stared back at me and said, "No."

God and country. My way or the highway.

Skepticism was part of our family conversation—questioning back and forth over wine, my ancestors on bended knees, and me pedaling to school, furiously debating the shape of the earth. Like Galileo, my family thought this mattered and that Popes would not excommunicate us. God did and did not matter. As I stared out my dorm window on tear-gas streets, I did not see gods stopping bad wars, helping addicts in back alleys with needles in arms, or giving a hand to mothers wailing in the dark. I turned pages, searching for answers, slipping into casual atheism.

IV. Death almost

The God question stayed with me as I crawled 60 miles through the Craters of the Moon desert at 21 with my girlfriend. We did not pray for salvation or ask for forgiveness when we were about to die. I looked at the sky, the planes overhead, and thought of the fickleness of fate. And much later when my prostate was full of cancer—discovered just in time. No, no turning to God, or the gods, when death raised the scythe's shadow high over my head. Asking for help from God was not in my cards. Yes, I saw those that believed prayed and were kind. But I did not give in. So stubborn.

What is the meaning of your life?

In college, the existentialists left too many words ricocheting around my head with no clear answer. *Being and Nothingness* was Sartre's way to bed Simone de Beauvoir. Beckett too wanted someone to warm him at night while he waited for Godot. For me, the Renaissance was full of too many priests selling favors and supporting the tyranny of the Church, while saints burned at the stake. Still, I stayed with the God question as Dante journeyed deep into the depths of Hell with Virgil, trying to unravel the persistent, sometimes deadly, sins of man and woman. Why so many circles? Were our sins so neatly catalogued? And who meted out the punishment? And the great spinner of tales, Shakespeare, confounded me with Hamlet's musing and Prospero's tempestuous dreams.

I left college confused with bookshelves of learned tomes. Poets played better with life's riddles than prophets. Better to walk barefoot in the desert, lost, than wait for the burning bush to speak.

> *"I prefer moralists*
> *Who promise me nothing...*
> *I prefer the hell of chaos to the hell of order...*
> *I prefer keeping in mind even the possibility*
> *That existence has its own reason for being"*
> —*"Possibilities," by Wislawa Szymborska*

V. Don't you believe in the spirit of Life?

No, of course not. I knew that for years, since I was four, maybe five, when I saw Einstein wrestle with the God question—hair on end, not able to tell us why God played dice with the universe, or why his quantum theory did not quite work. If Einstein could not get the God question right, why should I?

Later, when I was not so young—with my father reading on the window seat in the evening light as he walked us through the myths in the Golden Bowl, and Homer telling of the trials of Odysseus—I prayed to all the gods. Such capricious, jealous gods, fighting wars over Helen, a woman who loved too many great warriors. Hector and Achilles were vulnerable men and not gods, manipulated by spirits beyond them.

The capricious fates unnerved me. Why, why, why? No Old Testament God struck me down for praying to golden images. I had no proof for those miracles, those stories. At 11, Carl and I argued about the order of the world. There was no turning back and no one burning at the stake in my town. I was free to say no. I was lucky.

Early on, I felt the God question was a trick. Ministers and elders gathering their flock to do deeds for them. Of course, I didn't believe in those myths, those wars, that set of tablets, or Abraham sacrificing his boy, the sea separating for Moses, and Jesus turning water into wine. How could a young boy who heard such stories—whether by my father or preacher on high—how could I believe in God? The questions were a ruse to lead me astray.

Like Galileo, I drew circles of the moons and knew we were not the center of the universe. No, God made the world in seven days. Still, I read the stories and marveled at Satan's cleverness, his sophistry. I read how Dante descended through the circles of Hell, a lost man at 40, sliding down and down with an inscrutable guide to places he could not see, searching for Beatrice. I saw this Hell pictured on church walls, across frescoes and framed paintings in patrons' palaces, and brothels full of fun.

And John Milton, justifying the beheading of King Charles I, sang of the beauty of Paradise and the reasons for our fall. He argued that it was better to wallow in our free will than taste the fruit of God's imagined garden in a place with no seasons—no wind, snow, or rain—just sun, and no sin or death. Better to fall and try to believe, I muttered.

Milton's blind protestations resonated. Where was God? How do we love? I wandered with these tomes hoping for light, for a way to break my disenchantment. There must be some way out of here.

VI. How did you escape purgatory?

At 20, in dark theaters, I saw men, forlorn, walking down black-and-white streets, muttering to passersby about the meaning of life. My movie characters were happy to play chess with the grim reaper or cavort with the devil. Injustice and the hard, mean ways of the world were broken by wistful eyes; the ties of tyranny and cruelty did not strangle hope, wars played out on the screen, the sun rose.

ART moved my heart. Michelangelo's finger pointing. Van Gogh's starry night. And a late-night trumpet breaking my blues. Many wrestled with the God question and why bad stuff happened. Cinema did not serve up easy answers. But even lost in the movies and the castles of learning, I could not say I believed in the Supreme Being, or some master of the universe.

Why did it matter? Why the existential questions?

I knew that killing was bad, that going into a senseless war in Vietnam was not for me. But this was me, not God speaking. I pretended some voice said, "This war is bad," but this didn't work. No communism for me, no peace from them that want war. Better, I muttered, to run from the bad wars that my elders, my parents' friends guided and then say okay to God. Better to choose what war, what fight is right, and what war is not.

So when asked point blank, I could not say I believed in God. I saw, instead, the destruction that such beliefs bring. I felt the opprobrium of them that believed, the patriots, the fighters and the soldiers going to war. Maybe they had God on their side, yet I saw the casualties of war.

> *"I have met them at close of day*
> *Coming with vivid faces...*
> *We know their dream; enough*
> *To know they dreamed and are dead...*
> *Are changed, changed utterly*
> *A terrible beauty is born."*
> *—"Easter 1916," by William Butler Yeats*

VII. And what about death?

It was easy for me—at 5, 11, and 20, I could say, "No, I don't believe in God." But at 70, the question rises again. An archangel, one of the diaphanous ghosts, tells me of cancer and my fate—death not so soon, but closer than I imagined. Yes, I visit the dying, take serums and pills, am poked with needles. Around me pallid figures, brave hands holding fast, and the light of day shines on all who greet the waning light. Sadness and brave, happy smiles fill cancer wards. There is no surprise here; all our days are numbered. But no god will save me, or you.

Kind, soft hands, pills, and "How are you today?" greet me. The smile of caregivers fills my heart.

I am lucky to have come so far without God, to have sidestepped bad wars, and to have learned what? To be kind, thoughtful, and not mean? To breathe and listen to the spirit of the morning. The sun, the birds, the cold winds of winter snows. To take in the love offered and be thankful for love so close.

Why the smile? Why the bounce in your step?

Standing atop the mountain, I see not the struggles of men and women oppressed or diverted from goodness. No, I see more mountains, hills, and valleys, peaks painted with snow, the wind howling, and the hardness of each day. I see the early morning rays reflecting light from broken branches. I feel the rain, shifting jet streams, and the April weather ushering in spring. I hear the hawk up high, the bear crashing through the forest, and the coyote howls. I see, hear, and feel the shifting fortunes of nature surrounding me, not the honking horns or impatient looks.

I see me, a tiny silhouette against the mountain, the plain stretching to the sea—calm and heaving with much effect. I imagine all the creatures trying to make their way. I pause and hold my breath. What are we doing here? I feel the breath nearby, next to me.

How is it that I am so important, so special, waiting for the forces—gods, if you will— that made earth, sea, sun and moon, day and night to do better? We spin the stories, make myths that explain why we are, why I am, so important; but this is not so. I am a speck standing in our great universe. I know little more than the hawk above, or bluebird signaling another magnificent spring. I am barely visible.

Now that you have walked and played chess with death, do you not believe?

No, not yet. I touch the harsh beauty that surrounds. I ask questions, find words, and see all that surrounds me. I breathe in and am quiet. I walk lightly, ask fewer questions, have no answers. I do not gasp as the air fills my lungs, and I give thanks. I hold the love that surrounds.

Even when death stares at me from afar, even as others fade, lost to memory, I do not bend to the God question. Like a stubborn child, I cannot say, "Yes, I believe." I try to do good. One day I am here, the next gone. A stone, a memory, even a picture smiling, but then we are gone.

So why do I continue to wrestle with the God question, to pedal faster on my bike, to stare at the draft board men, to be touched by the dying, the brave, the caring? Why do I read, listen to music, and recite poetry? The puzzle of each day has walked with me since I rolled out of the crib and watched Einstein wander. Why did I just not say, "Yes?" I stay up late at night, wondering still at the questions that persist. I am amazed each day as the sun rises and the songs fill the air. I embrace the unknown.

> "*Someone who does not run*
> *toward the allure of love*
> *walks a road where nothing lives*"
> —*Rumi*

Fabrizia Faustinella

In the Eye of the Beholder

The plane trip was painfully long and sleepless. Many thoughts were darting in and out of her head and then swirling like dust devils, making it hard to calmly sift through them in an organized fashion. It was a true brain storm, associated with waves of palpitations, chest tightness, and irregular breathing. Francesca was heading to her parents' house. Her father's health had been deteriorating, and he was now wheelchair-bound. Help was needed, as they were planning to keep him home, and her mother, an older woman herself, was certainly not strong enough to take care of him. Francesca had planned a long leave of absence from work to sort things out and be present for more than the usual couple of weeks. While sitting uncomfortably squeezed between two large men, she was taking stock of her own life, revisiting all of her choices and questioning her deep sense of dissatis-faction. What was that about? She was an accomplished professional, after all, with a number of awards to her name, but had never felt successful. Why would that be? What was a successful life then? One of her friends, who shared similar feelings, came to the conclusion that in our society, success is measured mainly in terms of fame and money. Therefore, as their accomplishments made them neither popular nor rich, they couldn't possibly feel successful. Of course, success had been defined in many different ways, in-cluding "living a happy life," "liking yourself and what you do," "having a sense of purpose," "having a passion," and "following your dreams"; countless books had been written about it; countless *successful* people had talked about it and its secrets, but the proposed recipes seemed always elusive and confusing, as success and happiness didn't necessarily seem to go hand in hand.

With all those thoughts still crowding her head, she boarded the bus to get to her hometown. The countryside looked beautiful and peaceful, hilly, dotted with ancient villages, churches, and bell towers, surrounded by woods and green fields filled with bright yellow wildflowers. Sights so welcomed after the claustrophobic plane trip. Her breathing became deeper and more regular, her eyelids heavy, and she fell asleep.

Hiring a caregiver, that's what Francesca decided to do, the very moment she was awakened by the noise at the bus terminal, upon arrival in her city. All the consuming thoughts about her life and seemingly meaningless accomplishments dissipated in the fresh air, like morning mist under the sun, replaced by new needs and concerns.

She soon started interviewing several women who applied for the job, which entailed taking care of her father, helping him with the various activities of daily living, and cleaning the house as well. The chosen candidate would have to move into the house, where a bedroom with bathroom would be provided for the stay. She talked to a number of women, all of them from foreign countries. It was a tough job, and no woman from her home country would sign up to do it, despite the good pay. The choice was dictated by a number of criteria, not only good letters of reference. She needed someone strong enough to handle her father. He was a seventy-five-kilo man, and although a hoister lift was available to facilitate the various transfers from bed to chair and around the house, that was not an easy operation, and it still required physical strength. She also needed someone with at least some knowledge of the language so that she could communicate with her father and the other family members. Francesca needed to know that she had a good work ethic and was trustworthy, as she would have access to everything in the house. She wanted a woman with pleasant features as well. Her father had always appreciated beauty, and she thought it would lift his spirits to have a nice face to look at. For one reason or the other, many candidates had to be turned away. Then she was told that a woman from Eastern Europe was looking for a job because the person she was taking care of, in a small village close to the city, had died and she needed to move on.

Radana was her name. She traveled by train to come and talk to Francesca. They met in a park close to the train station, where she arrived with a friend who was also working as a caregiver for a family in town.

Radana grew up in a small Eastern European village where she married very young, raised two children, and worked in a clothing factory, all the while taking care of farm animals, big and small; milking cows and sheep; making cheese, by hand, out of the milk; tending the fields; planting and harvesting fruits and vegetables, processing and canning them in preparation for the long winter months ahead; mending clothes; cleaning the house; cooking, and doing whatever necessary to keep the household going. Hours and hours of intense physical labor, day in and day out. She would get up at four in the morning to complete all the farm chores and make breakfast for her family prior to walking to the factory, no matter the weather conditions, scorching heat or freezing winds, with snow up to her knees during the harsh winter times. Then she would go home and continue working at whatever needed to get done, with only a few hours of sleep at night. She would tell you now that, looking back, she didn't know how she could do it all. Eventually, she left her country to find a better life and a better source of income to help her family out. Francesca didn't learn any of this until much later in their relationship.

When they first met in that park outside the train station, Radana looked serious and quiet. Pretty face, early fifties. Dark short hair and dark eyes, with a deep gaze. Didn't smile much. She was well built, about five-foot-five, appeared to be physically strong; could have lifted Francesca with one of her arms, or at least that's what Francesca's impression was. There was something about Radana that felt reassuring. Francesca liked her instinctively, although she said very little. She had the look of the hard worker, the person who knows what to do and how to get things done, without having to be told twice. The kind of woman who seemed to know everything about difficult circumstances and was fully aware of the hardships of life.

The day after the meeting, Radana rang the doorbell and moved in with two pieces of luggage. That was the beginning of twenty months of faithful service. Radana had Thursday afternoons off, Sundays off, and one summer month off, during which she would go back to her country and visit her family. Otherwise, she was available at the house.

This was one of her typical days: Starting in the morning, she would help Francesca's father get out of bed; take care of his personal hygiene; move him to the breakfast table, where he would eat on his own; take him back to the bathroom; get him dressed for the day; move him to a large, comfortable chair in the den; read to him a book chapter or a newspaper article, as his eyes would tire easily; take him back to the bathroom every time it was needed; then bring him back to the table for lunch; take him back to bed for an afternoon nap; put him back in the chair to watch a TV show; take him back to the table for dinner; and eventually take him back to bed for the night. She would entertain him by showing him photos of her home country and her family, telling him folktales and also singing for him. She had a beautiful voice.

Francesca's mother would do the grocery shopping and the cooking. Radana would occasionally go to the store as well, to spare her from the extra trip, if something was missing. She would also clean the house and make herself useful in whatever way possible.

Holidays and birthdays came and went, seasons passed, and Radana kept on working diligently, day in and day out, for approximately twenty months.

Then the day arrived when Francesca's father started to quickly deteriorate. He knew the end was close. Radana reminded him to have courage and faith, which he did, as he had accepted with kindness and grace the chair-bound life of the past many months. For three nights in a row, the owl sang on the pine tree outside his bedroom balcony. Radana heard it too and said that the time had come. On the fourth day, Francesca's father passed away. Radana helped to get his body ready for the funeral and dressed him, one last time, in his favorite suit, before rigor mortis settled in.

After that, she spent two more weeks at the house, working quietly, cleaning, cooking, making those cold winter days less dark and difficult.

Eventually, she had to move on, as she accepted a similar job, taking care of another elderly man, not far away from Francesca's home.

Radana made a big difference in Francesca's life and in the life of her entire family. Radana was in fact the reason why Francesca's mother didn't go insane and fall ill herself. She was the reason why Francesca was able to maintain a job and keep on living her life in a different country, traveling back and forth, of course, but with some peace of mind. The same also was true for Francesca's brother, who lived in another city and certainly could not have quit his job to help out at the house.

Radana's dedication and hard work made their lives bearable during the hardship of those many months.

She came into their lives with a purpose. Her purpose was not to be successful or find happiness or riches. Yes, she was paid well for her services but certainly did not become wealthy. Her purpose was to do her job the best she could and to be helpful. And she did it with integrity, compassion, and commitment, carrying her strong work ethic, her honesty, and her giving nature into every single task at hand.

And that's what a successful life must be about, it occurred to Francesca. It's when you've made yourself useful to your fellow humans, when you have done good and left the world a better place than you found it. It's when you are concerned not about what you lack, but what good you can do for others.

Susan Eve Haar

Mediation

"Nine fifty-five," Alexa says. How can it be 9:55? I have to be in court at 10:00. My eyes won't focus. I fumble for my phone, remembering my lawyer sent me the address and his cell. I squint and call. He asks for my ETA.

"Twenty-five minutes." I leap from the bed, tearing a gray dress, drab, tried and true, from the hanger. Boots—I yank them on. Not too ladylike but I need them for protection.

"I'll tell counsel." He says nothing more. I'm grateful for that.

•••

I dreamt my house in a fever dream. It took nigh on to forever to actually get it built. I obsessed over tile, hunted for hinges, hired and fired contractors. The entryway looked like a California spa or the tomb of a wastrel fairy, replete with a carpet of Ming-green mosaic. Home, perhaps not large, but a foothold in the post-apocalyptic world of divorce. Family pictures on the wall, chocolate fondant in the fridge. I wanted the house to be beautiful for my children, an externalized perfection in the midst of an imperfect life. And that's what I built.

When the sewage floods began, it was hard to believe, as it must have been for the Egyptians when locusts plummeted from the heavens. There was no killing of the firstborn, not that, but there was a whole lot of shit. Excrement if you prefer. Sewage up to my ankles and then my knees, rising above the garbage bags I rubber-banded around my thighs. After the shock there was that terrible first cleaning. I did it on my own, dumping gallons of Mr. Clean into the fetid water to combat the stench before I began. And then came the second flood, the third, the fourth, ever and anon, as I hunted for the source, assisted by a kindly DEP inspector to whom my daughter fed rhubarb pie. Many explorations, many experts, much perplexity.

Up on the roof doing reconnaissance, we spotted a cattycorner meeting in the back of my house, the other building almost touching mine, though it faced the avenue. I knew the place, deserted and demolished except for the second floor. Climbing its dark staircase, the walls spotted with light like pox, you came to Sexy Boutique, a place replete with fantasy and fake phalluses. The inspector and I investigated. There were tubs of condoms and rubber gloves in the bathroom in the back, also a little sink. The inspector took a vial out of his pocket and poured red dye down the drain. He ran the water and we raced back to my basement. The dye bubbled up from the floor drains, red plumes billowing into the brownish sludge.

I knew the source but the sewage continued to flow into my home. I hired lawyers. I got a TRO, an order restraining the sewage, I suppose, from entering my house. But that was hardly the end of it.

There's a cab outside my door when I swing open the gate. I want to believe that it's a sign of forgiveness from the universe, or at least mercy, but I don't believe it.

"Eighty State Street." I slam the door.

The driver nods; I start to read him directions.

"I know, I know." He shakes his head.

"I'm late for court," I explain.

"Twenty-seven minutes," he says.

•••

The traffic is moderate. I take seven deep breaths. This is what is meant by visceral: a darkness I experience in the gut, my brain having forsaken me. I'm being sucked into some existential void, hoping for an alien invasion. I consider going home and crawling back into bed. But this is the legal system I am tangling with. There's no throwing in the towel or even hurling the racquet. I review all my evil deeds and serious mistakes made in the course of a lifetime. This is my very own catastrophe. There is no denying it; I have visited it upon myself. I am the moving party, and if I don't get what I need, I am totally screwed. Groping through my bag, I encounter a long-forgotten piece of gum. I unwrap it, a substitute for morning ablutions, raking my fingers through my hair. For a horrible moment I think I am wearing knee-highs, but then I see I've managed baggy tights, though a pattern of loops around the thigh reveals a shock of skin. I tug the hem down over my knees. The minutes trickle by inexorably. I look out the window at the city sliding by. The day is unseasonably warm, the sun beneficent. I consider buckling my seatbelt. I tell my body this is where we are, this is the day, there is nothing else.

•••

We arrive. The road next to the court is blocked by construction. A cop stops the cab.

"She's late for court," the driver says, now my ally in an indifferent universe. Unmoved, the cop waves us on.

"End of the block." The cabbie pulls over to the curb, pointing. I get out and run.

•••

Pushing through the revolving door, I see the metal detector and, next to it, a row of little white tubs like cake boxes awaiting keys, wallet, or weapon, should you have one. A woman blocks the line, investigating the contents of her capacious bag. I whisk in front of her, setting off the alarm as I head through.

"Take off your boots and hold up your hands," the cop says.

"Maybe wouldn't have happened if you'd waited," a man remarks, and I am washed away by a river of shame. It is in the nature of things that this is the wrong building.

•••

I don't look at the time as I exit the building; it's not going to help. While running into traffic, my goal to cross the street, I consider the possibility of getting hit, I haven't even brushed my teeth. I wonder how I have gotten this far in my life, survived to this august age, raised children, paid not-insubstantial taxes, buried lovers, chosen china patterns, and now am at the mercy of justice and my own incompetence.

•••

A woman with Brazilian-straightened hair is sitting on a bench as I get off the elevator.

"That way," she points to the left. It's one way or the other; I follow her directions. Around the bend of the atrium, I see my lawyer hanging out with a pointy-nosed man. They stop talking as I approach. My lawyer greets me, drawing me aside.

"His client hasn't showed up." His suit is an unlikely blue, the color of a robin that has taken a nosedive into ink, and he's wearing classy, horn-rimmed glasses. His hair, more coifed than mine, rolls back in a perfect wave. He looks like a gigolo attending university. I breathe a sigh of relief.

"Got here fast," he winks.

•••

I am debating washing my face in the bathroom when we're called into the conference room. The woman from the elevator bench is already seated at the long table, scrolling through her phone. She looks up.

"Just not here," she shrugs. I realize she's the lawyer for the defendants. I should have recognized her; after all, she'd inspected my house. All of it, even my bedroom. I remember my indignation. Did she think I was hiding sewage under my bed, rafting out of my room on a pillow? Looking up, she taps the edge of the table with impeccable nails. The mediator looks up at the clock, frowning.

"We're going to start." Well, I can't believe it. Neither the sex shop guys nor the slumlord have shown up. I am once again a model citizen, despite my many abject failures and lack of a shower. It's all relative. The mediator is telling us something about the process, the ways in which it is being replicated statewide; she speaks carefully, as if explaining sex to a child. Her model, she says, is a proven success. All her clerks are out for the holidays, she tells us, so the lawyers will have to do some writing on the whiteboards that cover one wall. No one looks very happy.

The pointy-nosed man with the Russian mafia eyebrows tells us he is a substitute for the building's lawyer—there are personal reasons he won't go into that she can't be present. At this he wiggles his eyebrows suggestively but he's very well prepared. He pulls a sheath of papers out of his briefcase and sits. There's an embroidered runner down the center of the table scattered with dyed shells and inscribed stones. I expect the one in front of me to say "retrograde" but it is mute. My lawyer sits too. I sit beside him.

The mediator asks my lawyer to speak first. He pushes back, rising athletically from his chair. The room is small but he paces, modifying to suit the confines, holding his hands interlaced behind his back. Now he stops, pivots, and begins to speak.

"Write on the whiteboard," the mediator urges. He hesitates, then, taking the cap off a green marker, he begins to write.

"The backflow began," he says, "sometime in November." Thanksgiving to be exact, my children fleeing the house and the tidal wave of sewage. He writes, then puts the cap back on the marker. Now he rolls onto the balls of his feet, tipping back and forth. There's a quick and quiet knock on the door. A small man with pixie ears tipped forward on his head slips in and sits next to the pointy-nosed lawyer. His skin is dusky; his black hair is cut stylishly and combed back flat. He sits down next to the woman lawyer. She looks exas-perated rather than pleased to see him. He looks at his lap. Is this really the man I left messages for in Brooklyn and called in Pakistan, politely asking for his attention? For whom I left begging notes both at Sexy Boutique and its sister shop, Rainbow Station, while inspecting the dildos and crack pipes by the counter? Him or maybe his father, I really don't know; he looks pretty young to be hosting transgendered sex liaisons in the basement.

•••

My lawyer covers most of the story pretty matter-of-factly. He notes that the sewage rose to six feet, and the pointy-nosed man shakes his head with disbelief. That's what grabbed the press, the sheer volume of sewage, that and the confluence of money, sex, and shit. I listen. I want my lawyer to do more, to describe the fouling of my gem, the dark clots floating through the living room downstairs. And then the Augean task of cleaning it, knee-deep in water opaque with disintegrating excrement. But what does he know? He wasn't there.

The door opens. A man sits down next to Pointy Nose. His skin is a blue-black, not tall but totally jacked. He wears a cap-sleeved shirt, though this is November, displaying his biceps. I can't help but look. He's sexy like his boutique; perhaps the name is eponymous. My lawyer's droning on. There's a smattering of law and various dates. The mediator is paying attention, as is the pointy-nose lawyer. His client is looking at his fingernails.

I ask to speak; I want to tell my story and I rise. The horror of finding the toilet erupting with fluid feces into the murky sewage that lapped at my Wellington boots. Bailing feces, disintegrating personal wipes, and free-floating condoms. How we fought the flooding, keeping the windows open November, December, all the way to April to combat the stench. To protect the home I had dreamt of and laboriously built. My lawyer folds his hands over his stomach.

"The home I thought I'd live in the rest of my life," I add. Well, there's a certain theatricality to that, I'll admit it, but it's fueled by righteous truth. I'm surprised when the mediator, looking nonplussed, asks what I paid for the house. Now she's interested. She raises her eyebrows. Foreclosure, I say.

•••

Throughout the proceeding the blue-skinned men sit impassive. They don't seem particularly concerned. The mediator smiles slightly, turning to the men. Her face breaks into practiced wrinkles. She nods at me and turns to the men.

"Can you acknowledge her feelings?" she says, leaning forward on the embossed green blotter that covers her desk. Even I am stunned. There's a long silence. I look at the man who sits across from me. He looks back, his eyes silent pools, reflecting nothing. Now he smiles. That's when I see that he's a natural-born killer, wily and wary. He's done things I can't imagine to get to this day and to this table. What was I thinking? That this guy who owns four sex shops with their concomitant business of prostitution and drugs would be a fellow traveler? He stretches and the muscles of his forearms ripple. It's nothing personal; it's just another hit-and-run to him, and he's wondering if he's dented the fender.

•••

That's when I understand that I have to settle. There's no solace to be had here, only lawyers' fees to accrue. I will never be made whole, as if money can do that. The cash that I've watched flood into the registers of Sexy Boutique—no one charges a cock ring—none of that will ever surface. I see it all in that moment as he smiles at me with his flat, black eyes. There is no choice. I will bend my knee, I will take my lumps. This is what it is to be born into the world. This is what it is to be a homeowner.

The mediator pushes back her chair and stands.

"Back in February," she smiles, benign as a Hadassah mother. "We've made a lot of progress."

Cynthia Lewis

My Time on Our Time (Where Couples Meat)

Hello,
I apologize.
I just committed the worst offense.
I called you by the wrong name.
That's a great way to start off.
Well if you're still interested, let me know.
        —Jake

Predictably, people who use OurTime.com often get confused. After all, it's a dating site for people over 50. Jake was confused about plenty. He'd mistakenly called me "Echo," despite the fact that it's the name of the site's administrative function, not of a person, so he hadn't really gotten me confused with another woman. Jake's worst offense, though, was failing to notice that I listed myself on my profile as a political liberal, while he admitted to being a conservative. (The majority of men safely refer to themselves as "middle of the road.") Once I assured Jake that my politics would immediately drive him nuts, he high-tailed it to more promising territory.

At least Jake wasn't confused enough to forget he'd ever approached me and we were now a done deal. I lost count of the number of guys whom I politely declined, but who, a few weeks later, wrote to me again as if they'd never seen my profile before. All they had to do was scroll far enough down the page with my picture on it, where our past correspondence was archived, plain as day. "Silver Fox"—so named for his full gray mane—expressed his interest in hearing from me on four separate occasions, even though, after each time, I'd responded that, much as I appreciated hearing from him, I didn't think we were a match.

I myself ventured onto Our Time as a result of a conversation I'd had with my twenty-three-year-old son, Hal. "Mom," he asked me one day just after New Year's, "can we talk about dating?"

"Sure," I responded. "You mean *your* dating, right?" I love it when he brings me into his confidence about someone he's seeing.

"No, yours," he said, then continued, "Mom, how would you feel about a dating site that was *totally free*?"

I cleared my throat before answering, "Probably not as good as you would."

The site, as anyone under 30 could guess, was Okay Cupid, and Hal was convinced it was the answer to my lonesomeness. Although hesitant, I tried to remain open-minded. It was a new year, after all, and Hal was right: I'd been solo long enough. So I registered on Okay Cupid, but without initiating any filters. When my first round of "matches" popped up with a nineteen-year-old, tattooed and pierced bisexual in far-away New York City, I retreated and threw in my lot with other baby boomers on Our Time.

Not long after I'd paid my $75.93 for a six-month subscription, I realized I could go into business advising guys on their pictures and profiles. Ubiquitous salt-and-pepper beards, mustaches, and goatees—seemingly attempts to compensate for partial or complete baldness—are only the beginning. Selfies, especially those that distort the subject's face and those taken in poor light, abound, although without apparent reason. Don't these guys have any friends who can take a picture, outside or next to a window, with a cell phone? And, fellas, ditch the cowboy and baseball hats for the profile, whose purpose is to let women see *what you look like.* Women will discover sooner or later that you're missing hair underneath. Merely *smiling into the camera* doesn't seem to occur to many of these guys, who must think that contemplatively staring off into space enhances their mystery.

The most extreme case of photographic cluelessness I came across involved a guy—I'll call him Max—who lived far enough away from me that I felt okay casually corresponding with him so long as we stayed on the site, as opposed to migrating to our personal email accounts. From the start, I'd noticed that in his main profile picture, the vestiges of a cropped-out woman were visible to Max's right, her elegant hand on his left shoulder, her blond hair and chin up against his cheek. I thought it must be his daughter. Surely, I told myself, it couldn't be his last significant other.

Emboldened to ask him about her, I wrote, "Who's the lady in the picture?" "The lady (that's no lady—just kidding)," he responded, "is my estranged wife." An apology ensued, but, uninterested in any kind of follow-up, I stopped writing. Several days later, he wrote me back. "i guess i said too much??" "No, Max," I replied, "you told the truth, which is that your wife, however estranged she may be, is both literally and figuratively in the picture."

Attempts to invent cool and fetching screen names, though they often flounder, are among the most entertaining features of Our Time. Monikers like "Dialectic Voyeur," "Goldenboy," "Johnny Rockit" (whose way-too-close-up photo surrounded by a weirdly yellow glow makes his head look like a reflection in a funhouse mirror), "Lookin4You371," and "bubba6006" put the observer's guess work to the test. What might 371 and 6006 denote? What does "Dialectic Voyeur" even mean?

Careful reading on Our Time is no more the norm than decent photos or compre-hensible screen names. In my profile, I stated, "Gents, I don't respond to people without a picture and a profile." In trying to give my warning a light touch, I'd apparently failed to convince the several guys a day who, without picture, profile, or both, invited me to "chat" with them. Could they possibly believe that the women whose pictures and profiles they were perusing were displaying themselves for the pleasure of men entitled to choose them without being chosen themselves? Really, guys? Without a picture and / or a profile, you appear to be hiding something, and the very women you're trying to lure won't be fooled. They'll just think you're desperate.

Careful writing, like careful reading, is also spotty on Our Time. Bad and ill-advised photos are an easy fix compared with illiteracy. My squeamishness as an English teacher aside, the lack of attention to such basics as where one sentence ends and another begins is shocking. Oh, the editing favors I could do these men if they'd let me near their profiles! Or if they'd simply begin by drafting their profiles on a word-processing program, note the red squiggly lines under typos, and cut and paste their corrected draft onto the site. Such a procedure wouldn't catch the difference between, say, "your" and "you're," or, more urgently, the problem with writing, "I'm hoping to meat someone special" or "I gust enjoy life in general." Nor would it address the bewildering and nonsensical overwriting in a salutation like "Ms. One Who Has Transformed, that'sReal, Positive, Strong, Youthful, Committed and Intelligent lady of a woman...." But it would catch doozies like "Some one to spend quality time with.no" (in reference to what the guy is looking for in a woman) or "I WILL ALWAYS STAND BY MY, HONESTY IS THE BEST POLICY. GROWING UP, I LEARNED TO GIVE MORE THAN I RECEIVED."

As a writer, I'm intrigued by the terrible prose on certain profiles the way some drivers are drawn to gazing at road-side wrecks. Here's someone whose faith in words to represent him accurately is, to say the least, scant:

> In my profile you may gleem a glance of the things in which I enjoy and have intrests in. It's alot like a snapshot, reveals some but one dimensional. To describe myself to you, may read like alot of others "in my own words"! If my profile has sparked a intrest, perhaps it would be best for you to make your own assessment. After all, is it not your opinion of who I am that counts when it comes to you! So if you perfer to draw your own conclusions based on meeting me vs reading, I look forwarded to hearing from you. For I am who I am and do not wish for my "in my own words" to become "fiction" for you.

In contrast, sometimes a few plain words prove ample, even if they're left improperly punctuated. I was approached by "Tennessee lover," who confessed in his profile to being a smoker. I replied, "I'm a reformed, three-pack-a-day smoker (over 25 years), so I'm afraid smoking is a deal-breaker for me," to which I received the eloquent response, "baby my loss honey."

Not every verbal entanglement ends so elegantly. Attempting to extricate myself from flirtatious, forward "Calabasas," I wrote, "I think I'm way too nerdy for you. My loss. I'm a school marm." When he responded, "What do you mean by nerdy?" I had to admit it was a fair question.

Far more challenging was dissolving the glue that kept me adhered to "Speechless 76." His overture was a suggestion that we meet for dinner, accompanied by helpful advice. "The dinner can be the entire date," he assured me. "Therefore, if one of us does not like the other after the meal we can allow the date to end." When I hadn't responded to him within a couple of hours, he plunged into further self-advertisement. "Lady, I am the most honest human being on the surface of this earth.... I am compassionate, kind, caring, loving, trustworthy, reliable, careful, thoughtful, a true gentleman, dedicated, wishes to treat you like an angel, very romantic, modest, gentle, patient, respectful, compatible, your best friend, loyal, committed, respectful, helpful, humble, faithful, loves to laugh and make you laugh too, committed to only one lady, loves to show you affection, loves to show you off, feels lucky to be with you, never gets angry, plus an excellent listener." Following this litany were promises to treat me like a "princess," his name, his phone number, his email address, and the closing "Hugs & Kisses."

When I hadn't responded within the next couple of hours, his impression of me as vain and heartless had worked him into a lather. "Since, I have yet to hear from you, I can only guess what kind of woman you are," he castigated me. "The type of personality, if you have a temper, if you fuss or argue." Mind you, he had yet to hear word one from me. Despite his suspicions about my "type of personality," he closed this third message with "I look forward to hearing from you." On the next day, he did. "For someone who refers to himself as 'speechless,'" I wrote, "you sure do say a lot!" When I asked him not to be in touch with me again, he retorted, "you are the one loosing the only honest gentleman you ever met." We can cut him some slack, owing to his perturbation, for not realizing that I'd never met him. His frenzy, however, was considerable and continued to play havoc with his grammar. "I knew you has problems by the way you acted when I tried to make a move toward you." Finally, the crushing blow. "Honestly, you scared me away from you the time you never responded"—that was the time I was away from my computer for a few hours while he was piling one message onto another.

After I'd been on OurTime.com for a while, one of my best friends cautioned me about scammers and low-lifes lurking on the site. I responded that I had modest expectations. "I don't think I'm going to meet a husband, probably not a boyfriend, either," I wrote to her in an email. But I was feeling as if I'd finally recovered from a very painful break-up two years earlier, and I was ready to have some fun for a change. "If I spend a Friday evening having dinner and conversation with a guy at a restaurant," I wrote to my friend, "that's plenty for now. In my situation, it beats going home and watching another episode of *Mad Men*. He doesn't have to be my soul mate. Besides, I'm fascinated by the culture of the thing."

As predicted, I didn't meet a long-term love interest, though I did form a friendship with a guy I met on the site who wasn't really my type. For a while, we went to movies and ate out together. Also as predicted, I became absorbed by the way mature adults present themselves and address others on a site that preserves anonymity indefinitely.

On occasion, I was genuinely enraptured by somebody's quirkiness, never more so than in the case of the fellow who went by the screen name "Hogstuff." William, as I'll call him, was a farmer with a very big heart. His profile photo made him seem to be laughing hysterically and inexplicably at something unseen, but my guess is that he was simply shy about taking himself seriously enough to pose for a real portrait.

As his screen name suggested, "Hogstuff" was refreshingly free of pretention. Like so many other hopefuls on OurTime.com, he held on to the rails of literacy for dear life. Yet his prose, though riddled with grammatical errors and misspellings, had a peculiar charm about it. It too was without pretention—transparent and, despite lack of formal correct-ness, clear enough. Vulnerable too. In reference to why he was on the site, he wrote:

I am really not sure there's a reason I have not been in any relationships after a few dates these ladies start talking about being in a relationship, What has ever happened to spending quality time with a quality person, I am not a possession guy I don't need to own or possess something very secure in who I am. No where I want to live after I have finished risen my kids that's a different color horse.

I was so taken by William's peculiar expression that I would reply with a sentence or two so that I could read what he wrote back.

"Hogstuff" was, surprisingly, a meaningful choice of aliases. Humble though he was, William had invented a feeding contraption that would prevent reproduction in feral hogs, which, you may know (as I did not), are a world-wide menace. In the U.S. alone—which has the fifth largest population on the globe—feral hogs destroy 11.8 billion dollars' worth of crops per year. He had patented the machine and, at the time I was corresponding with him, was about to unveil it at the world feral pig conference, where he'd been asked to join the world council on the basis of his invention.

When I exited Our Time for good, I dropped William a note telling him I'd like to stay in touch by email, although I didn't want to mislead him in the romance department. I've yet to meet him, but I hear from him once a year, at college basketball tournament time, when, as an avid Duke fan, he checks in about my college's Division I prospects. He sends me a photo of his adorable granddaughter and sounds ever cheerful, ever hopeful. His message usually coincides with an email promotion from Our Time, offering me a renewed membership for (their FINAL OFFER!) 65% off. Not even the lure of new writing material tempts me.

To the sweet, pretty, gray-haired lady who says on the television commercial for Our Time, "On-line dating? I know people meet that way, but where would I even start?" I say only, "*caveat emptor.*"

Kathleen Zamboni McCormick

Daddy's Girl

I recall being a relatively happy child of the sixties, until we discovered I was "exceptional." Testing occurred in third grade, and they said they'd never seen scores like mine. My parents were contacted and told I was outstanding, possibly a genius. Apparently, Father's first reaction was disbelief. "How can that be? She's a girl." Mother was less surprised. "Well, she's a Virgo, so she's always been a perfectionist."

Before the revelation, I'd mostly spent time with Mother, cooking, cleaning, shopping, and sewing, though always surrounded by books. Also, of course, developing lovely little friendships involving jump rope, Beatles cards, and Barbies. They said I was too young for sleepovers. Sometimes Father tried enlisting my interest in Red Sox games, though since I'd been taught nothing about baseball, our interactions were mutually disappointing and, to him, further proof of female defectiveness. A boy would have just known.

But now, after Father accepted that I was (highly) intelligent, attention began. Initially just questions on what I was studying. Pleasant, if unused to. Explaining long division, I imagined it was like I'd become a boy. But too much to hope for. "Someone has to look after her mind," Father proclaimed, and it was understood only he was up to the task. No one, including me, even thought to recognize I'd been doing just fine looking after my own mind.

Father developed new rules. With implications. He'd examine all homework directly after dinner. Which meant: 1. No longer helping Mother clear the table or wash dishes. I protested at unfairness to Mother. 2. Homework had to be completed before dinner. In fact, immediately after school. Mother protested at unfairness to me. "She needs time for fun and fresh air." And listening with friends to growing collections of 45s.

"She needs to learn to excel."

"She needs to be a regular kid."

"She needs discipline. Test scores won't last without hard work."

What *she* needed was to not be discussed in the third person while in the room. What she needed was recognition that she already excelled, without Father, that she soaked up knowledge naturally, maybe like boys with baseball. Of course, I had no words like those for years.

My stomach tightened with every argument, like claws squeezing inside, forcing me to throw up. Which went unnoticed.

No surprise Father got his way. So Mother worked alone in the kitchen, and Father and I toiled in the living room, as he "reviewed" my work. Spelling lists were easy, but his insistent and repeated pronunciations made me nervous—"brreck-fahsst," "ah-ro-mah"— and I stumbled. He recorded every hesitation, even if I spelled the word correctly. His list lengthened, and every night I had to spell what seemed like a hundred words, even if only three were assigned for the next day.

After kitchen work, Mother made me Mary Quant dresses from Simplicity patterns and Jordan Marsh's exquisite remnants we'd bought on sale together before we knew I was intelligent. Father and I drudged on. He sighed at how Mother's cleaning up and sewing machine noises distracted us from "our work together." I loved Mother's Mary-Quant-on-the-cheap but wanted her to make more noise, make him stop rather than make me that "Daddy's Girl" white dress with neck and wrist ruffles.

Father couldn't complain about my exceptional reading comprehension answers, but he berated my left-handed penmanship. Finger banging on my history homework, he yelled, "How will anyone know this says, 'Kateri Tekakwitha spent most of her time in prayer'?" He obviously could read it. I wrote neatly, painstakingly bearing down on always-sharpened pencils, yet it never crossed my mind to defend myself. Instead, because I'd made him angry, I felt responsible for calming him down.

"I'll write more carefully the next time, Dad," I said softly, head lowered. "You'll write more carefully now. Do it again. I said now," and he threw my notebook at me.

I had to erase all those crisp, thin words and write over them since homework had to be done in bound notebooks where no pages could be torn out. But the indentation of my first writing wouldn't completely disappear, so the rewrite looked messy. Once when a page ripped after I'd erased it for the third or fourth time and I got so upset (typical girl!), Mother made him stop.

"You're torturing the child and teaching her nothing. She does her work well on her own," Mother finally screamed and pulled the notebook and me away from him. Why hadn't Mother helped me before if she understood? I asked her the next day, but she said arguing with Father would simply prolong our review time. She felt sorry for me, but it was best to let him be. My mind heard her say, "I cannot defend you every night." My stomach heard, "He is in control, and he needs you, only daughter, because you are his single pleasure." Only when vomiting over the toilet bowl years later did I ask, "What about my needs? My pleasure?"

My grades gradually declined. Teachers' comments focused on new faults. Loss of confidence. Unusual reticence to speak. Inability to concentrate. Stomach pains. Stubborn refusals to see the nurse.

"Told you those tests were a fluke," Father admonished Mother. "She can't maintain her grades, even with my help. She needs more attention from me." And it seemed I'd be stuck reviewing homework forever, with him continually finding fault, proving my weaknesses, and then my need for him.

I got sicker. My mother sensed the pain my stomach was in. He put it down to "female hysteria." But when I couldn't stop vomiting for three days and had to be hospitalized, Mother used all the kitchen money to buy me a small desk at the secondhand store on the corner. The owner gave her a chair for free.

She set the desk up in my bedroom and told Father I'd do my homework alone now. I went into my room directly after dinner but could still hear him.

"Her grades'll go down further. She needs me to do well."

I told myself I'd work until everything was perfect, that it would be better than what I did with Father. Though, by then, I wasn't sure how. I kept worrying what Father would think. Whether I could be prepared for that spelling test in the morning without reviewing his long list. If my handwriting was clear enough. My answers sufficiently detailed. It was years before I could admit that what Father had really taught me was to doubt myself at every turn, to wonder if the tests had gotten it wrong, to imagine that I was as average as any other girl.

It took many more years to discover there was a whole set of literature on father-daughter relationships that were just like ours. There I was imagining myself to be simply a garden-variety neurotic—a little anxious and a perfectionist perhaps because of my star sign—when, in fact, I was suffering from the consequences of what is called "covert emotional incest." No wonder I couldn't stop vomiting.

Scott Minar

Flying Saucers

"So, I have a question only a physicist can answer." Steve's eyebrows rise. I'm telling him the story of a college friend and I standing in the grass at an outdoor concert. We are heads-up and stargazing, searching the night sky when we are startled by an enigma: a distinctive flash of light, a bright shooting star making a perfect right angle in the dark expanse overhead. We are sure it's a UFO.

After explaining, I ask Steve, a NASA scientist who specializes in solar winds, "Was that a UFO?"

"A perfect right angle?" Steve echoed.

"Sure! It was perfect."

Before I utter the last syllable though, he adds, "From what perspective?"

That pulls me up short, mind slower than tongue, one on earth and one in a spaceship travelling at the speed of light. I understand what he is suggesting, but can't stop myself from asking anyway, "What do you mean?"

Steve explains that in a three-dimensional world, if we shift perspective—i.e. the particular point of view from which we observe—then the degree of angle also shifts. He tries to let me down easy—offering that patient, kindly look physicists use when they realize the rest of the world isn't seeing things accurately. "It was a meteor. They split when entering the atmosphere. It happens all the time."

•••

The conversation changed me.

Despite my short career as a philosophy major at university, I had to admit that I'd failed to ask the right questions or to consider the limits of subjectivity in a grand universe of unfathomable scale.

When it came to inquiry, I had to start over—even though I'd graduated from college long ago and was a teacher myself.

•••

I've loved every sci-fi film I've ever seen (though I've skipped a few on principle), every sci-fi story or novel or investigative journalism book I've ever read. Pitiful, I know. I've worked hard to earn the *nerd* label. All sci-fi fans will tell us their love is based on three things: escapism, escapism, and escapism. The world backs you up against a figurative adolescent dumpster in the alley, and this is the way out—perfect, unassailable. Fantasy can't be disproven as narrative reality. It is itself. It is "what it is": a nice way to get away to a nicer place—sealed, positive ending secured and locked down. I've been like this since I was a child, and I'm not alone. The Star Trek franchise's apparent immortality is evidence of sci-fi's power and appeal—to a large number of a certain predisposition anyway. I was reading Kurt Vonnegut's novels in high school study hall, while taking a C in English. Raised on Ursula Le Guin, Isaac Asimov, and Ray Bradbury, I read books like *The Dispossessed* and *The Left Hand of Darkness*; or *The Martian Chronicles, Stranger in a Strange Land,* and *Dune.* I gobbled speculative narratives up, a voracious reader of what Steven King's mother called "trash," as distinguished (by her) from the even more pejorative term, "bad trash." I binge-read Erich von Däniken's *Chariots of the Gods* in an afternoon. My friends and I were on a journey. It was the 1970s; everyone was.

In one of the Golden Era science fiction stories I consumed back then—I can't remember the title or who wrote it—two children are being raised by their grandparents on a recently terraformed Jupiter. When an intergalactic social worker comes to check on them, she discovers that the children are receiving letters from their space-travelling, circus-performer parents once a week. But, as it turns out, the parents haven't really written a missive in years. They gave up shortly after dropping the kids off in their flying saucer. The grandfather started writing the parents' weekly letters for them, out of pity for the children. When the social worker confronts him about this, she says, "You have to tell them what's going on! You can't treat your grandchildren this way. I've always believed that the truth will set you free."

He responds, "And I have always believed it is the dreams that keep us going."

In retrospect, I was more like the social worker in that story, I suppose, but also, in truth, had the qualities of both. It's not easy to say which character in the tale is right— because of course both of them are. This little dialogue gem was one of the turning points that reset my perspective. Sometimes a question or a debate can be a Proteus moment. It can wake us up.

•••

The term "flying saucer" was probably invented around 1930, a year after my parents were born. But by 1952, the year before I came into this world, it had been replaced by the Air Force term, "UFO," the abbreviation for "unidentified flying object." The term "flying discs" is also sometimes used. Contrary to popular belief, sightings of disc-shaped flying objects may have been recorded as early as the late medieval period. Imagine Arthur and Lancelot riding toward Camelot only to be accosted by the giant robot *Klaatu* from the 1950s version of *The Day the Earth Stood Still.* This is even crazier than Mark Twain's gambit in *A Connecticut Yankee in King Arthur's Court.* Hank Morgan, the main character of Twain's time travel novel, merely brings nineteenth century technology to Camelot in order to save himself and to prosper, at least for a while, as Arthur's advisor and a replacement for Merlin.

I used to live and teach in Elmira, New York where Sam Clemens and his family are interred. I would sometimes ride a bicycle to the Clemens/Langdon gravesite at Woodlawn

Cemetery—a sprawling, old New England graveyard of immense natural beauty—to sit on a stone bench nearby and eat my lunch while meditating on literature's limitations beneath the giant oaks and maples shading that hillside. The school where I taught, Elmira College, was steeped in Twain studies and Clemens lore. A tour bus pulled up to campus several times a day. Visitors would get out, walk thirty yards or so across our college green filled with elms, cottonwoods, and oaks—their leaves' fluttering an atonal but nonetheless beautiful paean to upstate New York's unique and pleasant ambiance—and arrive at Twain's study to hear a brief lecture about its history. The construction is an octagon, a faceted circular geometry, and was built for him by his liberal and somewhat wealthy in-laws, the Langdon's. The study was originally placed at Quarry Farm on a promontory overlooking the Chemung River valley, where Sam and Livy, his wife, spent their summers and where many of his most famous novels were written. *A Connecticut Yankee in King Arthur's Court* is often referred to as a "groundbreaking" science fiction novel. But there were earlier versions of a time travel story—H.G. Wells' *The Chronic Argonauts,* for example, was published in 1888, a year before Twain's novel.

In those days, I often used to think of Twain's study as a kind of flying saucer. Ridiculous, I know, but sometimes one kind of imagining provokes another. It was fun to think of Twain taking off in that thing, winging west toward the Mississippi. What kind of innocence story—preserved or lost—would that be? Once during a seminar on teaching *Huck Finn* conducted by Vic Doyno of the University of Buffalo, we argued for a week over the question of whether or not Huck Finn changes over the course of his eponymous novel.

I mused then, and still do, that an abused child always needs a generous eye, so I have often thought for reasons I would learn much later in my own life.

•••

A funny thing happened to me once involving memory. My friend, bio-psychologist Patrick Drumm, has always warned me that memory is highly unreliable. I already knew a bit about that from reading a bundle of books about well-known criminal trials. Manson Family prosecutor Vincent Bugliosi famously argues that eyewitness testimony is largely misunderstood as evidence and is in fact often either dubious or simply wrong. Memory is typically recursive, a process involving subjective recovery of objective events, with emphasis on the word *subjective.*

I told a story for years about my father's illness and early death. He died of massive heart failure in the 1970s brought on by complications from adolescent diabetes. I often talked about the events that led to his illness. I told the story this way:

He had a car accident when he was sixteen. He was gravely injured and suffered a collapsed lung that needed to be re-inflated via the insertion of a tube through an incision just below his rib cage, a silver-dollar sized pucker on his skin there for the rest of his life. It looked like someone had poked his side with a giant, invisible pencil and then left it embedded there. A telephone pole had collapsed on top of his car. Electrical wires everywhere, it took some time to get him out. He was rushed to the hospital where he became so ill that he lost all of his hair and teeth over the following weeks. He eventually dropped to 93 lbs. and was given his Last Rights by a priest. The cross they gave him had a skull-and-crossbones on it, the kind reserved for those about to die. Then a day came when doctors told his family he wouldn't last the night. He recounted a marvelous dream he had then in which he was floating in outer space and had a choice to leave earth or return to it. He decided to return, and when he woke the next morning his condition had improved. He defied remarkable odds and lived—but his pancreas was gone. He took two shots of insulin a day for the rest of his life and hid his condition from most people —afraid it would make him unemployable. Eventually, he became a cop though and told thrilling stories about his adventures in law enforcement, the dangers he faced routinely.

I was talking with my mother a few years ago about this story, and I said to her. "You know, when dad got his diabetes, after the car accident."

She said, "What accident?"

Memory reset.

"There wasn't an accident?" I asked.

"No. He had appendicitis. They botched his surgery. After he came home, he became more and more ill. It was your Aunt who suggested he had to go back to the hospital. That's when they discovered they left something inside his abdomen and he developed sepsis from it."

Memory is useless. Why had I turned that narrative around in my head toward this elaborate, more-than-a-little absurd version? I instantly knew she was right.

I'd heard the story before. But why reinvent it over time? What mechanism inside me wanted it to be a car accident? What film was I watching inside my own head, changing the narrative to suit what or whom exactly? Of course, sometimes people simply omit the truth and lie by omission.

One of the more comic stories I tell involves how I didn't know my mother's first name until I was fifty years old.

My father was a tall German/Scots- or -English American, depending on how we trace the tree—fair-skinned, dirty blonde hair and striking gray eyes. We are Von Heller's on the German side, and part of the Virginia/West Virginia Byrd's on the Scots-English side. Apparently, my ancestor William Byrd I was the founder of Richmond, Virginia, and our tree includes Byrd the explorer and Byrd the senator, among others. My mother, on the other hand, is a short Sicilian woman—from the Leta and Frascona clans—whose first language was Italian. She was born at home on Cleveland's east side and is a great keeper of secrets. She would never tell me her birth date. My sister-in-law finally got it out of her: March 25, 1929.

We were at lunch with my mother's side of the family, Aunt Jean and cousin Rose. My aunt was talking about how they had moved from the Collinwood area of Cleveland to

Murray Hill, or Little Italy as it was and is still called. Aunt Jean said, "Yeah, that's when we stopped calling you Anna."

My mother said, "I hated that name. They always called me Anna Banana."

I interrupted. "Wait, what do you mean they called you *Anna*?" My mother's name is Nancy.

Nancy said, "That's what they called me in the neighborhood."

I said, "So your name is Anna?"

Aunt Jean chimed in for her, "Nope."

I was really confused. I looked at my Aunt, whose real name is Mary (every Italian family understands why a middle name is sometimes needed in cases like these—too many Mary's) and said, "What's her name?" a smile of shock now creeping into my expression.

Nancy, my mother, answered, "*Annunciata.*"

"Annunciata?" I parroted in absolute disbelief.

"Yeah, that's why they called me *Anna*. But then my Aunt told my mother, 'Call her Nancy. That's a good name in America.'"

I was floored. "So, I'm fifty years old and just learning that my mother's name is Annunciata?"

I had intimations about my mother's propensity to keep things secret before, but here was definitive proof—and a mystery. Why keep that from your children for so long? Without my aunt, I might never have known my mother's name.

But the years have taught me a few things. Who's to say what that truth or those omissions really indicate? The past itself is much more of a mystery than we may know.

Annunciata is for the Annunciation, when Gabriel came to the Virgin Mary and told her she would be the mother of the Son of God. He told Mary to name her son Yeshua. Many Christians observe the Feast of the Annunciation on March 25th—my mother's birthday. My grandmother named her daughter as a good Catholic should, for the feast associated with her appearance in the world. This is also an approximation of the northern vernal equinox, nine full months before the birth of Christ in December. I was born on December 22nd. So my mother and I are a small reflection of a much bigger picture, a longer story. Aren't we all in one way or another. How strange the days unravel over time. What lessons hide inside them waiting to be relearned and unfolded, unearthed or unwrapped like a present.

• • •

There's one more flying saucer I have to tell you about.

When I was a boy, our family had trouble. It was one of the things that led me—along with so many others, under what I'm sure are similar circumstances—to seek the solace of science fiction and fantasy. One day, my mother came home as usual, and my parents had their typical knock-down, drag-out fight. This kind of thing happened, to the best of my imperfect recollection, a few times a week for roughly five years—from the time I was eleven till I was sixteen. These were epic screaming matches, and my mother, a classically trained singer and stage actress, could really belt it out to the air. My father, who was paradoxically high-tempered and jovial, typically sat for a while and listened before chiming in. Then they'd be done for the evening. On this occasion though, my father, was more quiet than usual. Eventually, when he'd had enough, he picked up the saucer underneath his coffee cup and threw it across the room toward my mother where it shattered against the wall above the stove.

My mother went apoplectic with rage.

He wasn't trying to hit her. It was just a reflection of something else that was coming apart, something else that was broken.

The chronic angers of that house were a firing range, a dumping ground, a laboratory where forensic scientists might map the troubles of a family constituted too early by people who were too young and full of life's fire. Whatever it was that was broken then, however, was not to remain so, even though the effects of it would go on for a long time. Hope springs eternal. As an adult, I recognize how difficult our lives can sometimes be under stress and strain, dreams deferred or absent or impossible to reach from here.

What to do with all of that. I am still asking the question most days.

So I used my flying-saucers narratives to lift me away.

It took a long time, but I figured out years later, that I was one of those pieces of shattered ceramic, splintered by impact against the wall. Our family's physics were not a solitary thing or a unique event. Many of us have similar stories. I was split first in two, and then into many pieces by the anger I was raised with and under. Then I tried to add to it myself, but it wasn't in my nature. I learned later in life, when I had to, that young children absorb rage as guilt for their own wrongdoing, which is of course a chimera. We blame ourselves—because we can't face the fact of such anger, its visceral face, and we don't have the tools to manage it the way an adult might. It seems to us a black hole, a huge breach in the psyche where truth can't be faced, can't be denied—trapped at the edge of the singularity, an orbit we will never break. I tried unsuccessfully for a long time to understand and manage these things. I ran from and then into the walls and ceilings around me like some trapped, frantic bird. But in the end, I couldn't escape myself—or by myself. I needed help and I got it. Someone opened a door for me, and I went out—left with only the puzzle of memories like a giant jigsaw on the living room floor.

I ran toward those other flying saucers as a way of running away from the one flying across our kitchen. It's a small truth perhaps, but it means a lot to me.

•••

Memory is like an old VCR. We have a tape that we occasionally rewind. But every time we do, the replay is different. The narrative changes, things shuffle—are reset or reimagined. Imagination may be part of that. It is a kind of Jungian shadow following our recall and presenting, as it were, a different picture, one that is moving along with us. If I see the flying saucers one way, my parents are coming to get me, to take me back home to love and safety. If I see them another way, it's the opposite. But what is the truth? Grappling with the truth or the past is like lying down on a granite slab and wrestling with it.

We can't change it, there's nothing to win, and it doesn't fight back. So as the shrinks say, we are left with a choice and the ability to choose.

That's the point of the story I love best, when the character chooses goodness and love even in the depths of space and at the cost of her/his own life. There's a bigger picture here, a widescreen we all sit in front of. The projected light is behind us, but there's nothing to see if we stare into it. Only the story and its beauty make the difference.

Christopher Woods

Comings, Goings

On any trail, there is always someone ahead or behind. I thought about this as my wife and I hiked in Point Lobos State Park reserve, just outside Carmel. As we followed the North Shore Trail, we would occasionally encounter other hikers. Some came up from behind us, while others came to meet us.

The day was perfect. The sun was out, undeterred by the infrequent banks of fog drifting over us. The fog vanished quickly into the rocks and foliage.

Already we had come face to face with two deer. They stood on a large boulder and watched us with as much curiosity as we did them. There was no trace of fear in their dark, moist eyes.

We soon saw a couple walking toward us. It was a woman and a young man we soon learned was her son. Friendly, they stopped to talk. My wife and I stood bunched together with them on the narrow trail, on the lookout for poison oak on either side. The woman was out of breath. She announced quickly that she had emphysema, but was surprised that she could walk so well on the park trails. Better than walking in the city, she declared. "No exhaust here," I said. She nodded in agreement, then patted her shirt pocket. I have my trusty inhaler if I need it, she told us.

We went our separate ways. My wife and I chose to follow the Sea Lion Point Trail. Through the trees, the barks of seals seemed to float on the air. But before we got to the place where we might see the seals, a woman suddenly appeared behind us.

"I'm truly lost," she said, but there was a smile on her face. We understood. If one could choose a place to be lost, this might as well be it. After comparing maps for a few moments, the woman took off in the opposite direction. Watching her disappear into the landscape of flowers and trees and rocks, I wondered how it would be to walk these trails alone. I mean, there is the peace of solitude, and then there can also be loneliness. Given the woman's smile, my guess is that she was enjoying the peace. Who knows what she encountered in the months and years that led to this trail, on highways and through relationships.

An hour or so later, we found ourselves at Moss Cove, a peaceful place with large rocks rising from the water to break the stronger waves. The result was a tranquil place from which to watch the sea. Two years before, we had come to this same spot. There is a serenity, and perhaps sacredness, about it. We stayed a good while looking out over Moss Cove. I could stay here forever, my wife said. I agreed. Maybe, when the time came, we would have our ashes scattered here. One of us would do this for the other. Or, perhaps a relative or a friend could bring both our ashes here in due course. Who could know when? But it would be a way of staying, forever.

Walking away from Moss Cove was like leaving a shrine, or maybe departing a very special ceremony. We walked with a new kind of exhilaration. We did not want to leave, but for now it was time to go. Later, maybe later, we thought as we walked.

On Granite Point Trail, I could see a couple coming our way. They wore backpacks with easels strapped across them. I was not surprised when we all paused in our tracks. The man asked, "Is there anything to paint over there?" He was pointing over our shoulders in the direction of Moss Cove. His wife looked at us expectantly.

"You'll find much to paint," my wife said. "Well," the man told us, "I do landscapes, but my wife is looking for a building to paint."

"Then she won't be disappointed," I told him. I explained that, while the husband painted the land and rocks and water, his wife could paint the Carmelite Monastery, easily seen from Moss Cove.

Seeming pleased, they walked on. And we walked away. But we hoped we would be back, for a short visit, or maybe for always. On any trail, there is always someone ahead or behind. Perhaps some trails just go on and on. So much depends on memory and time.

Contributors

CB Adams, MFA, is an award-winning fiction writer and fine art photographer based in the Greater St. Louis area. Adams works with a collection of more than 60 film-based and digital cameras in a wide range of formats from 4x5 to 35mm and toy cameras to create images. In addition to works accepted to more than 30 nationwide exhibitions, recent photographs have been published in *Midwest Review, Genre Urban Arts 7, Heirlock Literary Magazine,* and *Tiny Seed.* His fiction has been published in *River Styx, Zoetrope All-Story Extra,* and elsewhere. Adams is the recipient of the Missouri Arts Council's highest writing awards, the Writers' Biennial and Missouri Writing!. The independent weekly *Riverfront Times* named Adams, "St. Louis' Most Under-Appreciated Writer." His website is qwerkyphotography.com.

Alex Aldred (he/him) lives and writes in Edinburgh, Scotland, where he is currently studying towards his PhD in creative writing. His poetry has previously appeared in the Cordite Poetry Review, In Parentheses, and Cathexis Northwest, among others. You can find out more about his work by visiting his site, alexaldred.co.uk, finding him on twitter @itsmealexaldred, or by summoning him to speak with you in person, provided you have access to the necessary runes.

Evan Balkan is the author of three novels, including the PEN/Faulkner nominated *Independence,* and seven books of nonfiction, including *The Wrath of God: Lope de Aguirre, Revolutionary of the Americas,* as well as many essays and short stories in an array of publications. His screenplays have won multiple fellowships and awards, and he is a co-writer for the television series *Wayward Girls.* He coordinates the English Department at the Community College of Baltimore County, where he runs the creative writing program, and is an adjunct instructor in the Johns Hopkins University's graduate Teaching Writing program. He holds degrees from Towson, George Mason, and Johns Hopkins universities and has served as a guest lecturer at Yale, Johns Hopkins, Bryn Mawr, and many other institutions.

A professor at Brandeis University, **John Ballantine** took his Bachelor's degree in English at Harvard, with an M.A. in Policy Studies from the University of Chicago and a Ph.D. in Economics from NYU Stern. He has published economic commentary in Salon and the Boston Globe. His literary work has appeared in *Cobalt, Crack the Spine, Existere, Forge, Green Hill Review, Lime Hawk, Oracle, Penmen Review, Ragazine, Rubbertop Review, Saint Ann's Review, Santa Fe Literary Review, Slippery Elm, Steetlight* and *SNReview.* He writes to understand the world we walk in and touch our complicated lives.

Maria Berardi's first poetry collection, *Cassandra Gifts,* was published in 2013 by Turkey Buzzard Press, and she is currently at work on her second, *Pagan,* from which these poems are excerpted. Her work has been published widely online and in print as well as at the Arvada Center for the Arts and Humanities as part of an installation by fabric artist Bonnie Ferrill Roman. She lives in the foothills west of Denver at 8,888 feet above sea level.

After receiving his B.A. in English from Colorado State University, **C. W. Bigelow** lived in nine northern states, both east and west, before moving south to the Charlotte, NC area. His short stories and poems have appeared in *The Flexible Persona, Literally Stories, Compass Magazine, FishFood Magazine, Five2One, Crack the Spine, Sick Lit Magazine, Midway Journal, Scarlett Leaf Review, Poydras Review, Cleaning Up Glitter, The Blue Mountain Review, Glassworks, Blood and Bourbon, The Courtship of Winds, Backchannels*, and *Drunk Monkeys,* among others.

Rose Mary Boehm is a German-born British national living and writing in Lima, Peru. Her poetry has been published widely in mostly US poetry reviews (online and print). Her fourth poetry collection, *The Rain Girl,* was published by Chaffinch Press at the end August 2020.

Karen Boissonneault-Gauthier is an Indigenous visual artist, writer, and photographer. Her photographic art has landed on the covers of *Pretty Owl Poetry, Wild Musette, Arachne Press, Nebo, Existere Journal of Art and Literature, Vine Leaves Literary Journal, Gigantic Sequins, Crack the Spine, Ottawa Arts Journal,* and others. She has been featured in New York's *WebSafe2k16, Lily Poetry Review, The Scarborough Big Arts Book,* Los Angeles' *The Lunch Ticket, Vox Voila, Understorey Magazine, Dek Unu,* and *A Caged Mind.* Karen presently designs custom face masks using her visual art at artofwhere.comrtists/kcbgphotography. Her website is kcbgphoto.com

Roger Camp lives in Seal Beach, CA where he gardens, walks the pier, plays blues piano, and spends afternoons with his pal, Harry, over drinks at Nick's on 2nd. When he's not at home, he's traveling in the Old World. His work has appeared in *Poetry East, Gulf Coast, Southern Poetry Review,* and *Nimrod.*

Abby Caplin's poems have appeared in *AGNI, Catamaran, Love's Executive Order, Manhattanville Review, Midwest Quarterly, Salt Hill, TSR: The Southampton Review, Tikkun,* and elsewhere. Among her awards, she has been a finalist for the Rash Award in Poetry, semi-finalist for the Willow Run Poetry Book Award, finalist for the Anna Davidson Rosenberg Poetry Award, and a winner of the San Francisco Poets Ecleven. She is a physician and practices mind-body medicine in San Francisco. Visit http://abbycaplin.com.

Judith Beth Cohen's novel *Seasons* was published in 1984 by The Permanent Press. Excerpts appeared first in *The New American Review.* The book was originally published in German translation by Rowohlt of Hamburg as part of their international New Woman Series and has recently been reissued as an ebook. Her short fiction, reviews, and articles have appeared in numerous magazines including *The North American Review, New Letters, High Plains Literary Review, Sojourner, The Northern New England Review, The Christian Science Monitor, The Boston Herald, The Boston Review,* among others. She has had residency grants to Provincetown Fine Arts Work Center, Yaddo, MacDowell and other artist's colonies and has recently become a yoga teacher.

Mike Cohen, a retired lawyer, lives in Seattle. He is the author of the novel *Rivertown Heroes* (2017,) and the short story collection *The Three of Us* (2018) published by Adelaide Books. His short stories have appeared in *Streetlight, Adelaide, STORGY, Umbrella Factory, FRiGG, Litbreak, The Furious Gazelle Magazines, The North Dakota Quarterly,* and *The American Writers and Penman Reviews.* His short story "The Cantor's Window" was a Winner Nominee in *Adelaide Magazine's 2018 Literary Voices* and was anthologized in *Streetlight Magazine's Best Stories of 2017.*

Thomas DeConna has taught English for thirty-nine years and has now turned his focus towards writing fiction. His work is published or forthcoming in *The Long Story, Mobius, Wild Violet,* and *The Write Launch.*

Fabrizia Faustinella is a physician and film maker. She grew up in Italy and now practices as an internist in the Texas Medical Center in Houston, Texas. The care of the undeserved and the homeless has inspired her to write about her experiences in several patient-centered essays which have been published in academic and literary journals alike. Dr. Faustinella is also a film writer, producer and director with an interest in social problems. She has received national and international recognition for her short movie productions. She recently wrote, directed, and produced *The Dark Side of the Moon,* a feature length film-documentary about the root causes of homelessness and the hardship of street life.

Doris Ferleger—winner of the *New Letters Poetry,* Songs of Eretz Prize, Montgomery County Poet Laureate Prize, Robert Fraser Poetry Prize, and the *AROHO* Creative Non-Fiction Prize, among others—is the author of three full volumes of poetry: *Big, Silences in a Year of Rain* (finalist for the Alice James Books Beatrice Hawley Award), *As the Moon Has Breath,* and *Leavened*; and a chapbook entitled *When You Become Snow.* Her work has been published in numerous journals including *Cimarron Review, L.A. Review,* and *South Carolina Review.* She holds an MFA in Poetry, a Ph.D. in psychology, and maintains a mindfulness-based therapy practice in Wyncote PA.

Jack Foster is a writer and artist living in Los Angeles. He is the creator of the comic book *GUN.* His work in comics and poetry explores similar terrain—a word balloon is a kind of poem in itself, metered and economical with a careful eye for shape. More of his work can be found at RecklessEyeballs.com.

Malisa Garlieb is a writer, teacher, mother, and metalsmith. Her poems have appeared in *Painted Bride Quarterly, Calyx, Rhino,* and *Rust + Moth,* among others. *Handing Out Apples in Eden,* her first collection, was published by Wind Ridge Books in 2014. She is working on a second book.

Carolyn Geduld is a mental health professional in Bloomington, Indiana. Her fiction has appeared in numerous literary journals and anthologies. Her novel, *Take Me Out The Back,* was published by Black Rose Publishers in 2020.

Irving A. Greenfield has published in *Amarillo Bay, Runaway Parade, Writing For Tomorrow, eFictionMag, The Stone Hobo, Prime Mincer, The Note and Cooweescoowee (3X),* and *The Stone Canoe,* electronic edition. He is cited in Wikipedia. He and his wife live on Staten Island.

Susan Eve Haar is a member of The Actor's Studio, Ensemble Studio Theater, and the Writer's Guild East. Her plays have been produced at Primary Stages, The Women's Project and the Edinburgh Fringe Festival. Recent theater publications include *Best Short Plays 2018, Best Men's Monologues 2018,* and *Best Women's Monologues 2018.* In 2019 her monologue "Waiting at The Bodyshop" was included in *Monologues for Headspace Theatre,* edited by Michael Bigelow Dixon. Her fiction has been published in the *Columbia Journal, The North Dakota Quarterly, the Saint Ann's Review, CRAFT* and *bioStories.* She is a graduate of Harvard Law School. susanevehaar.com

Meredith Davies Hadaway is the author of three poetry collections: *Fishing Secrets of the Dead, The River is a Reason,* and *At The Narrows* (winner of the 2015 Delmarva Book Prize for Creative Writing). She has received fellowships and awards from the Virginia Center for Creative Arts and the Maryland State Arts Council. She holds an MFA in Poetry from Vermont College of Fine Arts and was, for ten years, poetry editor for *The Summerset Review.* Hadaway is a former Rose O'Neill Writer-in-Residence at Washington College where she taught ecopoetry and served as chief marketing officer for 30 years.

John Haugh lives in Greensboro, NC where he works in finance and is trying to assemble his first chapbook, *Repurpose Those Ghosts.* Recent publishing credits include poems in *Main Street Rag, Kackalack, The Roanoke Review, Peregrine, North Carolina Literary Review,* and *The Tipton Poetry Review.* Mr. Haugh was a finalist for the Applewhite poetry award recently, was a NCAA national champion in fencing years ago, and spent untold hours browsing Oxford Books in Atlanta and Powell's City of Books in Oregon when young.

John Calvin Hughes holds degrees from the University of Southern Mississippi and the University of South Florida. His work appears in *Dead Mule, Southern Indiana Review, Autumn Sky Poetry, The Timberline Review, The American Journal of Poetry,* and *Mississippi Review,* among others. His publications include a critical study, *The Novels and Short Stories of Frederick Barthelme* (The Edwin Mellen Press); two poetry chapbooks, *The Shape of Our Luck* (Sargent Press) and *Cul-de-sac Agonistes* (Black Bomb Books); a full-length poetry collection, *Music from a Farther Room* (Aldrich Press); and three novels, *Twilight of the Lesser Gods* (CreateSpace), *Killing Rush* (Second Wind Publishing), and *The Lost Gospel of Darnell Rabren* (Bowen Press Books). He lives and works in Florida.

James Croal Jackson (he/him/his) is a Filipino-American poet. He has a chapbook, *The Frayed Edge of Memory* (Writing Knights Press, 2017) and recent poems in *DASH, Sampsonia Way,* and *Jam & Sand.* He edits *The Mantle* (themantlepoetry.com). He works in film production in Pittsburgh, PA. (jamescroaljackson.com)

Sharon Kennedy-Nolle, a graduate of Vassar College, holds an MFA in poetry from the Writers' Workshop and a Ph.D. in English from the University of Iowa. Her chapbook *Black Wick: Selected Elegies,* which concerns the loss of her son, was a semi-finalist for the 2018 Tupelo Snowbound Chapbook Contest. It was chosen as the 2020 Chapbook Editor's Pick by Variant Literature Press and will appear in print in February 2021. Her poetry has appeared or is upcoming in a variety of print and online journals. She lives and teaches in New York.

Mary Kipps writes poetry for all age groups, in traditional forms as well as in free verse. A former Pushcart Prize nominee, her work has appeared regularly in poetry journals and anthologies across the U.S. and abroad since 2005. She is also the author of three humorous paranormal Kindle books: *All in Vein, A Sucker for Heels,* and *Bitten: A Practical Guide to Dating a Vampire.*

Ellen Tovatt Leary spent twenty years acting on the professional stage. She performed in theaters from the Ahmanson in LA to the State Theatre in Lincoln Center, including four Broadway, many off-Broadway and regional theaters. She worked with Hal Prince, Maureen Stapleton, and James Hammerstein, among others. She graduated from Antioch College and was a Fulbright scholar at LAMDA. Her first book, a memoir, *Mother Once Removed,* details her childhood growing up on Bleecker Street in Greenwich Village in the 1940s with an eccentric, divorced mother. She was on the writing staff of the Carnegie Hill News in New York for fourteen years. She has published short stories, poems, and a novel entitled *The Understudy.* She is a native New Yorker who currently resides, with her husband, in LA.

Cynthia Lewis is Charles A. Dana Professor of English at Davidson College, where she has been teaching Shakespeare, Renaissance literature, and creative nonfiction since 1980. She has published numerous articles and two books on Shakespeare and his contemporaries, the latest recently out: *"The game's afoot": A Sports Lover's Introduction to Shakespeare.* Her creative nonfiction has been published in such venues as *The Hudson Review, New Letters, The Antioch Review, Southern Cultures, The Massachusetts Review,* and *Charlotte Magazine.* Between 2006 and 2016, four of her essays have been cited as a "Notable Essay" in the *Best American Essays* series. Her essay "Return Engagement: The Haunting of Hamlet and Dale Earnhardt, Jr." won *Shenandoah*'s Thomas Carter Essay Prize for 2016, and her essay "Body Doubles" won the Meringoff Prize for nonfiction from the Association of Literary Scholars, Writers, and Critics.

Lisa Low's poetry, reviews, interviews, and academic essays have appeared in or are forthcoming from *The Massachusetts Review, The Boston Review, Cross Currents, Woolf Studies Annual, Phoebe, The Potomac Review, Crack the Spine, Delmarva Review, Broken Plate, Tusculum Review, Lit Break Magazine, Boomer Lit Mag, Evening Street, Spillway, The Virginia Normal,* and *Streetlight Magazine,* among others. She is one of the editors of *Milton, the Metaphysicals, and Romanticism* (Cambridge University Press in 1994). She received her doctorate in English Literature from the University of Massachusetts and spent 20 years as an English professor at Cornell College, Colby College, and Pace University. In addition to her work as an educator, Low has been a film and theatre critic for Christian Science Monitor Broadcasting. You can learn more at Lisa's website, lisalowwrites.com.

Katharyn Howd Machan, author of 39 collections of poetry (most recently, in 2020, *A Slow Bottle of Wine,* winner of the Jessie Bryce Niles Chapbook Competition), has lived in Ithaca, New York, since 1975 and, now as a full professor, has taught Writing at Ithaca College since 1977. After many years of coordinating the Ithaca Community Poets and directing the national Feminist Women's Writing Workshops, Inc., she was selected to be Tompkins County's first poet laureate. Her poems have appeared in numerous magazines, anthologies, textbooks, and stage productions, and she has edited three thematic anthologies, most recently, with Split Oak Press, a tribute collection celebrating the inspiration of Adrienne Rich. *Katharyn Howd Machan: Selected Poems* (FutureCycle Press) was awarded the 2018 FutureCycle Poetry Book Prize.

Thomas Mampalam is a neurosurgeon in private practice in Northern California. He writes poetry informed by my medical, immigration, and family experiences. He has poems published or forthcoming in the *Journal of the American Medical Association,* the journal *Neurology, The Healing Muse, Intima Journal of Narrative Medicine, The Avalon Literary Review, California Quarterly, The Cortland Review,* and *Metonym.*

DS Maolalai has been nominated for Best of the Web and twice for the Pushcart Prize. His poetry has been released in two collections, *Love is Breaking Plates in the Garden* (Encircle Press, 2016) and *Sad Havoc Among the Birds* (Turas Press, 2019).

Kathleen Zamboni McCormick is Professor of Literature and Writing at Purchase College, SUNY. Her creative work has been published in *Sweet Tree Review, Green Hills Literary Lantern, South Carolina Review, phoebe, Italian Americana, Zone 3, CAYLX, Paterson Literary Review, Kestrel, Crack the Spine,* and many others. Her novel, *Dodging Satan: My Irish/Italian Sometimes Awesome but Mostly Creepy Childhood* (Sand Hill Review Press, 2016) won the 2017 Foreword Reviews Gold Medal in Humor and the 2017 Illumination Bronze Medal for Catholic Books (Pope Francis won the Gold!). In 2019, She received the Elena Lucrezia Cornaro Award: named for the first woman in history to receive a PhD, this award recognizes outstanding Italian American scholars for their significant contributions to their profession and their communities. "Daddy's Girl" will appear in her next book dealing with social class and feminism.

A former writer and editor for several sports publications, **Patrick McEvoy** has stories in various comic book anthologies such as *Emanata, Uncanny Adventures, Indie Comics Quarterly,* and *GuruKitty's Once Upon a Time and Gateway to Beyond.* A short story he wrote has also appeared on Akashic Books' website. His short plays have been performed at the Players Theatre in New York as part of their various festivals (Sex, NYC and BOO) in 2013, 2014, 2015, 2016 and 2019. Another short play was accepted into Emerging Artists Theatre New Works series in 2020. Photography has also been exhibited at Greenpoint Gallery.

Zoe Messinger's writing has been published in *ONTHEBUS, Hobart, Litbreak, (mac)ro(mic), Good Works Review, Penumbra,* and *Peter Greenberg Worldwide.* She's also published a cookbook, *Foodie Two Shoes: 46 Taste Tips from a Traveling Teenager* (Small Batch Books, 2011). Zoe has a Bachelor of Science degree from the School of Hotel Administration at Cornell University. As a chef she has cooked in two award-winning LA restaurants and for two years ran a food truck in both Milan and Amsterdam. Zoe is a graduate of the Upright Citizens Brigade (UCB) and has performed stand-up in venues from LA to New York City to Paris. One day she hopes to eat caviar while taking a long, hot bath. Today is not that day.

Scott Minar is Contributing Editor/Poetry Translations for *Crazyhorse* (College of Charleston —South Carolina). His poems and essays have appeared in *The Paris Review, Poetry International, Poetry International Online, Crazyhorse, Terrain, Ninth Letter, The Laurel Review, The Newfoundland Herald, Eton 77, Map Literary,* and elsewhere in the US and abroad. He is the former Director of the Songwriting Workshop at the Chautauqua Writers' Festival in upstate New York. His poetry and prose have been translated into several languages. He has published four books of poetry, the most recent of these are *Cymbalism* (Mammoth Books 2016; Arabic version by Linda Books, Al Sweida Syria 2017) and *Gilgamesh and Other Poems* (Arabic version by Linda Books, Al Sweida Syria 2018; English version by Mammoth Books forthcoming in 2020). His translations and co-translations have appeared in *The Laurel Review, Crazyhorse, Poetry International, Terrain,* and a number of other international publications. He teaches at Ohio University Lancaster Campus.

Charlene Stegman Moskal is a Teaching Artist for The Alzheimers Poetry Project under the auspices of the Las Vegas Poetry Promise Organization. Charlene is a visual artist, a performer, a voice for NPR's *Theme and Variations,* and a writer. She is published in numerous anthologies, magazines and online, most recently, *Connecticut River Review, Sandstone & Silver; an Anthology of Nevada Poets, Southwestern American Literature, Oyez Review,* and *Humana Obscura.* Zeitgeist Press is the publisher of her second chapbook, *One Bare Foot.* Charlene is in her seventh decade, loves laughter and coffee ice cream hot fudge sundaes.

Suzanne O'Connell's recently published work can be found in *North American Review, Poet Lore, The Menacing Hedge, Steam Ticket, Typishly,* and *Forge.* O'Connell was awarded second place in the *Poetry Super Highway* poetry contest, 2019, and was nominated twice for the Pushcart Prize. She received Honorable Mention in the Steve Kowit Poetry Prize, 2019. Garden Oak Press published her two poetry collections, *A Prayer For Torn Stockings* and *What Luck.*

Kenneth Pobo has a new book, *Uneven Steven,* now out from Assure Press and another, *Opening,* forthcoming from Recto Y Versos Editions. He recently retired from his teaching job at Widener University. His work has appeared in *North Dakota Quarterly, Atlanta Review, Nimrod, Mudfish, Hawaii Review,* and elsewhere.

Emily Rubin's debut novel, *STALINA* (Mariner Books 2011), was a selection from the Amazon Debut Novel Award Contest. Her short stories and essays appear in *The Red Rock Review, Conjunctions, SmartSet, LitBreak, Poets & Writers Magazine, NY Observer,* and *HAPPY.* Since 2005 Rubin has produced the reading and performance series, *Dirty Laundry: Loads of Prose,* in working laundromats around the country, and she also founded the Write Treatment Workshops, creative writing workshops for Mount Sinai Hospital Cancer Centers in NYC. With an MFA from St. Jospeh's College Writers' Foundry, Rubin has taught fiction for Bard College's Life Long Learning Institute and as faculty in Columbia University's Narrative Medicine Program. She lives in NYC and Columbia County, NY with husband, Leslie, and dog Sebastian. emilyrubin.net

David Salner's latest collection is *The Stillness of Certain Valleys* (Broadstone Books, 2019). His stories and poems have appeared in many journals including *Threepenny Review, Ploughshares, Beloit Poetry Journal, Carve,* and *The Moth* (U.K.). He worked as iron ore miner, steelworker, machinist; now as librarian. His first novel, *A Place to Hide,* will appear in 2021 from Apprentice House. His website is DSalner.wix.com/salner

Nick Sweeney's stories are scattered around the web and in print. *Laikonik Express,* his Poland-set novel, came out with Unthank Books. US Publisher Bards and Sages published his speculative novelette *The Exploding Elephant* in 2018, and his novella *A Blue Coast Mystery, Almost Solved,* about the swingin' sixties and genocide, is out in November 2020 with Histria Books. He is a freelance writer and musician, and lives on the English coast.

Philip Terman is the author of six full-length book of poetry and four chapbooks. His most recent collection is *Our Portion: New and Selected Poems.* A selection of his poems, *My Dear Friend Kafka,* was translated into Arabic and published in Damascus, Syria. His poems appear in numerous journals and anthologies, including *Poetry Magazine, The Kenyon Review, The Georgia Review,* and *The Sun Magazine.* He's a professor of English at Clarion University and is the coordinator of The Bridge Literary and Arts Center in Franklin, PA. He has collaborated with other artists, including composers, painters, and sculptors, and performs his poetry with the jazz band, *The Barkeyville Triangle.* More information can be found at philipterman.com.

Dealt homosexuality, Arabic, and rhythm, **Intesar Toufic** is playing his hand notoriously. After drumming in punk bands and working with Syrian refugees in Lebanon, he ventured east where he now studies international politics with hopes of influencing them one day. His fiction has appeared in *Haunted Waters Press, gayflashfiction.com, Every Day Fiction, The New Smut Project,* and others. His nonfiction has appeared in *The Gay & Lesbian Review, Bull Men's Fiction,* and *From Whispers to Roars.* He is seeking representation for an LGBT romance novel about obsession, a straight frat boy, a gay painter, domination, and money. He is dead serious about this book business, goddamnit. Facebook.com/ScandalousArab

John Tustin is a writer of love letters and poetry and is currently in exile. His poetry has appeared in many disparate literary journals, and fritzware.com/johntustinpoetry contains links to his published poetry online.

Victor Walker is a former teacher and a full-time writer. His short stories have appeared in *New Black Voices, The Wisconsin Review, The Long Story, The MacGuffin, Red Rock Review, The Baltimore Review, Great Lakes Review, West Trade Review,* and other literary publications. A Chicagoan, he is presently living in Easton, Pennsylvania.

Will Walker lives in San Francisco with his wife and their dog. He is a former editor of the *Haight Ashbury Literary Journal.* He has two collections available on Amazon: *Wednesday after Lunch* (winner of the 2008 Blue Light Press Book Award) and *Zeus at Twilight.* He has attended many poetry workshops over the years, most notably with Marie Howe.

Christopher Woods is a writer and photographer who lives in Chappell Hill, Texas. He has published a novel, *The Dream Patch*; a prose collection, *Under a Riverbed Sky*; and a book of stage monologues for actors, *Heart Speak.* His photographs can be seen in his gallery at christopherwoods.zenfolio.com. His photography prompt book for writers, *From Vision to Text,* is forthcoming from Propertius Press. His novella, *Hearts in the Dark,* is forthcoming from Running Wild Press.

About FutureCycle Press

FutureCycle Press is dedicated to publishing lasting English-language poetry books and anthologies in both print-on-demand and Kindle formats. Founded in 2007 by long-time independent editor/publishers and partners Diane Kistner and Robert S. King, the press incorporated as a nonprofit in 2012. A number of our editors are distinguished poets and writers in their own right, and we have been actively involved in the small press movement going back to the early seventies.

The FutureCycle Poetry Book Prize and honorarium is awarded annually for the best full-length volume of poetry we publish in a calendar year. Introduced in 2013, our Good Works projects are anthologies devoted to issues of universal significance with all proceeds donated to a related worthy cause. Our Selected Poems series highlights contemporary poets with a substantial body of work to their credit; with this series we strive to resurrect work that has had limited distribution and is now out of print.

We are dedicated to giving all of the authors we publish the care their work deserves, making our catalog of titles the most diverse and distinguished it can be, and paying forward any earnings to fund more great books.

We've learned a few things about independent publishing over the years. We've also evolved a unique, resilient publishing model that allows us to focus mainly on vetting and preserving for posterity the most books of exceptional quality without becoming over-whelmed with bookkeeping and mailing, fundraising activities, or taxing editorial and production "bubbles." To find out more, come see us at futurecycle.org.

www.ingramcontent.com/pod-product-compliance
Lightning Source LLC
Chambersburg PA
CBHW080720020726
47502CB00009B/2485